THE
GREATEST
HUNTING
STORIES
EVER
TOLD

Also By The Author

Classic Hunting Tales
Tales of Woods and Waters
Complete Outdoors Encyclopedia
The American Fisherman's Fresh and Salt Water Guide
The Outdoor Sportsman's Illustrated Dictionary
Complete Guide to Fresh and Saltwater Fishing
Complete Guide to Camping and Wilderness Survival
Game Birds and Gun Dogs
Hunting Dangerous Game

THE
GREATEST
HUNTING
STORIES
EVER
TOLD

Tales of Big Game Hunting

EDITED BY
Vin T. Sparano

Skyhorse Publishing

Library of Congress Cataloging-in-Publication Data is available on file.

Cover design by Richard Rossiter
Cover artwork © Terry Doughty

Print ISBN: 978-1-63450-284-9
Ebook ISBN: 978-1-63450-846-9

Printed in the United States of America

To all my hunting and fishing buddies
and the camps we shared. May our
memories always remind us of the
wonderful life we have lived.

Contents

Introduction

More than thirty years ago, I collected what I considered to be the greatest hunting stories of all time. I wanted these memorable hunting tales to be preserved forever in a book to be read by generations of hunters, young and old. That personal goal has not changed. I now cherish the opportunity to once again bring you those same classic hunting tales that I selected many years ago.

There have been many changes in the game fields and hunting camps around the world, but what I miss most are the vivid hunting tales written by some of the greatest hunters and writers in the golden history of the outdoors. I've had the pleasure of knowing some of these men, whose hunting skills may well be overshadowed by their gift of storytelling. I have even hunted with several of these authors.

I am frequently faced with the fact that this kind of outdoor literature is rapidly disappearing. In the face of a changing hunting culture, I fear it no longer recognizes that its precious history must be preserved and is in danger.

As a boy and as a young editor at *Outdoor Life* magazine, I grew up reading outdoor books and magazines. Every month I would hunt sheep with Jack O'Connor or hunt Cape buffalo in Africa with Robert Ruark. I learned a lot from these men. More importantly, I shared their adventures. Even today, I can smell the barbequing of sheep ribs on a mountain with Jack O'Connor. I can recall memorable grouse hunts with my old friend Jerry Gibbs and a truly scary caribou hunt in the Arctic Circle with Jim Zumbo.

There were other adventures, too. People in the wilderness with a once-in-a-lifetime tale that they somehow managed to get into words. Olive Frederickson is an example, the remarkable women from British Columbia who had to pick up a rifle and hunt to save her children from starvation. These were real stories and I wonder why I see so few of them today.

Not all stories are ordeals. Jim Carmichel, for example, will bring laughter to your heart as he tells how pigeon scat brought justice to a screeching halt in the town of Jonesboro. Jerry Gibbs will bring tears to your eyes when he remembers his dog Gypsy.

Every so often, along comes a gem of a story, one that you can read ten times and it will always be an entertaining adventure. That's what this book is all about. Here is my favorite selection of outdoor stories, culled from many years of reading outdoor tales. Some will make you happy, some will make you sad. But all the stories will stay with you forever.

I want to thank *Outdoor Life* for granting me permission to reprint the stories I know so well. Finally, I want to thank the authors of these stories. To those who are still alive I say "keep writing and give us more stories we can carry in our hearts." To those who have passed on to happier game lands, I can only express admiration and a promise to tell their stories and toast their names in hunting camps.

Vin T. Sparano, Editor Emeritus, *Outdoor Life*.
April 2015

SUICIDE MADE EASY

by Robert C. Ruark

S ome people are afraid of the dark. Other people fear airplanes, ghosts, their wives, death, illness, bosses, snakes or bugs. Each man has some private demon of fear that dwells within him. Sometimes he may spend a life without discovering that he is hagridden by fright—the kind that makes the hands sweat and the stomach writhe in real sickness. This fear numbs the brain and has a definite odor, easily detectable by dog and man alike. The odor of fear is the odor of the charnel house, and it cannot be hidden.

I love the dark. I am fond of airplanes. I have had a ghost for a friend. I am not henpecked by my wife. I was through a war and never fretted about getting killed. I pay small attention to illness, and have never feared an employer. I like snakes, and bugs don't bother me. But I have a fear, a constant, steady fear that still crowds into my dreams, a fear that makes me sweat like a Spanish fighting bull. I have killed Mbogo, and to date he has never got a horn into me, but the fear of him has never lessened with familiarity. He is just so damned big, and ugly, and ornery, and vicious, and surly, and cruel, and crafty. Especially when he's mad. And when he's hurt, he's always mad. And when he's mad, he wants to kill you. He is not satisfied with less. But such is his fascination that, once you've hunted him, you are dissatisfied with other game, up to and including elephants.

The Swahili language, which is the lingua franca of East Africa, is remarkably expressive in its naming of animals. No better word than *simba* for lion was ever constructed, not even by Edgar Rice Burroughs, Tarzan's daddy. You cannot beat *tembo* for elephant, nor can you improve on *chui* for leopard, *nugu* for baboon, *fisi* for hyena or *punda* for zebra. *Faro* is apt for rhinoceros, too, but none of the easy Swahili nomenclature packs the same descriptive punch as *mbogo* for a beast that

3

will weigh over a ton, will take an 88 millimeter shell in his breadbasket and still toddle off, and that combines crafty guile with incredible speed, and vindictive anger with wide-eyed, skilled courage.

From a standpoint of senses, the African buffalo has no weak spot. He sees as well as he smells, and he hears as well as he sees, and he charges with his head up and his eye unblinking. He is as fast as an express train, and he can haul short and turn himself on a shilling. He has a tongue like a wood rasp and feet as big as knife-edged flatirons. His skull is armor-plated and his horns are either razor-sharp or splintered into horrid javelins. The boss of horn that covers his brain can induce hemorrhage by a butt. His horns are ideally adapted for hooking, and one hook can unzip a man from crotch to throat. He delights to dance upon the prone carcass of a victim, and the man who provides the platform is generally collected with a trowel, for the buffalo's death dance leaves little but shreds and bloody tatters.

I expect I have looked at several thousand buffalo at close range. I have stalked several hundred. I have been mixed up in a herd of two hundred or more, and stayed there quietly while the herd milled and fed around me. I have crawled after them, and dashed into their midst with a whoop and a holler, and looked at them from trees, and followed wounded bulls into the bush, and have killed a couple. But the terror never quit. The sweat never dried. The stench of abject fear never left me. And the fascination with him never left me. Toward the end of my first safari I was crawling more miles after Mbogo than I was walking after anything else—still scared stiff, but unable to quit. Most of the time I felt like a cowardly bullfighter with a hangover, but Mbogo beckoned me on like the sirens that seduced ships to founder on the rocks.

For this I blame my friend Harry Selby, a young professional buffalo —I mean hunter—who will never marry unless he can talk a comely cow mbogo into sharing his life. Selby is wedded to buffalo, and when he cheats he cheats only with elephants. Four times, at last count, his true loves have come within a whisker of killing him, but he keeps up the courtship. It has been said of Selby that he is uninterested in anything that can't kill him right back. What is worse, he has succeeded in infecting most of his innocent charges with the same madness.

Selby claims that the buffalo is only a big, innocent kind of he-cow, with all the attributes of bossy, and has repeatedly demonstrated how a madman can stalk into the midst of a browsing herd and commune with several hundred black tank cars equipped with radar and heavy artillery on their heads without coming to harm. His chief delight is the stalk that leads him into this idyllic communion. If there are not at least three mountains, one river, a trackless swamp and a cane field between him and the quarry, he is sad for days. Harry does not believe that buffalo should be cheaply achieved.

Actually, if you just want to go out and shoot a buffalo, regardless of horn size, it is easy enough to get just any shot at close range. The only difficulty is in shooting straight enough, and/or often enough, to kill the animal swiftly, before it gets its second wind and runs off into the bush, there to become an almost impregnable killer. In Kenya and Tanganyika, in buffalo country, you may almost certainly run onto a sizable herd on any given day. I suppose by working at it I might have slain a couple of hundred in six weeks, game laws and inclination being equal.

As it was, I shot two—the second better than the first, and only for that reason. Before the first, and in between the first and second, we must have crawled up to several hundred for close-hand inspection. The answer is that a 42- or 43-inch bull today, while no candidate for Rowland Ward's records, is still a mighty scarce critter, and anything over 45 inches is one hell of a good bull. A fellow I know stalked some 60 lone bulls and herd bulls in the Masai country recently, and never topped his 43-incher.

But whether or not you shoot, the thrill of the stalk never lessens. With your glasses you will spot the long, low black shape of Mbogo on a hillside or working out of a forest into a swamp. At long distances he looks exactly like a great black worm on the hill. He grazes slowly, head down, and your job is simply—simply!—to come up on him, spot the good bull, if there is one in the herd, and then get close enough to shoot him dead. Anything over 30 yards is not a good safe range, because a heavy double—a .450 No. 2 or a .470—is not too accurate at more than 100 yards. Stalking the herd is easier than stalking the old and wary lone bull, which has been expelled from the flock by the young bloods, or stalking an old bull with an askari—a young bull that serves as stooge and bodyguard to the oldster. The young punk is usually well alerted while his hero feeds, and you cannot close the range satisfactorily without spooking the watchman.

It is nearly impossible to describe the tension of a buffalo stalk. For one thing, you are nearly always out of breath. For another, you never know whether you will be shooting until you are literally in the middle of the herd or within a hundred yards or so of the single O's or the small band. Buffalo have an annoying habit of always feeding with their heads behind another buffalo's rump, or of lying down in the mud and hiding their horns, or of straying off into eight-foot sword grass or cane in which all you can see are the egrets that roost on their backs. A proper buffalo stalk is incomplete unless you wriggle on your belly through thornbushes, shoving your gun ahead of you, or stagger crazily through marsh in water up to your rear end, sloshing and slipping and falling full length into the muck. Or scrambling up the sides of mountains, or squeezing through forests so thick that you part the trees ahead with your gun barrel.

There is no danger to the stalk itself. Not really. Of course, an old cow with a new calf may charge you and kill you. Or the buffs that can't see you or smell you, if you come upwind in high cover or thick bush, might accidentally stampede and mash you into the muck, only because they don't know you're there. Two or three hundred animals averaging 1,800 pounds apiece make a tidy stampede when they are running rump to rump and withers to withers. I was in one stampede that stopped short only because the grass thinned out, and in another that thoughtfully swerved a few feet and passed close aboard us. If the stampede doesn't swerve and doesn't stop, there is always an out. I asked Mr. Selby what the out was.

"Well," he replied, "the best thing to do is to shoot the nearest buffalo to you, and hope you kill it dead so that you can scramble up on top of it. The shots may split the stampede, and once they see you perched atop the dead buffalo they will sheer off and run around you."

I must confess I was thoroughly spooked on buffalo before I ever got to shoot one. I had heard a sufficiency of tall tales about the durability and viciousness of the beasts—tall tales, but all quite true. I had been indoctrinated in the buffalo hunter's fatalistic creed: Once you've wounded him, you must go after him. Once you're in the bush with him, he will wait and charge you. Once he's made his move, you cannot run, or hide, or climb a tree fast enough to get away from a red-eyed,

6

rampaging monster with death in his heart and on his mind. You must stand and shoot it out with Mbogo, and unless you get him through the nose and into the brain, or in the eye and into the brain, or break his neck and smash his shoulder and rupture his heart as he comes, Mbogo will get you. Most charging buffalos are shot at a range of from 15 to three feet, and generally through the eye.

Also, we had stalked up to a lot of Mbogo before I ever found one good enough to shoot. We had broken in by stalking a herd that was feeding back into the forest in a marsh. Another herd, which had already fed into the bush and which we had not seen, had busted loose with awful series of snorts and grunts and had passed within a few feet, making noises like a runaway regiment of heavy tanks. This spooked the herd we had in mind, and they took off in another direction, almost running us down. A mud-scabby buffalo at a few feet is a horrifying thing to see, I can assure you.

The next buff we stalked were a couple of old and wary loners, and we were practically riding them before we were able to discern that their horns were worn down and splintered from age and use and were worthless as trophies. This was the first time I stood up at a range of 25 yards and said ''Shoo!'' in a quavery voice. I didn't like the way either old boy looked at me before they shooed.

The next we stalked showed nothing worth shooting, and the next we stalked turned out to be two half-grown rhino in high grass. I was getting to the point where I hated to hear one of the gun bearers say, ''Mbogo, Bwana,'' and point a knobby, lean finger at some flat black beetles on a mountainside nine miles away. I knew that Selby would say, ''We'd best go and take a look-see,'' which meant three solid hours of fearful ducking behind bushes, crawling, cursing, sweating, stumbling, falling, getting up and staggering on to something I didn't want to play with in the first place. Or in the second place, or any place.

But one day we got a clear look at a couple of bulls—one big, heavily horned, prime old stud and a smaller askari, feeding on the lip of a thick thorn forest. They were feeding in the clear for a change, and they were nicely surrounded by high cane and a few scrub trees, which meant that we could make a fair crouching stalk by walking like question marks and dodging behind the odd bush. The going was miserable underfoot, with our legs sinking to the knees in ooze and our feet catching and tripping on

7

the intertwined grasses, but the buff were only a few thousand yards away and the wind was right; so we kept plugging ahead.

"Let's go and collect him," said Mr. Selby, the mad gleam of the fanatic buff hunter coming into his mild brown eyes. "He looks like a nice one."

Off we zigged and zagged and blundered. My breath, from overexertion and sheer fright, was a sharp pain in my chest, and I was wheezing like an overextended pipe organ when we finally reached the rim of the high grass. We ducked low and snaked over behind the last bush between Mbogo and us. I panted. My belly was tied in small, tight knots, and a family of rats seemed to inhabit my clothes. I couldn't see either buffalo, but I heard a gusty snort and a rustle.

Selby turned his head and whispered: "We're too far, but the askari is suspicious. He's trying to lead the old boy away. You'd best get up and wallop him, because we aren't going to get any closer. Take him in the chest."

I lurched up and looked at Mbogo, and Mbogo looked at me. He was 50 to 60 yards off, his head low, his eyes staring right down my soul. He looked at me as if he hated my guts. He looked as if I had despoiled his fiancée, murdered his mother, and burned down his house. He looked at me as if I owed him money. I never saw such malevolence in the eyes of any animal or human being, before or since. So I shot him.

I was using a big double, a Westley-Richards .470. The gun went off. The buffalo went down. So did I. I had managed to loose off both barrels of this elephant gun, and the resulting concussion was roughly comparable to shooting a three-inch antiaircraft gun off your shoulder. I was knocked as silly as a man can be knocked and still be semiconscious. I got up and stood there stupidly, with an empty gun in my hands, shaking my head. Somewhere away in Uganda I heard a gun go off and Mr. Selby's clear Oxonion tone came faintly.

"I do hope you don't mind," said he. "You knocked him over, but he got up again and took off for the bush. I thought I'd best break his back, although I'm certain you got his heart. It's just that it's dreadfully thick in there, and we'd no way of examining the wound to see whether you'd killed him. He's down, over there at the edge of the wood."

Mbogo was down, all right, his ugly head stretched out. He was lying sideways, a huge, mountainous hulk of muddy, tick-crawling, scabbyhided monster. There was a small hole just abaft his forequarters, about three inches from the top of his back—Mr. Selby's spine shot.

"You got him through the heart, all right," said Mr. Selby cheerfully. "Spine shot don't kill 'em. Load that cannon and pop him behind the boss in the back of his head. Knew a dead buffalo once that got up and killed the hunter."

I sighted on his neck and fired, and the great head dropped into the mud. I looked at him and shuddered. If anything, he looked meaner and bigger and tougher dead than alive.

"Not too bad a buff," Selby said. "Go forty-three, forty-four. Not apt to see a bigger one unless we're very lucky. Buff been picked over too much. He'd have been dead twenty yards inside the bush, but we didn't know that, did we? Kidogo! Adam! Taka head-skin!" he shouted to the gun bearers and sat down on the buffalo to light a cigarette. I was still shaking.

As I said, I was shooting a double-barreled Express rifle that fires a bullet as big as a banana. It is a 500-grain bullet powered by 75 grains of cordite. It has a striking force of 5,000 foot-pounds of energy. It had taken Mbogo in the chest. Its impact knocked him flat—2,500 pounds of muscle. Yet Mbogo had not known he was dead. He had gotten up and had romped off as blithely as if I had fired an air gun at his hawser-network of muscles, at his inch-thick hide that the natives use to make shields. What had stopped him was not the fatal shot at all, but Harry's back breaker.

"Fantastic beast," Selby murmured. "Stone-dead and didn't know it."

We stalked innumerable buffalo after that. I did not really snap out of the buffalo fog until we got back in Nairobi, to find that a friend, a professional hunter, had been badly gored twice and almost killed by a "dead" buffalo that soaked up a dozen slugs and then got up to catch another handful and still boil on to make a messy hash out of poor old Tony.

I am going back to Africa soon. I do not intend to shoot much. Certainly I will never kill another lion, nor do I intend to duplicate most of the trophies I acquired on the last one. But I will hunt Mbogo. In fear and trembling I will hunt Mbogo every time I see him, and I won't shoot him unless he is a mile bigger than the ones I've got. I will hate myself

9

while I crawl and shake and tremble and sweat, but I will hunt him. Once you've got the buffalo fever, the rest of the stuff seems mighty small and awful tame. This is why the wife of my bosom considers her spouse to be a complete and utter damned fool, and she may very well be right.

Field & Stream
January 1954

MY FIRST DEER, AND WELCOME TO IT

by Patrick F. McManus

F or a first deer, there is no habitat so lush and fine as a hunter's memory. Three decades and more of observation have convinced me that a first deer not only lives on in the memory of a hunter but thrives there, increasing in points and pounds with each passing year until at last it reaches full maturity, which is to say, big enough to shade a team of Belgian draft horses in its shadow at high noon. It is a remarkable phenomenon and worthy of study.

Consider the case of my friend Retch Sweeney and his first deer. I was with him when he shot the deer, and though my first impression was that Retch had killed a large jackrabbit, closer examination revealed it to be a little spike buck. We were both only 14 at the time and quivering with excitement over Retch's good fortune in getting his first deer. Still, there was no question in either of our minds that what he had bagged was a spike buck, only slightly larger than a bread box.

You can imagine my surprise when, scarcely a month later, I overheard Retch telling some friends that his first deer was a nice four-point buck. I mentioned to Retch afterwards that I was amazed at how fast his deer was growing. He said he was a little surprised himself but was pleased it was doing so well. He admitted that he had known all along that the deer was going to get bigger eventually although he hadn't expected it to happen so quickly. Staring off into the middle distance, a dreamy expression on his face, he told me, "You know, I wouldn't be surprised if someday my first deer becomes a world's-record trophy."

"I wouldn't either," I said. "In fact, I'd be willing to bet on it."

Not long ago, Retch and I were chatting with some of the boys down at Kelly's Bar & Grill and the talk turned to first deer. It was disgusting. I

11

can stand maudlin sentimentality as well as the next fellow, but I have my limits. Some of those first deer had a mastery of escape routines that would have put Houdini to shame. Most of them were so smart there was some question in my mind as to whether the hunter had bagged a deer or a Rhodes scholar. I wanted to ask them if they had tagged their buck or awarded it a Phi Beta Kappa key. And big! There wasn't a deer there who couldn't have cradled a baby grand piano in its rack. Finally it was Retch's turn, and between waves of nausea I wondered whether that little spike buck had developed enough over the years to meet this kind of competition. I needn't have wondered.

Retch's deer no longer walked in typical deer fashion; it "ghosted" about through the trees like an apparition. When it galloped, though, the sound was "like thunder rolling through the hills." And so help me, "fire flickered in its eyes." Its tracks "looked like they'd been excavated with a backhoe, they were that big." Smart? That deer could have taught field tactics at West Point. Retch's little spike buck had come a long way, baby.

At last Retch reached the climax of his story. "I don't expect you boys to believe this," he said, his voice hushed with reverence, "but when I dropped that deer, the mountain trembled!"

The boys all nodded, believing. Why, hadn't the mountain trembled for them too when they shot their first deer? Of course it had. All first deer are like that.

Except mine.

I banged the table for attention. "Now," I said, "I'm going to tell you about a real first deer, not a figment of my senility, not some fossilized hope of my gangling adolescence, but a real first deer."

Now I could tell from looking at their stunned faces that the boys were upset. There is nothing that angers the participants of a bull session more than someone who refuses to engage in the mutual exchange of illusions, someone who tells the simple truth, unstretched, unvarnished, unembellished, and whole.

"Even though it violates the code of the true sportsperson," I began, "I must confess that I still harbor unkind thoughts for my first deer. True to his form and unlike almost all other first deer, he has steadfastly refused to grow in either my memory or imagination; he simply stands there in original size and puny rack, peering over the lip of my consciousness, an insolent smirk decorating his pointy face. Here I offered that thankless creature escape from the anonymity of becoming someone else's second or seventh or seventeenth deer or, at the very least, from an old age presided over by coyotes. And how did he repay me? With humiliation!"

The boys at Kelly's shrank back in horror at this heresy. Retch Sweeney tried to slip away, but I riveted him to his chair with a maniacal laugh. His eyes pleaded with me. "No, don't tell us!" they said. "Don't destroy the myth of the first deer!" (which is a pretty long speech for a couple of beady, bloodshot eyes).

Unrelenting and with only an occasional pause for a bitter, sardonic cackle to escape my foam-flecked lips, I plunged on with the tale, stripping away layer after layer of myth until at last the truth about one man's first deer had been disrobed and lay before them in all its grim and naked majesty, shivering and covered with goose bumps.

I began by pointing out what I considered to be one of the great bureaucratic absurdities of all time: that a boy at age 14 was allowed to purchase his first hunting license and deer tag but was prevented from obtaining a driver's license until he was 16. This was like telling a kid he could go swimming but to stay away from the water. Did the bureaucrats think that trophy mule deer came down from the hills in the evening to drink out of your garden hose? The predicament left you no recourse but to beg the adult hunters you knew to take you hunting with them on weekends. My problem was that all the adult hunters I knew bagged their deer in the first couple of weeks of the season, and from then on I had to furnish my own transportation. This meant that in order to get up to the top of the mountain where the trophy mule deer hung out, I had to start out at four in the morning if I wanted to be there by noon. I remember one time when I was steering around some big boulders in the road about three-quarters of the way up the Dawson Grade and a Jeep with two hunters in it came plowing up behind me, I pulled over so they could pass. The hunters grinned at me as they went by. You'd think they'd never before seen anyone pedaling a bike 20 miles up the side of a mountain to go deer hunting.

I had rigged up my bike especially for deer hunting. There were straps to hold my rifle snugly across the handlebars, and saddlebags draped over the back fender to carry my gear. The back fender had been reinforced to support a sturdy platform, my reason for this being that I didn't believe the original fender was stout enough to support a buck when I got one. My one oversight was failing to put a guard over the top of the bike chain, in which I had to worry constantly about getting my tongue caught. Deer hunting on a bike was no picnic.

A mile farther on and a couple of hours later I came to where the fellows in the Jeep were busy setting up camp with some other hunters. Apparently, someone told a fantastic joke just as I went pumping by because they all collapsed in a fit of laughter and were doubled over and rolling on the ground and pounding trees with their fists. They seemed like a bunch of lunatics to me, and I hoped they didn't plan on hunting in the same area was I headed for. I couldn't wait to see their faces when I came coasting easily back down the mountain with a trophy buck draped over the back of my bike.

One of the main problems with biking your way out to hunt deer was that, if you left at four in the morning, by the time you got to the hunting place there were only a couple of hours of daylight left in which to do your hunting. Then you had to spend some time resting, at least until the pounding of your heart eased up enough not to frighten the deer.

As luck would have it, just as I was unstrapping my rifle from the handlebars, a buck mule deer came dancing out of the brush not 20 yards away from me. Now right then I should have known he was up to no good. He had doubtless been lying on a ledge and watching me for hours as I pumped my way up the mountain. He had probably even snickered to himself as he plotted ways to embarrass me.

All the time I was easing the rifle loose from the handlebars, digging a shell out of my pocket, and thumbing it into the rifle, the deer danced and clowned and cut up all around me, smirking the whole while. The instant I jacked the shell into the chamber, however, he stepped behind a tree. I darted to one side, rifle at the ready. He moved to the other side of the tree and stuck his head out just enough so I could see him feigning a yawn. As I moved up close to the tree, he did a rapid tiptoe to another tree. I heard him snort with laughter. For a whole hour he toyed with me in this manner, enjoying himself immensely. Then I fooled him, or at least so I thought at the time. I turned and started walking in a dejected manner back toward my bike, still watching his hiding place out of the corner of my eye. He stuck his head out to see what I was up to. I stepped behind a small bush and knelt as if to tie my shoe. Then, swiftly I turned, drew a bead on his head, and fired. Down he went.

I was still congratulating myself on a fine shot when I rushed up to his crumpled form. Strangely, I could not detect a bullet hole in his head, but one of his antlers was chipped and I figured the slug had struck there with sufficient force to do him in. "No matter," I said to myself, "I have at last got my first deer," and I pictured in my mind the joyous welcome I would receive when I came home hauling in a hundred or so pounds of venison. Then I discoverd my knife had fallen out of its sheath during my frantic pursuit of the deer. Instant anguish! The question that nagged my waking moments for years afterwards was: Did the deer know that I had dropped my knife? Had I only interpreted it correctly, the answer to that question was written all over the buck's face—he was still wearing that stupid smirk.

"Well," I told myself," what I'll do is just load him on my bike, haul him down to the lunatic hunters' camp, and borrow a knife from them to dress him out with." I thought this plan particularly good in that it would offer me the opportunity to give those smart alecks a few tips on deer hunting.

Loading the buck on the bike was much more of a problem than I had expected. When I draped him crosswise over the platform on the rear fender, his head and front quarters dragged on one side and his rear quarters on the other. Several times as I lifted and pulled and hauled, I thought I heard a giggle, but when I looked around nobody was there. It was during one of these pauses that a brilliant idea occurred to me. With herculean effort, I managed to arrange the deer so that he was sitting astraddle of the platform, his four legs splayed out forward and his head drooping down. I lashed his front feet to the handlebars, one on each side. Then I slid up onto the seat ahead of him, draped his head over my right shoulder, and pushed off.

I must admit that riding a bike with a deer on behind was a good deal more difficult than I had anticipated. Even though I pressed down on the brake for all I was worth, our wobbling descent was much faster than I would have liked. The road was narrow, twisting, and filled with ruts

15

and large rocks, with breathtaking drop-offs on the outer edge. When we came hurtling around a sharp, high bend above the hunters' camp, I glanced down. Even from that distance I could see their eyes pop and their jaws sag as they caught sight of us.

What worried me most was the hill that led down to the camp. As we arrived at the crest of it, my heart, liver, and kidneys all jumped in unison. The hill was much steeper than I had remembered. It was at that point that the buck gave a loud, startled snort.

My first deer had either just regained consciousness or been shocked out of his pretense of death at the sight of the plummeting grade before us. We both tried to leap free of the bike, but he was tied on and I was locked in the embrace of his front legs.

When we shot past the hunters' camp, I was too occupied at the moment to get a good look at their faces. I heard afterwards that a game warden found them several hours later, frozen in various postures and still staring at the road in front of their camp. The report was probably exaggerated, however, game wardens being little better than hunters at sticking to the simple truth.

I probably would have been able to get the bike stopped sooner and with fewer injuries to myself if I had had enough sense to tie down the deer's hind legs. As it was, he started flailing wildly about with them and somehow managed to get his hooves on the pedals. By the time we reached the bottom of the mountain he not only had the hang of pedaling but was showing considerable talent for it. He also seemed to be enjoying himself immensely. We zoomed up and down over the rolling foothills and into the bottomlands, with the deer pedaling wildly and me shouting and cursing and trying to wrest control of the bike from him. At last he piled us up in the middle of a farmer's pumpkin patch. He tore himself loose from the bike and bounded into the woods, all the while making obscene gestures at me with his tail. I threw the rifle to my shoulder and got off one quick shot. It might have hit him too if the bike hadn't been still strapped to the rifle.

"Now that," I said to the boys at Kelly's, "is how to tell about a first deer—a straightforward factual report unadorned by a lot of lies and sentimentality."

Unrepentant, they muttered angrily. To soothe their injured feelings, I told them about my second deer. It was so big it could cradle a baby grand piano in its rack and shade a team of Belgain draft horses in its shadow at high noon. Honest! I wouldn't lie about a thing like that.

They Shoot Canoes, Don't They?
Holt, Rinehart & Winston, 1977

"DUCKS? YOU BAT YOU!"

by Gordon MacQuarrie

T onight is the end of summer. A needle-fine rain is pelting the shingles. Autos swish by on wet concrete. Until now summer has been in full command. This full, cold rain is the first harbinger of autumn.

Maybe the cold rain started me off. A flood of recollections of my first duck-hunting trip crowds everything else from my mind. Just such a rain—only colder—was falling from northern Wisconsin skies that night in late October, many years ago, when the President of the Old Duck Hunters' Association, Inc., rapped at my door.

It was an impatient rap. I found him standing in the hall, quizzical, eager, in his old brown mackinaw that later was to become his badge of office. As always, only a top button of the mackinaw was fastened. His brown felt hat dripped rain. Below the sagging corners of the mackinaw were high tan rubber boots. He danced a brief jig, partly to shake off the rain and partly to celebrate an impending duck hunt.

"Hurry up!" he said.

"Where?"

"You're going duck hunting."

That was news. I had never been duck hunting. Not once in a varied life devoted to fishing and hunting had I ever hunted ducks. For some reason, ducks had not appealed to me. They had just been something that flew over a lake where I was fishing late in the year. I didn't know it then, but I was much like a person who has grown to maturity without having read *Robinson Crusoe*.

"Shut the door!" a voice cried from within my house.

It was my wife, the daughter of the President, the only person who awes Mr. President. He shuffled through the door with alacrity and took a tongue-lashing for sprinkling water on the floor.

18

"Who's going duck hunting?" demanded the lady, adding, "and who says who can go duck hunting? Isn't it enough that he spends all his idle moments fishing?"

"It's like this," began Hizzoner. "I told him last summer that now, since he was more or less one of the family, I ought to take him duck hunting. He's been at our house eating ducks and currant jam for years. Why shouldn't he contribute to the—er—groaning board?"

"I see," said the daughter of the President cannily. "You want someone to row the boat."

"I do not!" he replied indignantly. "I even borrowed a gun for him."

"You'll find he won't row. He won't even put up curtain rods. He looks like a dead loss for both of us."

"I'll take a chance on him."

From a closet she helped me resurrect heavy clothing, including an old sheepskin coat. When I was ready, the President advised his only heir that he would return the body safely some time the next evening. It was then about eight P.M. The lady whom I had wed only some four months previously sat down resignedly with a magazine. Her parting injunction was: "Mallards. Get some mallards."

A loaded car was at the curb. Wedged in a corner of the backseat beside duffel and a crate of live duck decoys was a huge figure that answered to the name of Fred. Later I was to learn that better duck shots have seldom displayed their wares on any of our local waters.

Down sandy Highway 35 with the rain streaking the windshield, off to the right at the store in Burnett County, over the humpbacked hills, then into a yard beyond which a light from a house gleamed among huge oak trees. As we drove up, a floodlight came on as though someone within the house had been waiting for us.

It was Norm. Always there is a Norm for duck hunters who really mean it, some vigilant sentinel of the marshes who phones to say, "The flight is in." Norm was apprehensive. As we stored things in our allotted cabin we did not have to be reminded by him that it was growing colder. The rain was abating, and a northwest wind was rocking the oaks. "Little Bass may be frozen over," said Norm. "You should have come when I first phoned, two days ago. The temperature has fallen from fifty-five to forty since sunset."

We occupied the cabin. There were two full-sized beds. Norm built up a roaring jack-pine fire in the little airtight stove. There was much palaver along instructional lines for my benefit. Later my two bene-factors prepared for bed.

"We'll give you the single bed," said the President magnanimously. "Fred and I are used to sleeping together. We'll put this extra blanket between the beds. Whoever gets cold and needs it can just reach over for it. Good night."

In five minutes they were asleep. Outside the wind rose. Even before I fell asleep, only half warm, I contemplated the probability of grabbing that blanket. Later I woke. I was somewhat congealed. I reached for the blanket. It was gone. I tried to fall asleep without it, but the cold was steadily growing worse.

Teeth chattering, I got up, lit a kerosene lamp and discovered the blanket carefully tucked around the two sleeping forms in the other bed. Sound asleep and snoring gently lay my two kind old friends. I wouldn't for the world snake that blanket off their aging bones. Not me.

I piled all available clothing on top of my own thin blanket and tried again to sleep. At times I almost succeeded, but it was along toward 3:30 A.M. when I got up, lit a fire in the stove and thawed out. Then I dozed in an old rocking chair, to be awakened soon by a loud thumping on the single wall of the cabin.

It was Norm delivering his summons to his hunters. I turned up the wick on the lamp. The President and Fred awakened languorously. The President sat upright, threw his legs over the edge of the bed and studied the top of the table where the blanket had rested.

"Just looking for scratches in the varnish," he said. "Dreamed last night I heard someone reaching for that blanket. Wasn't you, was it? Surely a young man with your abounding vitality wouldn't be needing an extra blanket?"

"Why, we've got the blanket ourselves," chimed in Fred. "Now isn't that funny? Do you know, I had a dream too. Dreamed I was cold in the night and got up and took the derned blanket."

Since then I have learned to get that extra blanket in a hurry.

In Norm's kitchen there was a beaming platter of eggs and bacon. When it was empty, the platter was refilled with sour-cream pancakes, such as people often talk about but seldom can get. And after that a big white coffeepot was passed around as the Old Duck Hunters', Inc., washed down layer after layer of toast.

Outside it was bitter cold. The first real arctic blast had helped to dry the sand roads. Where it did not dry them the cold froze them, so that the car lurched and bumped along the ruts. There was the faintest hint of dawn as the car turned through a cornfield, plunged over rough ground a hundred yards and came to a stop near the base of a long point thrusting into the middle of a narrow, shallow lake.

This point on Little Bass Lake was—and still is—one of the most sought-after ducking points in northwest Wisconsin. Situated north of Big Yellow, this shallow lake with its swampy shores is a natural haven for ducks escaping bombardment on the bigger lake.

From a nearby patch of scrub oak the President hauled at something until, in the faint light, I saw he had hold of a duck boat. I helped him drag it to the water. He paddled off through thin ice inshore to spread the decoys in open water. While he was busy at this morning ritual the searing slash of duck wings came down to us a half dozen times. Fred called to him to hurry, but no one hurries the President when he is making a set.

Finally he came ashore and occupied the small scrub oak blind alongside mine. Even then he was not content to sit and wait, as was Fred in the nearby blind, but counted over and over again the wooden decoys. And was dissatisfied when he had 32. "Anyone knows you've got to have an uneven number. Why, thirteen is better than any even number!" he chafed.

I just sat. Said I to myself, "So this is duck hunting." Just sit and wait.

Then there was a searing roar in back of us. I was about to raise my head to see what it was, but the mittened hand of Mr. President seized my shoulder and pulled me down to the sand floor of the blind. He himself seemed to be groveling in the sand, and from the nearby cover where Fred skulked I heard him stage-whisper: "Don't move. They're flying in back to look us over."

Twice again the sound of many wings cleaving the frosty air was borne down to us. At no time did I dare look up. The sound faded, disappeared entirely, then swelled again, louder and louder. When it seemed it could grow no louder, it changed to a hissing diminuendo. That sound was my first introduction to the music of stiff, set wings on a long glide down.

"Now!" Maybe it was Fred who said it, maybe it was Mr. President.

Before I had thrust my head over the parapet of scrub oak Fred's 32-inch double had sounded and the President, who shot a pump in those

21

days, had fired once and was grunting and straining to operate the action for the next shot. He had to catch that old corn sheller of his just right to make it throw the empty out and a new shell in. Always, whether it worked smoothly or not, the President gave off a groaning, whining sound between shots, like an angry terrier held back from a square meal. He got off three shots before I could make out a low-flying squad of dark objects hightailing across the lake.

"Bluebills," said the President.

On the open water beyond the rushes and in the quieter water on the very thin ice were five objects. I dragged the duck boat from its thicket and retrieved them. One of them had green on its wings. "What the—?" said Fred. "Look, Al! One greenwing among those bluebills."

So this was duck hunting. Well, not bad. Not bad at all. Indeed not!

The sounds of swift wings and booming guns were good sounds. The smell of burned powder was a good smell. The feel of those birds, warm in a bare hand, was a good feeling. My toes had been cold; now they were tingling. I knew those five ducks would go best with wild rice and currant jelly. They made a nice little pile at our feet in the blind.

After a while Gus Blomberg, who owned the point and lived in a little house 500 yards back of us, came down through the oaks to see what was going on. He took a chew of snuff and said: "Halloo-o-o! How iss it, eh? Nice docks, you bat you!"

Great guy, Gus. Fred gave him a dollar. That was for the use of his point. Gus said "Tenk you," and also, "How 'bout leetle coffee at noon, eh? Goes good cold day. You bat you!"

Gus went away. The President stood up occasionally and beat his mitts together to warm his fingers. Fred just sat. He had enough fat to keep him warm. I never saw him wear gloves in a blind, even on frightfully cold December mornings. All Fred wore was his old shooting jacket and a cigarette. He could keep his cigarette lit in a cloudburst.

Other ducks came in. Some went on, and some stayed. After a while it occurred to me that I might try a shot at a duck myself.

"Haven't you had your gun here all this time?" asked the President. And he meant it; he had been too busy to think of anything but that early-morning flight. He took me back to the car and unearthed a short-barreled hammerlock, the fore piece of which was held firm by close-wrapped wire.

"It's the best I could find around the neighborhood," he said. "The choke has been sawed off. Don't shoot at anything unless it's on top of you.''

So I had a gun. This duck-hunting business was getting better and better.

Back in the blind, Fred had a couple more down. A flock of four bluebills came in. They were trusting souls. They neither circled nor hesitated. They came spang in, from straight out in front, low. They set their wings. I picked out one and fired—both barrels. One fell at the second shot.

My first duck! Lying out there on the thin ice, white breast up, dead as a doornail. The President and Fred had declined to shoot. They were furthering the education of a novice. They were, in fact, letting the duck-hunting virus take full effect. They laughed at me and pounded me on the back and kidded me, and all day after that they seemed to get an awful kick out of just looking at me and grinning.

About noon it began to snow. The wind fell off. The decoys froze in tightly. Fred stirred and said, "Coffee!" Hizzoner explained to me that it was necessary to pull in the blocks before leaving the blind. I was glad for the exercise. After coffee and some of the other things had been duly consumed, we returned to the blind, Fred to his motionless waiting. Hizzoner to his quick, birdlike neck craning.

The President usually saw the ducks first and signaled Fred. It did not perturb Fred much. The only sign of excitement from him was a gradual drawing-in of his neck, turtlelike. Then he would stamp out the last quarter inch of his cigarette and wait. At the crucial moment he didn't stand to fire; he just straightened out his legs and sort of rared up. He was by far the best duck shot I have ever seen.

Maybe I killed another duck; I am not sure. From then on I shot with the others. They had let me have my chance. I had killed a duck. It had been an easy shot. They knew that. So did I. But they did not speak of it. They just kept grinning, for they must have known I had been ordained to love the game and they were glad to help a natural destiny work itself out.

They grinned when I threw myself into the small chores that beset the duck hunter. Dragging the duck boat from the thicket for a pickup, cutting new boughs for the blind, walking around the sedgy shore of Little Bass to pick up a cripple that had drifted over, driving back for a package of cigarettes for Fred.

To all these tasks I set myself eagerly. They came as part of the game.

23

Those two rascals had frozen me the night before; but they had introduced me to something new and something good, and I was grateful.

Since then, while hunting with these two I have felt this obligation to do my part. Both are many years older than I, and they have appreciated it, but, of course, never mentioned it. They would prefer to guy me with mild rebuke, criticize my shooting and otherwise continue the good work already well begun.

Of such stuff are the recollections of that first ducking trip. Diverse images, grateful peeks back at two wise and capable practitioners of what has become for me the most dramatic thing in outdoor sports.

The outdoors holds many things of keen delight. A deer flashing across a burn, a squirrel corkscrewing up a tree trunk, a sharptail throbbing up from the stubble—all these have their place in my scheme of things. But the magic visitation of ducks from the sky to a set of bobbing blocks holds more of beauty and heart-pounding thrill than I have ever experienced afield with rod or gun. Not even the sure, hard pluck of a hard-to-fool brown trout, or the lurching smash of a river smallmouth has stirred me as has the circling caution of ducks coming to decoys.

The afternoon wore on. Shortly before quitting time Gus came back, to stand with Fred for a chance at a few mallards. He took a brace and was satisfied. Mr. President said he thought he'd take a walk around the north end of Little Bass "just for the fun of it." Gus said he might find a mallard or two if there was open water, "but you got to sneak opp on dem. You bat!"

"You bat you, too, Gus," said the President. He buttoned the second button on the brown mackinaw and headed into the swirling flakes.

Fred lit a cigarette. We waited. Collars and mittens were now soggy with snow water. Fred's magic cigarette somehow managed to stay lit and in the waning light glowed more brightly. From the north end of the lake came four reports, muffled by the distance and the snow.

"Ay hope iss dem mollard," said Gus. "Al, he like dem mollard, you bat you!"

We were picked up and packed up when the President returned. The President had two mallards, of course. He dropped them in the car trunk with the other birds and unbuttoned the top button of the old brown mackinaw. We stood in the snow and said good-bye to Gus. Added to his

24

brace of birds were three more that Fred gave him. He turned and walked away through the rasping cornstalks with a final, "You bat you!"

The President addressed me: "How'd you like it?"

In those days I was very young. It took me a long time to try to say what I felt. I have never succeeded yet. I simply babbled.

We drove out of the cornfield, stopped to yell good-bye to Norm, who came out to his back door to wave, and then headed for the main highway. I drove. Fred reposed in the back, comfortable as the clucking ducks against whose crate he leaned. At my side sat the President. The light from the cowl partly illuminated his strong, sharp features.

Finally I said: "Wish you had let me in on this earlier in the season. There won't be another duck weekend after today."

The President flicked cigar ashes and replied: "I thought of that, but decided to break it to you gently. Too much of a good thing is bad for a growing boy."

Stories of the Old Duck Hunters & Other Drivel
Willow Creek Press, 1979

BEAR ATTACK!

by Ed Wiseman
AS TOLD TO
Jim Zumbo

The bear came at me with no warning. Ears flattened, neck hairs stiffly erect, it growled fiercely as it charged, full bore, right at me. I saw its flashing teeth as it came, and I knew in an instant it was a grizzly, although I'd never seen one in the wild before. There was no mistaking the hump on its back, the broad face and the guard hairs. I've seen a couple of hundred black bears in the woods, enough to know that this one was entirely different from the rest.

The grizzly's attack started about 30 yards away, and I had no time to raise my bow and arrow. For a brief moment I thought the bear would go around me. Maybe its charge was a bluff. I'd had close confrontations with black bears before, and even had them approach me, but they all eventually backed off, giving me nothing more than a good scare.

This bear kept coming, growling and snapping its teeth with each terrifying bound. When I realized it meant business, I shouted at the top of my lungs, but it was no use. In two more leaps, the bear would be all over me.

I'm 46, a full-time outfitter, and I make my living taking people hunting and fishing. I was raised in Colorado and live in Crestone, near Alamosa. Fourteen years ago, I decided to go into outfitting and I've been at it ever since. The country I hunt is one of the most remote regions in the Rocky Mountains of Colorado.

I had four elk hunters out that day, the last day of the 1979 bow season. The weather was balmy, with bright blue skies, and the warm temperature made for comfortable hunting, although it got chilly in the evening.

My hunters were W. C. Niederee and his son, Mike, from Great

26

Bend, Kansas, and Rick Nelson and Jim Latin, both from McPherson, Kansas. On that last day, Ace Calloway guided Rick and Jim, Chuck Gibbs guided Dr. Niederee, and I took Mike. Al Brandenburg, my cook, remained in camp.

Dr. Niederee decided to hunt on a slope opposite camp that day. The rest of us rode out of camp together and split up about three miles down the trail. Ace, Rick and Jim rode south to hunt the East Fork of the Navajo River; Mike and I headed west for the Main Fork.

Mike was the only hunter in the party who hadn't seen elk that week. Everyone had seen plenty of animals, and Rick said he'd looked at about 85. I figured the Main Fork would be a good place to show elk because I knew of some pockets that were always good. The area was just off the Continental Divide; it was rugged country that few people penetrated. It was about 11 miles by trail from camp to the place I wanted to hunt, about five miles overland.

About two P.M., we tied our horses in the timber and began to hunt on foot. We split up and planned to meet at the other end of the meadows, where I'd intercept Mike. Although I carried my bow, I wasn't really hunting intently. I figured on looking for elk sign and later meeting Mike.

I worked my way along and kept my eyes on some open meadows in the timber. I thought I'd see Mike as he traveled through them. He never appeared, so I wandered up toward the horses to see if he'd returned to meet me there. Freckles, my Apaloosa mare, and Buckshot, Mike's horse, stood quietly in the trees. Mike wasn't around.

I headed back down to look for more sign. We were in a small finger off the main ridge, and I knew there was a good chance that Mike and I would meet. About five o'clock, while walking across a small flat, I heard an ominous growl a short distance away.

For a moment, while the grizzly charged straight at me, I thought it might be trying to get around me. But I quickly discounted that possibility as the bear narrowed the distance to just a few yards, still coming full steam. At close range, I could easily see the hump on its back and the yellow guard hairs. The bear growled continuously, and its open mouth exposed a set of huge teeth. My shouts, which might have startled or turned another bear, had no effect. This grizzly was enraged, and I was in bad trouble.

The charge lasted only a few seconds. I was carrying my compound bow at my side, but there was no time to nock an arrow. My knife was in my day pack, well out of reach for the precious split second I had.

The bear was almost on top of me when I raised my bow, trying to fend off the attack. I shoved it in the grizzly's face, but it bowled me over. The bow clattered to the ground, and arrows scattered everywhere.

As soon as I hit the ground I curled up into a ball. I brought my knees up under my belly to protect my vitals, stuck my face into my chest as far as I could, and clasped both hands behind my head to cover my neck. My day pack was still on my back, and would offer some protection there. I had read many articles that said playing dead was the thing to do during a bear attack. I knew that no man is a physical match with an enraged bear.

The grizzly immediately started mauling my right leg with its teeth. I had little sensation of pain, but I vividly remember the sounds of flesh tearing as the bear ripped into me. As I lay there helplessly, my only hope was that the grizzly would tire of me and leave.

It kept biting and chewing at my leg, and I forced myself to lie as quietly as I could. I still felt that if I didn't present myself as a threat to the bear, it would quit and lumber off into the woods. Strange as it might seem, I never panicked, even as the grizzly continued to work over that right leg.

I felt the bear dragging me slightly, but most of the time it would bite into my leg, shake its head and bite into the leg again. It didn't use its huge claws, just its teeth.

Then the bear dropped my leg and bit into my right shoulder. It clamped down hard, and penetrated my flesh deeply with its powerful jaws. I didn't know it then, but the bear had bitten completely through my shoulder, from one side to the other. Later, at the hospital, doctors found puncture wounds all the way through. Clinical tests also showed it bit my shoulder twice, but there was no tearing, just deeply penetrating bites.

When the bear let go of my shoulder and started on my leg again, I remember telling myself, This could be the end.

At that point I realized that this was more than a passing attack. Playing dead was getting me nowhere, so I desperately started thinking about fighting back. If the mauling kept up, the grizzly would surely kill me.

28

In the blur of the ordeal, I saw an arrow lying close by. I reached for it, and because of good luck or providence, it was pointing toward the bear.

I'm convinced that my hunting background was a factor that weighed heavily in my survival. I always trained myself to instinctively shoot at one part of an animal rather than the whole thing. I focused all my attention on the grizzly's frontal portion and brought the arrow up with as powerful a thrust as I could muster, all the while concentrating intently on a small spot that I judged to be vital. I'm right-handed, but the arrow was in my left. I plunged it deeply into the bear. Years ago, I was a meat cutter. I know something about animal anatomy, but lying on the ground with a bear tearing into me, I wasn't sure I could drive it away before it killed me. Survival was all I could think of then, and I knew I must try.

The arrow I used, a new Bear razorhead fitted on a magnum aluminum shaft, is one of the strongest made. Somehow, the arrow snapped in half after I drove it into the bear. I remember reading about people who have by some incredible force lifted wrecked cars off their loved ones; the human brain in such cases goes momentarily haywire and the adrenalin flows. Maybe that's what happened to me. All my senses were fine-tuned to driving off that grizzly. There was no other choice.

After the shaft broke, I reached for the arrow and yanked it back out of the grizzly. A stream of blood flowed from the wound, and I rammed the broken arrow back in again as hard as I could. I remember thinking that the blood looked like it was coming from the jugular. I was convinced I had struck a pretty good blow. At that point I thought, Maybe I've got a chance.

The grizzly gave no indication of being hurt and kept biting and tearing at my leg. It kept on growling, just as it had done throughout the entire attack. Right after I stabbed it, it started on my left leg for the first time.

Suddenly, the bear stopped working me over and walked over the top of me. A great gush of blood from the bear's arrow wounds splashed over me as the animal stepped across. The grizzly loped off and stopped about 25 yards away. I saw it slowly lower itself to the ground. It lay still, and I knew it was dead.

I was off in a side finger of the drainage, and my only hope was to make it to the main trail where I might be found. I didn't realize it at the time, but Mike was only a couple of hundred yards away from me throughout the entire ordeal.

I got up slowly, unsure whether my mangled right leg could hold my weight. I tested it carefully and was relieved to find that I could walk. The main trail wasn't far, and I started for it standing up. The bleeding was starting to take its toll, though, and I felt myself going into shock.

I was about 90 yards from the scene of the attack when I heard Mike shout. I was surprised and relieved to hear him. I shouted back, and he appeared in the timber moments later.

Mike is 25 and a full-time farmer. He is tough and wiry, but when he walked out of the woods toward me, he looked like he'd seen a ghost. My physical appearance didn't help. I was covered with blood from the top of my head to the soles of my feet. Every square inch of my camouflage clothing was blood-soaked, and my face and hands were crimson.

Afterward, I learned that Mike had heard the bear growl as it charged me. He also heard my shouts. By the time he got to the scene, the attack was over, and all he could see was a great spot of blood-soaked ground, my bow and scattered arrows. He was convinced the bear had killed me and dragged me off. He moved slowly with a nocked arrow, figuring he'd be facing the bear too. Then he spotted the bear lying dead and realized I might be alive after all.

We used the limited supplies from a small first-aid kit to bandage my leg as well as we could, with strips of Mike's shirt for wrappings. I made myself as comfortable as possible, and Mike went for help. The sun was setting, and I knew I was in for a long, hard night.

By the time Mike returned with the horses, I had grown much weaker. He brought them over to where I lay, and they got jittery when they caught a whiff of the bear and the blood. Mike tied Buckshot by the reins, and when he led Freckles toward me, Buckshot reared back and shucked the bridle. The spooked horse took off.

Mike tried to position Freckles in a way that would be easiest for me to get aboard. But when I stood up, I lost consciousness. Mike eased me to the ground, and it was a while before I came to.

I tried a second time to get on the horse, with Mike pushing and lifting me. Freckles is a big horse, 17 hands high. That worked against me now. I got my foot into the stirrup, swung my mangled right leg over and grabbed the saddle horn. I talked to Freckles, who was still jittery, and she settled right down.

30

We started off, and Freckles got shaky again because of the strange smells. Mike was leading Freckles using only a lead rope and halter, so I told him to put the bridle back on. When he did, we had better control, and she calmed down some.

As we traveled, Mike led my horse, and he constantly looked back and said, "Ed, talk to me, talk to me." I was slumped over in the saddle, bent over to the front. That way I wouldn't pass out. If I tried to sit straight up, I'd feel myself getting dizzy and going under again. Mike tied my raincoat over the saddle horn to keep it from bouncing into my gut, but it was still painful to stay in the saddle. Riding wasn't helping my leg, which was still bleeding freely.

Mike wasn't sure of the country, and every once in a while, when my head cleared enough that I could look around, I'd give him directions to get us on the trail. I was having trouble maintaining full consciousness.

Finally we got to a large meadow, and I decided I could go no further. I knew it would be foolhardy to continue because camp was still some 10 miles away and I'd never make it. The meadow would serve as a good place for a helicopter to land. It was about seven in the evening, and I knew I had to rest and get my head down to where I could think straight. I was the only one who knew where we were, and I had to get Mike ready for what was in store for him. I had to describe in detail the overland route to base camp. If he took the trail, the way he had come, it would be an extra six miles or more, some of it with no visible trail. So he'd have to go across the mountains. It was the dark of the moon, and he had his work cut out for him.

Mike built a fire while I lay back and rested. He dragged wood to where I could reach it, but in his haste to get going for help, he didn't gather as much as I'd need. He piled all the extra clothes on top of me. I told him to follow a nearby stream bed up to a pond and then cross the Continental Divide. The ride downhill would be pretty steep going. But he'd come out about half a mile above camp.

I knew it was asking a lot of him to find camp during the blackness of the night, but I was confident that with the landmarks I'd described to guide him, along with trustworthy Freckles, he'd get there. All of my mountain horses are well oriented to the country, and they can find their way around as well as anyone.

After Mike left, I was as conservative as I could be with the firewood supply. As time wore on, though, I knew I was going to run out. The closest wood was some distance away, so I tried to burn a somewhat green log that Mike had inadvertently dragged over.

It started to get colder, and I knew I'd have to do something for warmth. I saw the outline of a log up the hill behind me, and it appeared there was some firewood around it. I rested again, did some isometric exercises to stimulate body heat a little, and covered my head with a jacket to retain as much heat as I could.

There was no way I'd be able to get up the hill and return to the original campfire with wood, so I started dragging myself along the ground, hoping to start another fire at the log. I used both arms and my left leg, and every move was a painful effort. I kept my head as low as possible to avoid passing out.

It was only 20 feet or so to the log. It seemed 10 times that far, but I kept myself from panicking. I concentrated on little things—like what I should do in the next hour, or two hours. I thought back about the sequence of events so far—I had survived a bear attack, my vital organs were intact, Mike was close by to assist me, I was at a point where I could be rescued, and now Mike was heading for help. I wouldn't entertain the thought that it wouldn't work. It would work. Help could be on its way by midnight, just an hour or so away. Dr. Niederee would be there with medical supplies and I'd have my sleeping bag to warm up in.

But help didn't come by midnight. The evening began to pass more slowly, and I wondered if the men might be having trouble finding me. I was in an area where we seldom hunted, and no one in the camp was familiar with that part of the country.

A new problem came up. The evening breeze grew stronger, and I began shivering. I had to find protection from the wind, and looked about for some kind of shelter. I saw a small pine tree not far off. Its thick boughs grew to the ground. It was my only hope for a windbreak, so I inched over to it, covered myself with the clothing I had available and tried to get comfortable. I didn't want to sleep, because if I slowed my body processes, I would only hasten hypothermia. The combination of shock and loss of blood made it dangerous to risk sleep. I had no choice but to stay alert.

While I lay there, I assessed my plight. I'm a practicing emergency medical technician, and I know something about vital life signs. If I could withstand the loss of blood and shock, hypothermia would be the only thing that could write the final chapter. Curiously enough, I was confident that I'd survive.

Suddenly, I saw two flashlights above me, coming off the ridge. I yelled and heard Mike shout back. He was alone, carrying a flashlight in each hand. It was about three in the morning. I'd been alone eight hours.

When he reached me, Mike immediately started a fire, but it was difficult because the wood was wet. Finally he got a good blaze going. I was eager for its warmth. He told me that his dad, Dr. Niederee, and Ace were on top of a high ridge. We spotted their flashlights, and they located us when they saw the fire. Mike hollered that he'd found me.

The position of their flashlights told me that they were too far down the canyon. They needed to go back to a patch of thick timber and then work their way down through it. Mike tried to warn them about a steep hillside near them, but they apparently didn't understand what he was saying.

About five A.M., Ace and Dr. Niederee appeared on foot, without medical supplies or sleeping bag. I learned that they had tried to work their way across some brush along the steep shale hillside when trouble began.

Ace's horse hit the shale, slipped and spun around. The doctor's horse, Puffer, slipped on the shale and slid about 10 feet down the mountain. Puffer somehow came to a stop, and Dr. Niederee eased out of the stirrups so as not to unbalance the horse. He got off, grabbed for a bush and fought his way up out of the loose shale. Puffer tried to get out but slid down another 100 feet. It was impossible for Ace and the doctor to get to the horse in the dark.

Later that morning some of my men tried to get Puffer out. They got the saddle, sleeping bag and medical supplies and planned to come back the next day with more help. But it was too late. In his attempt to get out, Puffer went over the edge of the cliff and fell 200 feet to his death.

Dr. Niederee looked my leg over and saw there was no immediate danger. He was concerned about hypothermia. The men built a fire to warm the length of my body.

After I was comfortable and somewhat warm, we spent the rest of the night waiting for the helicopter that was to come in at daybreak. Mike built a fire where he wanted the helicopter to land.

It began to get light, and we strained to hear the helicopter, but it didn't come. Time began to drag because of the anticipation, and for the first time, I was beginning to look forward to going to the hospital.

About a half hour after daybreak the helicopter broke the Continental Divide, and we all heard it at the same time. It was a beautiful sound, and it didn't come any too soon. I was starting to shiver uncontrollably.

The Medivac team performed flawlessly and got me to Alamosa Community Hospital without a hitch. The pilot flabbergasted passers-by when he put the ship down smack in front of the emergency room door.

After the doctors looked me over, they quickly got me under an electric blanket. My temperature was down to 95 degrees, and my blood pressure was low. Dr. Niederee thought I'd lost as much as three pints of blood. My right leg from knee to ankle looked like hamburger. One of the small bones was broken, and there was infection as well as possible nerve damage. I also suffered bites on my left leg, both arms, and my right shoulder. I expect to go back in for surgery to help mend the broken bone in my leg, and some skin graft and nerve repair.

Now that the ordeal is over, I can't help but think back on incidents in my hunting territory. Once I guided a hunter who watched over a horse carcass as a bait. During the night, a bear dragged the horse, which weighed about 400 pounds, to an area about 100 yards away to feed on it. I assumed it was a big black, but now, I wonder if it could have been a grizzly.

About seven years ago, while I was away from my base camp, a bear moved in and destroyed it. I found seven-inch wide prints in the dirt. Again, I thought it was a big black bear.

Three of my clients have insisted that they've seen grizzlies. I know there are plenty of blacks in my territory; my hunters saw five during the 1979 elk bow season alone. The blacks are blond, brown, fire-engine red, black, and shades in between. I always figured those "grizzlies" were big blacks, but now I'm not so sure.

With the grizzly encounter now a matter of history, one of my most sincere hopes is that experiences like mine will not make people fear the outdoors. As always, any bear is to be respected for its potential danger, not feared. I don't know why the grizzly attacked me, but I have no qualms about going right back into that country as soon as I can. You can be sure of one thing, though. The next time I come across huge bear tracks, I'm going to wonder just what made them.

Bear Attack!

Postscript—About the Man and the Grizzly

Ed Wiseman didn't survive the grizzly attack because of luck. He is a powerful man, and he was able to use his strength against the bear. He did not wish to kill the bear and tried to avoid taking an aggressive stand until he realized it was a matter of life or death. Since the incident, Wiseman has repeatedly stated that he does not want people to fear bears, only respect them.

Since the attack, biologists have learned that the grizzly that attacked Wiseman was an old sow, more than 20 years old and weighing about 400 pounds.

Until this attack, grizzlies were thought to be extinct in Colorado. Two were killed in 1951, before the bears were declared an endangered species. Both were about three years old. One of them was killed just a dozen miles or so from the place where Wiseman was attacked.

Wiseman owns Toneda Outfitters in Crestone, Colorado, and hunts year-round. He uses hounds for cougars and bears. Wiseman runs a clean camp, and wants only serious hunters. He doesn't allow alcoholic beverages, because he wants his hunters to be in their best physical shape each day in the mountains. Although he accommodates gun hunters, he is a bow hunter himself and specializes in archery hunts. He is an official measurer for the Pope and Young Club.

Mike Niederee, who was with Wiseman during the attack, says, "Ed is one of the finest outdoorsmen I've ever known. There's a local saying that nobody keeps up with Ed Wiseman in the woods. He's simply the toughest guy around."

One of his nephews sums up Wiseman's abilities this way: "Of course Uncle Ed won the bear fight. He wins every time."

Outdoor Life
January 1980

DE SHOOTINEST GENT'MAN

by Nash Buckingham

Nash's most famous story has had a long and glorious career.

1916: First published in Casper Whitney's magazine, *Recreation*, where the editor, Edward Cave, bought it for $75, a good fee at that time for an unknown writer.

1927: Reprinted in the first combined issue of *Outdoor Life & Recreation*.

1930: Used in the anthology, *Classics of the American Shooting Field*, by John C. Phillips (president of American Wildfowlers) and Dr. Hill; 150 copies signed by Phillips, Hill and the artist Frank Benson.

Between 1930 and 1934: Used in a gunning anthology by Harry McGuire.

1934: Derrydale edition of *De Shootinest Gent'man*. (950 copies)

1941: Scribner's edition of the single story, *De Shootinest Gent'man*.

1943: Putnam edition, *De Shootinest Gent'man*.

1961: Nelson collection, *De Shootinest Gent'man and Other Hunting Tales*. (260 copies signed; also regular edition.)

In *Wild Fowl Decoys*, 1934, Joel Barber mentions a Windward House edition of *De Shootinest Gent'man* that I have been unable to locate.

Finally, I was presented with a taped recording of "De Shootinest Gent'man," read in 1965 by Robert Reaves of Manning, North Carolina.

Few writers have had a story published when they were 36, used again when they were 47, 50, about 52, 54, 61, 63, and 81. If "De Shootinest Gent'man" is a true story—and who would doubt it any more than the existence of Lady Luck and the Happy Hunting—then Nash Buckingham has Horace to thank not only for his best title (among some great ones) but for his immortality as a writer. It is by this story that Nash is known to 80 percent of his readers, many of whom think subliminally of Nash, not Mr. Money, as "De Shootinest Gent'man."

Like other stories in that first Derrydale collection, this was written during a period in Nash's life when that rich flow of Buckingham narrative was bursting to pour out under the pressure of his prime gunning years in an environment stiff with game and abounding with opportunity to shoot. Nash being Nash, the story would have to open with Molly's goose stew recipe. Irma Buckingham

36

Witt describes Horace's helpmeet, Molly, as "the original five-by-five, and, oh, how she could cook up, 'vittles'!"

The club is Beaver Dam, identified by Horace's presence and by the "Han'werker" blind. "The Judge"—James M. Greer—was a charter member of Beaver Dam.

Horace, as Horace always does, approaches perfection. Old photographs show him medium in height, not heavy, with full mustache, dressed not in hunting clothes, other than a shooting coat, but always wearing a vest, frequently a long overcoat, almost invariably a felt hat. But to see him you need no picture other than Nash's words and Horace's mellifluous expressions. I came across a letter to Nash from his literary agent, relaying the opinion of one editor that Nash should simplify the Negro dialect in a certain story. I'll wager Nash's reply was: "But that is what he said!" Horace's difficulty with Harold Money's British accent—so "queer an' brief lak"—and his wistful contemplation of "dat ole big bottle wid de gol' haid" are painted from life.

If Uncle Tomism in this story—and it is there—is objectionable, try to view a parallel situation with a French Canadian or a Swedish guide who has a weakness for the bottle. I certainly object to placing any man, whatever his race, in the position of a dog performing for a biscuit, and to try to brush it aside because it is funny doesn't work. But the story is so real I end up accepting it simply as what happened.

The legendary Captain Harold Money turns up sporadically in shooters' conversations, especially in the East and South. Nash wrote the story in 1916, but according to his inscription on a photograph it took place in 1908. In his files I found a copy of a letter in which he wrote in 1954 about Harold Money:

Harold Money, younger son of an old and honored British family, came to this country with his father, Capt. E. C. Money, who produced the earliest smokeless powders. They were a wonderful pair. Harold first attracted attention by winning the famous Carteret Handicap at live birds in the East and went on to become a professional exhibition shot for the old Winchester Repeating Arms Co. For several years his rating headed many lists.

When the circuits closed he'd come here to Memphis during the winter to enjoy the duck-club life. If there was ever a better all-around game shot, plus unselfish, gentlemanly spirit that endeared him to all, I have yet to meet him. I shot with Harold for many years, until 1908, when he returned to England.

Brilliantly educated, he was as much at home in an Indian wicki-up as at the court of St. James. From Ceylon he rushed into World War I. Years later, he returned to America and was with Abercrombie & Fitch in New York. He married the widow of the late Douglas Franchot and they retired to a lovely home on the Severn near Annapolis. He contracted pneumonia in the Adirondack Mountains two years later and passed on.

37

John Olin described Harold Money to me as he saw him first in 1913, after John had left Cornell and was working at his father's Western Cartridge plant at East Alton, Illinois: "Money was tall—six feet four or five—and he had been loading and handling the Velox smokeless powder, which we obtained from his father. It was made with picric acid and he was as yellow as a Chinaman."

A faded photograph in Nash's collection shows Harold Money beside a horse in a sedge field, fondling the ears of a pointer standing with its forepaws on Money's waist; he is wearing a tweed cap and a shooting coat, and his celebrated Winchester Model 97 is in the crook of his right arm. The photo is inscribed in Nash's writing: "Capt. Harold Money, champion gunner and ace sniper in W.W.I., home on a brief vacation. A dear friend."

Describing a live-pigeon match at Rogers Springs, Tennessee, in January 1910, Nash wrote: "I was shooting Harold Money's marvelously choked 1897-model Winchester trap gun that he left with me when he returned to England in 1908." (Nash won the shoot-off with 33 straight at 35 yards.)

Nash told John Bailey he had met Harold Money about 1905. "Nash told me," John said, "that Money was a superb shot on any kind of game except a quail covey rise. Said he was death on singles but the covey rise always troubled him." (Horace should have been there then.)

Next to his role in "De Shootinest Gent'man," Captain Harold Money was probably best known as a trap shot and third as a personality in Abercrombie & Fitch's gun department. Charles Wicks wrote me:

I worked with Harold Money for a numbers of years. He came with Abercrombie & Fitch in 1926 or '27. He was typically English, a meticulous dresser and always appeared as if he were scrubbed clean. He was a wonderful mixer, well mannered and liked by everybody. He liked to drink and I think he made bathtub gin and usually had a bottle hidden somewhere in the department, but he never was drunk although the aroma followed him.

He represented A&F at various shoots, New York Athletic Club, etc. and always shot his old Winchester M/97. Why, I do not know (I had expressed surprise than an Englishman did not shoot a double) only that he was a wonderful shot and apparently the M/97 was the gun for him. He told me that he never cleaned it outside of wiping it off. He said that the dirtier the barrel got, the tighter it shot.

Money was a friend of the old actor, Fred Stone, who did quite some shooting himself. Abercrombie & Fitch merged with Von Lengerke & Detmold in 1929 and Money was still with A&F. He was a good friend of a very wealthy man by the name of Franchot—I do not recall his first name. Franchot died and Money married the widow, I think in 1930. After this he did not have to work. They had a big place as I remember in Tulsa, Oklahoma, and a summer residence in the Adirondacks. Whenever he was in New York we had lunch together. I do not know when he died but think it was not long after he married. I would guess he was in his 60's.

38

De Shootinest Gent' man

Nash placed Harold Money's age at one year older than his own. The photograph in *De Shootinest Gent' man* shows him as suave, with dark hair gray at the temples, mixed-gray mustache and heavy eyebrows, whimsical mouth, somewhat large British nose, a shooter's gray eyes, a cigarette in a hand that had never worked, and an easy manner evident through the camera. His father, Captain E. C. Money, should not be confused with Captain A. W. Money, a live-bird shot who wrote *Pigeon Shooting* in 1896 under the pseudonym "Blue Rock."

As God made ducks and Horace, here is the story that made Nash Buckingham.

S upper was a delicious memory. In the matter of a certain goose stew, Aunt Molly had fairly outdone herself. And we, in turn, had jolly well done her out of practically all the goose. It may not come amiss to explain frankly and above board the entire transaction with reference to said goose. Its breast had been deftly detached, lightly grilled and sliced into ordinary "mouth-size" portions. The remainder of the dismembered bird, back, limbs, and all parts of the first part thereunto pertaining, were put into an iron pot. Keeping company with the martyred fowl, in due proportion of culinary wizardry, were sundry bell peppers, two cans of mock turtle soup, diced roast pork, scrambled ham rinds, peas, potatoes, some corn and dried garden okra, shredded onions, and pretty much anything and everything that Molly had lying loose around her kitchen. This stew, served right royally, and attended by outriders of "cracklin' bread," was flanked by a man-at-arms in the form of a saucily flavored brown gravy. I recall a side dish of broiled teal and some country puddin' with ginger pour-over, but merely mention these in passing.

So the Judge and I, in rare good humor (I forgot to add that there had been a dusty bottle of the Judge's famous port), as becomes sportsmen blessed with a perfect day's imperfect duck shooting, had discussed each individual bird brought to bag, with reasons, pro and con, why an undeniably large quota had escaped uninjured. We bordered upon that indecisive moment when bedtime should be imminent, were it not for the delightful trouble of getting started in that direction. As I recollect it, ruminating upon our sumptuous repast, the Judge had just countered my remark that I had never gotten enough hot turkey hash and beaten

39

biscuits, by stating decisively that his craving for smothered quail remained inviolate, when the door opened softly and in slid "Ho'ace"! He had come, following a custom of many years, to take final breakfast instructions before packing the embers in "Steamboat Bill," the stove, and dousing our glim.

Seeing upon the center table, twixt the Judge and me, a bottle and the unmistakable ingredients and tools of the former's ironclad rule for a hunter's nightcap, Ho'ace paused in embarrassed hesitation and seated himself quickly upon an empty shell case. His attitude was a cross between that of a timid gazelle scenting danger and a wary hunter sighting game and effacing himself gently from the landscape.

Long experience in the imperative issue of securing an invitation to "get his'n" had taught Ho'ace that it were ever best to appear humbly disinterested and thoroughly foreign to the subject until negotiations, if need be even much later, were opened with him directly or indirectly. With old-time members he steered along the above lines. But with newer ones or their uninitiated guests, he believed in quicker campaigning, or, conditions warranting, higher-pressure sales methods. The Judge, reaching for the sugar bowl, mixed his sweetening water with adroit twirl and careful scrutiny as to texture; fastening upon Ho'ace meanwhile a melting look of liquid mercy. In a twinkling, however, his humor changed and Ho'ace found himself in the glare of a forbidding menace, creditable in his palmiest days to Mister Chief Justice himself.

"Ho'ace," demanded the Judge, tilting into his now ready receptacle a gurgling, man's-size libation, "who is the best shot—the best duck shot—you have ever paddled on this lake—barring—of course, a-h-e-m-m—myself?" Surveying himself with the coyness of a juvenile, the Judge stirred his now beading toddy dreamily, and awaited the encore. Ho'ace squirmed a bit as the closing words of the Judge's query struck home with appalling menace upon his ear. He plucked nervously at his battered headpiece. His eyes, exhibiting a vast expanse of white, roamed pictured walls and smoke-dimmed ceiling in furtive, reflective, helpless quandary. Then, speaking slowly and gradually warming to his subject, he fashioned the following alibi.

"Jedge, y' know, suh, us all has ouh good an' ouh bad days wid de ducks. Yes, my lawdy, us sho' do. Dey's times whin de ducks flies all ovah ev'ything an' ev'ybody, an' still us kain't none o' us hit nuthin'—

40

lak me an' you wuz' dis mawnin', Jedge, down in de souf end trails." At this juncture the Judge interrupted, reminding Ho'ace severely that he meant when the Judge—not the Judge and Ho'ace—was shooting.

"An' den dey's times whin h'it look lak dey ain't no shot too hard nur nary duck too far not t' be kilt. But Mistah Buckin'ham yonder—Mistah Nash he brung down de shootin'est gent'man whut took all de cake. H'its lots o' de members he'ah whuts darin' shooters, but dat fren' o' Mistah Nash's—uummp-uummpphh—doan nevuh talk t' me 'bout him whur de ducks kin' hear, 'cause dey'll leave de laik ef dey known he's even comin' dis way.

"Dat gent'man rode me jes' lak he wax er saddle an' he done had on rooster spurs. Mistah Nash he brung him on down he'ah an' say: 'Ho'ace,' he say, 'he'ahs a gent'man frum Englan',' he say, 'Mistah Money—Mistah Horl' Money,'—an' say, 'I wants you t' paddle him t'morrow an' see dat he gits er gran' shoot—unnerstan'?' I say—'Yaas, suh, Mistah Nash,' I say, 'dat I'll sho'ly do, suh. Mistah Money gwi' hav' er fine picnic ef I has t' see dat he do m'se'f—but kin he shoot, suh?'

" 'Mistah Nash,' he say, 'Uh-why-uh-yaas, Ho'ace, Mistah Money he's uh ve'y fair shot—'bout lak Mistah Immitt Joyner or Mistah Hal Howard.' I say t' m'se'f, I say, 'Uummmpphh—huummpphh w-e-e-l-l he'ah now, ef dats de case me an' Mistah Money gwi' do some shootin' in de mawnin'.'

"Mistah Money he talk so kin'er queer an' brief lak, dat I hadda' pay mighty clos't inspection t'whut he all de time a-sayin'. But nex' maw- nin', whin me an' him goes out in de bote, I seen he had a gre't big ol' happy bottle o' Brooklyn Handicap in dat shell box so I say t' m'se'f, I say, 'W-e-l-l-l, me an' Mistah Money gwi' git erlong someway, us is.'

"I paddles him on up de laik an' he say t' me, say, 'Hawrice—uh— hav' yo'—er—got any wager,' he say, 'or proposition t' mek t' me, as regards,' he say, 't' shootin' dem dar eloosive wil' fowls?' he say.

"I kinder studies a minit, 'cause lak I done say, he talk so brief, den I says, 'I guess you is right 'bout dat, suh.'

"He say, 'Does you follow me, Hawrice, or is I alone?' he say.

"I says, 'Naw, suh, Mistah, I'm right he'ah wid you in dis bote.'

" 'You has no proposition t' mek wid me den?' he say.

"S' I, 'Naw, suh, Boss, I leaves all dat wid you, suh, trustin' t' yo' gin'rosity, suh.'

41

" 'Ve'y good, Hawrice,' he say. 'I sees you doan' grasp de principul. Now I will mek you de proposition,' he say. I jus' kep' on paddlin'. He say—'Ev'y time I miss er duck you gits er dram frum dis he'ah bottle—ev'y time I kills a duck, I gits de drink—which is h'it?—Come—come—speak up, my man.'

"I didn't b'lieve I done heard Mistah Money rightly an' I says—'Uh—Mistah Money,' I says, 'suh, does you mean dat I kin hav' de chice whedder you misses or kills e'vy time an' gits er drink?'

"He say—'Dat's my defi,' he say.

"I says—'Well, den—w-e-l-l—den, ef dats de case, I gwi', I gwi' choose ev'y time yo' misses, suh,' Den I say t' m'se'f, I say, 'Ho'ace, right he'ah whar you gotta be keerful, 'ginst you fall outa de bote an' git fired frum de Lodge; 'cause ef'n you gits er drink ev'ytime dis gent'man misses an' he shoot lak Mister Hal Howard, you an' him sho gwi' drink er worl' o' liquah—er worl' o' liquah.'

"I pushes on up nur'ly to de Han'werker stan', an' I peeks in back by da' l'il pocket whut shallers offn de laik, an' I sees some sev'ul black-jacks—four of 'em—settin' in dar. Dey done seen us, too. An' up come dey haids. I spy 'em twis'in' an' turnin'—gittin' raidy t' pull dey freight frum dere. I says, 'Mistah Money,' I say, 'yawnder sets some ducks—look out now, suh, 'cause dey gwi' try t' rush on out pas' us whin dey come outa dat pocket.' Den I think—'W-e-l-l, he'ah whar I knocks de gol' fillin' outa de mouf o' Mistah Money's bottle o' Brooklyn Handicap!'

"I raised de lid o' de shell box an' dar laid dat ol' bottle—still dar. I say, 'Uuuuummmpp-huuummpph.' Jus' 'bout dat time up goes dem black-haids an' outa dar dey come—dey did—flyin' low to de watah—an' sorter raisin' lak—y' knows how dey does h'it, Jedge?

"Mistah Money he jus' pick up dat fas' feedin' gun—t'war er pump—not one o' dese he'ah afromatics—an' whin he did, I done reach fo' de bottle, 'cause I jes' natcherly knowed dat my time had come. Mistah Money he swing down on dem bullies—Ker-py-ker-py—powie-powie—slamp-slamp-slamp-ker-splasah—Lawdy mussy—gent'mens, fo' times, right in de same place h'it sounded lak—an de las' duck fell ker-flop—almos' in ouh bote.

"I done let go de bottle, an' Mistah Money say—mightly cool lak—say, 'Hawrice,' he say, 'kin'ly to examin' dat las' chap clos'ly,' he say, 'an obsurve,' he say, 'efn he ain' shot thru de eye.'

"I rakes in dat blackjack, an' sho' nuff—bofe eyes done shot plum out—yaas, suh, bofe on 'em right on out. Mistah Money say, 'I wuz—er—slightly afraid,' he say, 'dat I had done unknowin'ly struck dat fellah er trifle too far t' win'ward,' he say. 'A ve'y fair start, Hawrice,' he say. 'You'd bettah place me in my station, so that we may continue on wid'out interruption,' he say.

" 'Yaas, suh,' I say, 'I'm on my way right dar now, suh,' an' I say to m'se'f, I say, 'Mek haste an' put dis gent'man in his bline an' give him er proper chanc't to miss er duck.' I didn' hones'ly b'lieve but whut killin' all four o' dem other ducks so peart lak wuz er sorter accident. So I put him on de Han'werker bline. He seen I kep' de main shell bucket an' de liquah, but he never said nuthin'. I put out de m'coys an' den cre'p back wid' de bote into de willers t' watch.

"Pretty soon, he'ah come er ole drake flyin' mighty high. Ouh ole hen bird she holler t' him, an' de drake he sorter twis' his haid an' look down. I warn't figurin' nuthin' but whut Mistah Money gwi' let dat drake circle an' come 'mongst de m'coys—but aw! aw! All uv' er sudden he jus' raise up sharp lak an'—Kerpowie! Dat ole drake jus' throw his haid onto his back an' ride on down—looked t' me lak he fell er mile—an' whin he hit he throw'd watah fo' feet! Mistah Money he nuvver said er word—jus' sot dar!

"He'ah come another drake—way off to de lef'—up over back o' me. He turn 'roun—quick lak—he did—an' ker-zowie—he cut him on down, too. Dat drake fall way back in de willers an' co'se I hadda wade after 'im.

"Whil'st I wuz gone, Mistah Money shoot twice—an' whin I come stumblin' back, dar laid two mo' ducks wid dey feets in de air. Befo' I hav' time t' git in de bote agin he done knock down er hen away off in de elbow brush.

"I say, 'Mistah Money, suh, I hav' hunted behin' som' far-knockin' guns in my time, an' I'se willin', sho—but ef you doan, please suh, kill dem ducks closer lak, you gwi' kill yo' Ho'ace in de mud.' He say—'Da's all right 'bout dat,' he say, 'go git de bird—he kain't git er-way 'cause h't's daid as er wedge.'

"Whin I crawls back to de bote dat las' time—it done got mighty col'. Dar us set—me in one en' a-shiverin' an' dat ole big bottle wid de gol' haid in de far en'. Might jus' ez well bin ten miles so far ez my chances had done gone.

"Five mo' ducks come in—three singles an' er pair o' sprigs. An' Mistah Money he chewed 'em all up lak good eatin'. One time, tho'—he had t' shoot one o' them high-flyin' sprigs twice, an' I done got halfway in de bote—reachin' fer dat bottle—but de las' shot got 'im. Aftah while, Mistah Money say, 'Hawrice,' he say, 'how is you hittin' off—my man?'

" 'Mistah Money,' I say, 'I'se pow'ful col', suh, an' ef yo' wants me t' tell you de trufe, suh, I b'lieves I done made er pow'ful po' bet.' He say, 'Poss'bly so, Hawrice, poss'bly so.' But dat 'poss'bly' didn't get me nuthin'.

"Jedge, y' Honor, you know dat gent'man sot dar an' kill ev'ry duck whut come in, an' had his limit long befo' de eight o'clock train runned. I done gone t' watchin', an' de las' duck whut come by wuz one o' dem lightnin' express , teals. He'ah he come—look lak somebody done blowed er buckshot pas' us. I riz' up an' hollered—'Fly fas', ole teal, 'do yo' bes'—'caus' Ho'ace need er drink.' But Mistah Money just jumped up an' throw'd him fo'ty feet—skippin' 'long de watah. I say, 'Hol' on, Mistah Money, hol' on—you don' kilt de limit.'

" 'Oh!' he say, 'I Hav'—hav' I?'

"I say, 'Yaas, suh, an' you ain' bin long 'bout h'it, neither! '

"He say, 'Whut are you doin' gittin so col', den?'

"I say, 'I spec' findin' out dat I hav' done made er bad bet had erlot t' do wid de air.'

"An' dar laid dat Brooklyn Handicap all dat time—he nuvver touched none—an' me neither. I paddles him on back to de house, an' he come a-stalkin' on in he'ah, he did—lookin' kinda mad lak—never said nuthin' 'bout no drink. Finally, he say—'Hawrice,' he say, 'git me a bucket o' col' watah.' I say t' m'se'f, I say, 'W-e-l-l-l—dat mo' lak h'it—ef he want er bucket o' watah—you gwi' see some drinkin' now.'

"Whin I come in wid de pail, Mistah Money took offin all his clo'es an' step out onto de side po'ch an' say, 'Th'ow dat watah ovah me, Hawrice, I am lit'rully compel,' he say, 't' have my col' tub ev'ry mawnin'.' M-a-n-n-n! I sho' thow'd dat ice col' watah onto him wid all my heart an' soul. But he jus' gasp an' hollah, an' jump up an' down an' slap hisse'f. Den he had me rub him red wid er big rough towel. I sho' rubbed him, too. Come on in de clubroom he'ah, he did, an' mek hisse'f comfort'ble in dat big rockin' chair yonder—an' went t' readin'. I

44

brought in his shell bucket an' begin' cleanin' his gun. But I see him kinder smilin' t' hisse'f. Atta while, he says, 'Hawrice,' he say, 'you hav' los' you' bet?'

"I kinda hang my haid lak, an' 'low, 'Yaas, suh, Mistah Money, I don' said farewell to de liquah!'

"He say, 'Yo' admits, den, dat you hav' don' los' fair an' squar'—an' dat yo' realizes h'it?'

" 'Yaas, suh!'

"He say, 'Yo' judgmint,' he say, 'wuz ve'y fair, considerin',' he say, 'de great law uv' av'ridge—but circumstances,' he say, 'has done render de ult'mate outcome subjec' to de mighty whims o' chance?'

"I say, 'Yaas, suh,'—ve'y mournful lak.

"He say, 'In so far as realizin' on anything 'ceptin de mercy o' de Cote'—say—'you is absolutely on-est—eh! my man?'

"I say, 'Yaas, suh, barrin' yo' mercy, suh.'

"Den he think er moment, an' say, 'Verree-verree—good!' Den he 'low, 'Since you acknowledge de cawn, an' admits dat you hav' done got grabbed,' he say, 'step up'—he say, 'an' git you a tumbler—an po' yo' se'f er drink—po' er big one, too.'

"I nev'uh stopped f'nuthin' den—jes' runned an' got me er glass outa de kitchen. Ole Molly, she say, 'Whur you goin' so fas'?' I say, 'Doan stop me now, ol' woman—I got business'—an' I sho' poh'd me er big bait o' liquah—er whol' sloo' o' liquah. Mistah Money say, 'Hawrice—de size o' yo' po'tion,' he say, 'is primus facious ev'dence,' he say, 'dat you gwi' spout er toas' in honor,' he say, 'o' d' occasion.'

"I say, 'Mistah Money, suh,' I say—'all I got t' say, suh, is dat you is de king-pin, champeen duck shooter so far as I hav' done bin in dis life—an' ve'y prob'ly as fur ez I'se likely t' keep on goin', too.' He sorter smile t' hisse'f!

" 'Now, suh, please, suh, tell me dis—is you evah missed er duck—anywhar—anytime—anyhow—suh?'

"He say, 'Really, Hawrice,' he say, 'you embarrasses me,' he say, 'so hav' another snifter—there is mo', consider'bly mo',' he say, 'in yo' system, whut demands utt'rance.'

"I done poh'd me another slug o' Brooklyn Handicap, an' say—'Mistah Money, does you expec' t' evah miss another duck ez long ez you lives, suh?'

45

"He say, 'Hawrice,' he say, 'you embarrasses me,' he say, 'beyon' words—you ovahwhelms me,' he say—'get t' Hell outa he'ah, befo' you gits us bofe drunk!' "

The Best of Nash Buckingham
Winchester Press, 1973

THE RHINOCEROS

by Jack O'Connor

T he rhinoceros is one of the world's largest land animals. The familiar black rhino weighs about 3,000 pounds, and its larger cousin, the "white" rhino, about 4,000 pounds. By comparison the big black African Cape buffalo weighs about 2,000 pounds, and the larger Asiatic gaur, (largest of the world's wild cattle) weighs around 2,700 pounds.

The rhino is one of the dumbest of all animals. It cannot get it through its pea-sized brain that it is not the cock of the walk as it was 50,000, 100,000, 1,000,000 years ago. Yet it is a powerful animal, armored with heavy hide and a wicked lance on its nose.

For hundreds of thousands of years, the rhino has solved all difficulties by rushing at them and either tossing them or frightening them away. In Africa today, though a lion may pick off a rhino calf if it can do so with impunity, the lion wants no part of an adult animal. I am sure the larger cave lions and the sabertoothed tigers of Europe's Pleistocene felt the same way about the woolly rhinoceros of those distant days.

The rhino has a keen sense of smell and likewise hears very well. It is, however, extremely shortsighted and may see things only as vague shapes and shadows. Its bulk, strength and stupidity—combined with its curiosity and its habit of solving problems by running over them—make the rhino an exceedingly uncomfortable neighbor to have around. The animal is literally too stupid to be afraid. In the early days of the Uganda Railway that runs from Mombasa on the Kenya coast to Nairobi and on to Uganda, rhinos were very plentiful and it was common to have a rhino take on a train single-handed. The encounter sometimes actually derailed the small engines in use then. Often the rhino was killed, but sometimes it survived the encounter.

The rhino is a vanishing species and there are few in East Africa today where there were hundreds 50 years ago. Nevertheless, it is still common to hear of rhinos charging four-wheel-drive hunting cars, trucks, or anything else that moves in rhino country.

In the summer of 1963, Prince Abdorreza Pahlavi, brother of the Shah of Iran, was hunting in Angola with Mario Marcelino, the white hunter who had steered my wife and me around the previous year. The prince and Mario were tooling along early one morning through a section of the country where rhinos were often seen, when with no warning a rhino shot out of the bush and crashed into the front of the car, running its horn through the radiator and getting head and horn tangled up with the twisted metal of the car. As one could well imagine, the prince and Mario were a bit taken aback. How they managed to keep from being thrown from the car I have no idea. Anyway, they piled out shooting and that was the end of the rhino.

It is quite common for hunters after game in the brush—a lion, elephant, kudu—to be charged by a rhino. Often the rhino is just coming up to investigate at a nice brisk trot, but sometimes it means business. I was once hunting oryx and lesser kudu in the thorny brush of Kenya's Northern Frontier District when I saw a rhino trotting upwind toward me, snorting like a steam-switch engine. My gun bearer and I stood still, but I was set to shoot or dodge, whichever seemed best. But when the rhino got about 30 yards from us it slowed down and apparently forgot what had riled it. The head went down, the eyes closed, and the rhino appeared to have fallen asleep. My gun bearer and I sneaked off and that was the last I ever saw of the animal.

The funniest rhino story I have ever heard was told me by my friend Robert Chatfield-Taylor. He was hunting elephants in the Northern Frontier when, just about dusk, the hunting car got stuck in the sands of a dry wash the Somalis call a lugger. The two gun bearers and the white hunter were trying to get it out and Bob was standing by when he heard a tremendous snorting and crashing of brush, and here came a rhino trotting up to investigate.

Startled half out of his wits, Bob rushed to the hunting car, and grabbed his double .470 to defend himself. The white hunter, who had enough troubles just then anyway, was furious. He grabbed a handful of sand, threw it in the rhino's eyes and shouted: ''Bugger off, you bastard!'' The rhino buggered off.

The Rhinoceros

The rhino is a very ancient animal. In the incredibly remote Miocene and Pliocene, rhinos occupied both eastern and western hemispheres, and in the form of the now extinct woolly rhinoceros they ranged over Pleistocene Europe. Today they are found only in tropical Asia and Africa. The Indian form is now found only on the Assam plain. The "Javan" rhino inhabits Bengal, Burma, the Malay peninsula, Java, Sumatra and Borneo.

There are two species of rhino in Africa, the "black" and the "white." Actually, neither species is black or white—both are a dull gray. Rhinos, like hogs, like to roll in mud and dust—and often one sees red rhinos, white rhinos, blue rhinos, depending on the color of the mud they have wallowed in. A rhino I shot in Tanzania in 1953 looks in the movies I took to be so light gray as to be almost white.

The largest of the African rhinos is the square-lipped, or "white," rhino, which except for the elephant is the world's largest land mammal. It is called white because the early Dutch settlers referred to it as the *wyt* rhino, meaning the one with the wide square mouth, since *wyt* is the Afrikaans word for "wide." Because one type was called the white rhino, the other became the black rhino.

The black rhino is an odd enough animal, but the white rhino is such a strange-looking beast that it looks as if it belongs to another world and another era. The white differs in many ways from its black cousin. It has large, hairy ears, whereas those of the black rhino are round, small and naked. The white carries its tail looped over its back; the black holds its tail up in the air like a radio antenna. The white rhino is a grazer, the black is a browser. The white rhino is a much less nervous and irascible creature than the black.

The white rhino has longer horns than the black, and in both species the female has longer and more slender horns than the male. The record white rhino horn is a very old one from a beast shot in South Africa by Sir W. Gordon-Cumming, a British hunter, explorer and nobleman. It is 62½ inches long and the rear horn is 22¼. Another is recorded that is 56½ inches long. The record black rhino horn is 53½ inches long and is from Kenya.

There are two varieties of white rhino, the southern and the northern. The southern was at one time extremely common all over South Africa between the Orange River and the Zambezi. Many were killed by early settlers and hunters. By 1880 they were rare, and early in this century only about half a dozen remained in an isolated part of Zululand. A reserve was established for them. They slowly increased and now there may be about 500. The remaining northern white rhinos are scatterd over a wide area in Uganda, Chad, the Central African Republic and the southern Sudan. The entire population of the northern white rhinos is now believed to be about 1,100.

There are more black rhinos than any other existing species of rhinoceros, but in most areas of Africa where they were once common they are now rare. My wife has made safaris in northern and southern Tanzania, in Mozambique and in Angola and she has never laid eyes on one. The only place I have ever seen more than one or two in a day was in the Northern Frontier District of Kenya. On a short safari in Angola in the late summer of 1962, I saw two rhinos, one with excellent horns. My wife had chosen to sleep in that morning. Later the big rhino was shot by another hunter.

The black rhino is a browser, not a grazer, and instead of having the wide square mouth of the white rhino it has a hooked, triangular upper lip. The point is prehensile, used to strip off the leaves and twigs the animal feeds on.

The black rhino will stand around five feet high at the shoulder and weigh from 3,000 to 3,500 pounds. In spite of its great bulk it is light on its feet and a trotting rhino seems hardly to touch the ground. All rhinos carry a colony of half a dozen to a dozen tick birds, which I understand are a species of starling, around on their backs. The birds are supposed to make their living by eating the ticks from the rhino, for the folds of a rhino's skin, particularly around the lower parts, are generally crawling with ticks. The tick birds have better eyes than the rhino, and when they see something strange they fly chirping off their host's back. The rhino then charges around blowing and snorting to try to catch the scent and locate the danger.

Old Faro, as the beast is called in Swahili, is found from Ethiopia to the Zambezi and westward to Chad, the Central African Republic, Nigeria and the Cameroons. At one time the rhino was commonly found in quite open country, and was likewise seen abroad at all hours of the day. When Theodore Roosevelt hunted in Kenya and Uganda in 1910, he saw and shot many rhinos in the open, white as well as black.

Today the rhino has been so harried that it is more generally found in heavy thorn brush, and if it is seen in the open it is generally at dawn and at dusk. In fact in many areas, stirring up a drowsy rhino is one of the hazards of hunting the beautiful greater kudu, as both species like dry thorny hills.

The rhino is a slow breeder. One calf is born at a time after an eight-and-a-half-month gestation period. The calf is suckled for two years and the cows do not breed oftener than every two or three years. It is common to see a cow rhino with a calf several years old and almost as large as she is. Where modern man with his rifle does not enter into the ecological picture the rhino can increase even with its slow rate of breeding and lack of intelligence because it is just about without natural enemies. But if the rhino is hunted much, its numbers go down because the species is slow to replace itself.

In some areas rhinos have been killed off to make room for native settlements. In his book *Hunter*, J. A. Hunter, the Kenya white hunter, tells of having killed several hundred rhino in an area where some Wakamba were to be settled and which was being cleared of brush. Many have been shot in the Rhodesias along with thousands of head of other game because of the theory that game carries the tsetse fly. Now these areas have no game but they still have the tsetse fly.

Rhinos have decreased all over the world in modern times, however, because rhino horn is valuable, much more valuable pound for pound than ivory. And the reason that the horn is valuable is that the Chinese entertain the notion that it is a powerful aphrodisiac. The fact that the notion is completely without foundation does not keep the horn from being in great demand and fetching high prices. In East Africa, the horns of rhinos that have been poached are generally sold by African hunters to Indian traders and then smuggled out of the country on Arab dhows. The horn eventually reaches China. I understand that the way to use it is to cut a very thin sliver from the horn, powder it, and drink it in a cup of hot tea.

When rhinos were plentiful, they were slaughtered by the hundreds for their horns. In an old African book by Frederick Courtenay Selous, the explorer, museum collector and writer, I find the following: "One trader alone supplied 400 Matabili native hunters with guns and ammunition, and between 1880 and 1884 his store always contained piles of rhinoceros horns, although they were constantly being sold to traders and carried south. It sounded the death knell of white and black rhinoceros alike in all the country that came in reach of those Matabili hunters.''

The fatal horn of the rhino is actually not horn at all but hair that grows together, and the ''horns'' are attached to the hide instead of the skull. Unlike true horns, they have no core. As we have seen, the record black rhino horn comes from Kenya and is 53½ inches long with the second horn being 18½ inches long. This is the only black rhino horn over 50 inches, in the eleventh edition of *Records of Big Game*, but 12 are 40 inches or over. Forty-four are over 30 inches in length.

Many excellent rhino trophies have been taken by Americans, several fine ones by hunters I know. Dean Witter, the San Francisco financier and widely experienced hunter, has taken two rhinos that went over 30 inches in Tanzania. Frank Hibben, the anthropologist and writer, has a rhino trophy with a front horn of 31½ inches, and Elgin Gates took a 29⅜-inch rhino in 1956. Boyd Williams of the Williams Gun Sight Company has a rhino trophy with a very long front horn. I have never measured it but I'd guess it to be around 30 inches.

The horns of the cow rhinos are longer but more slender than those of the bulls. Almost always the front horn is longer than the rear horn, but occasionally the rear horn will be as long or longer than the front one. Many people simply want to be able to say that they have shot a rhino, and consequently some pretty small rhino horns have been brought back from Africa and proudly mounted. I have seen them as short as eight inches. My one and only rhino trophy is nothing to write home about as the front horn is only a bit over 20 inches.

Just how dangerous is a rhino? As is the case with the rest of Africa's dangerous game animals, opinions differ with the experience of individual observers. Some men who have spent years back in the bush say they would hardly consider them dangerous at all—that to be hurt by a rhino a man would have to be either careless, unlucky, or stupid. One white hunter I know was run over, badly frightened, and terribly bruised by a rhino. He considers Old Faro the most dangerous animal in Africa because, he says, the rhino is the only African animal that will habitually attack unwounded. He says you can be tossed, trampled, gored or killed by a rhino you were not hunting and didn't even know was in the country.

In the old days of foot safaris, when white hunters and clients took out for the bush followed by long lines of porters carrying burdens on their heads, it was routine to have some ill-tempered old rhino come charging down to rout the porters, put them up trees, and scatter tents, chop boxes and camp furniture all over the countryside. In those days of many rhinos, those leading safaris always loaded their rifles, watched nervously, and hoped for the best whenever a rhino was sighted.

A rhino is a creature of habit. It generally waters between eight and nine o'clock at night and always comes and goes by the same path. Woe to the safari that unwittingly camps on a rhino's path. One chap I know had just got to sleep one moonlight night when he heard a mixture of snorts, grunts, yells. An instant later he was knocked out of his cot and his tent vanished as if by magic. He has a vague recollection of seeing his tent, loosely draped around a fleeing rhino, disappearing into the bush. The members of the safari were upset, but no one was hurt. Then and there they moved camp 100 yards out of the rhino trail.

Powerful rifles and full-metal-jacketed (solid) bullets are usually recommended for rhino. They are big brutes and their hides are thick. Thin-jacketed, high-velocity bullets would probably go to pieces pretty badly on a rhino and most expanding bullets would probably give unsatisfactory penetration on a rhino's heavy shoulder blade. However, many rhinos have been killed with such mild rifles as the 7x57 Mauser, the 6.5mm Mannlicher-Schoenauer and the .303 British—if round-nosed full-metal-jacketed bullets are used and the shots well placed. D.W.M. Bell, that great Scottish ivory hunter, killed many with the round-nosed solid military 7mm bullet.

Syd Downey says a rhino is easy to kill with a bullet through the lungs or with one that breaks both shoulders. An old-time South African hunter said a rhino went down within a few yards with a shot that went through both lungs, but that if only one lung were hit, it could travel a long way even though bleeding heavily at the nose and mouth.

My one and only rhino didn't appear to me to be hard to bring down. This animal had been shot in the guts with an arrow on which the poison was not very strong. This made the rhino sick and mean. It had chased and hurt several Africans, and when my safari went through the Tanzanian town of M'Bulu a game ranger asked us to knock it off.

When we found the rhino standing under a tree I would not have been more surprised and excited if it had been a dinosaur. I tried for a heart shot at 125 to 150 yards, but my rhino fever must have made me jerk the trigger, as the rhino ran off. I found out later that the 480-grain solid from the .450 Watts (wildcat predecessor of the .458 Winchester) had struck a bit low and a bit behind the heart.

I had expected the rhino to come raging down on me like an avenging spirit, stick its horn into my quivering abdomen and throw me over a thorn tree. Instead it whirled and ran like a rabbit.

Right then I really distinguished myself. I stopped my rifle's swing and the bullet went right past the rhino's ample fanny. Then mentally I gave myself a swift kick, swung well ahead of the fleeing rhino and fired with the rifle moving. I heard the bullet strike and saw the rhino stumble. When it had run about 50 yards it fell and was dead when we got to it.

That was rhino that had to be shot and might very well have died anyway, as it had a bad abdominal wound. Yet I felt strangely guilty for having shot this visitor from out of the mists of time. I'll never shoot another.

I have known people who have been mauled by lions and knew one hunter whom a lion killed. I have known several who have been mauled by leopards and tossed by elephants and buffaloes. But I have never known anyone who was badly hurt by a rhino, perhaps because there are not many rhinos any more. Just the same, a rhino killed tough old Bwana Cottar, an American who was one of the best and bravest white hunters East Africa ever saw.

Outdoor Life
January 1965

THE PAINFUL MOOSE

by Clare Conley

H unts are memorable for many reasons—your first and, worse luck, your last; the most exciting; the most dangerous; the biggest trophy; the happiest; the one with special friends; and more. They can occur anywhere from a small-game thicket in the back pasture to a mountain in Tibet, and, of course, they can happen anytime. You most often only really know how great one was long after it is over.

But of all the memorable hunts I have had in near places and far and for whatever reasons, one that stands out in my memory occurred in Alaska in the fall of 1971. And the reason I remember it so well is the strange collection of things that happened to all of us, but mostly to me. I guess I'd have to say the reason I remember it is that there seemed to be no reason at all to the unusual collection of occurrences. And surprisingly, I know I would have to rate it as the most painful hunt I was ever on.

On September 4, Fred Bear, the father of modern-day bow hunting, Colonel Joe Engle, the astronaut, and I arrived at Bob Buzby's hunting camp on the Dry Creek, 80 miles by air south of Fairbanks, Alaska.

Since this was my first time in Alaska for hunting, and because I had read about it so much, I hurried to get started at the soonest opportunity on the first afternoon. But whereas I had expected to see big game, moose and caribou everywhere, I soon learned that Alaska on foot is even larger than it looks on the map, and game animals are not found in each and every little clump of willows and side draws. For the most part my afternoon became a kind of get-acquainted-with-the-area affair in which I learned that a mountain that looks close and easy to walk over is usually miles away and a tough climb.

The next day, now knowing better what to expect, I got away from camp early and alone, and with my bow clutched in my hand I left behind in the first hour the area I had poked around in the first afternoon out. In the meanwhile Joe Engle had elected to go for a Dall sheep with a rifle as his first choice and packed on out to a camp higher up in the mountains. Although we later kept daily contact with that camp by radio it would be a week before Joe returned with his trophy. Fred on that first day chose to scout some natural salt licks for fresh activity and to build blinds. He of all of us knew what he was doing.

I can't really do justice to describing what it is like to walk across a rolling sidehill in that part of Alaska. The slopes are covered with low brush, shin-high mostly, with occasional lines of taller brush along the route of every trickle of water. The valley bottoms are lined with evergreens, softwoods and willows, but the mountainsides are mostly short brush. And on these slopes I set off for some little rolling hills in the distance that looked promising. An hour later I didn't seem to be gaining on them much. A second hour's walking did make a noticeable difference, and while glassing the area where I was going during a rest stop I saw, wonder of wonders, what I considered to be a nice caribou. He was wandering without apparent motive in and around three little knobs which were strung out in a line. The same knobs had caught my eye when I first saw them at the start of the day.

I'd like to say that I performed a miraculous stalk on that bull caribou across the mile or so of open ground that separated us right to an eyeball-to-eyeball confrontation. And actually I didn't do too badly— except that the caribou didn't know or care where he was going and consequently never went in the same direction more than a minute or two, and he never stopped either. Finally I knew I had him figured out. I had cut the distance to the knobs down to a couple hundred yards, and when he went out of sight behind Knob No. 1 heading for Knob No. 3, I raced across the last open flat intent on ambush at Knob No. 3. I got there, got in position to draw and waited—and waited. Finally I decided I would chance a little peek around the knob just to find out what was taking the bull so long. All I saw was the tail end of a caribou vanishing in the wrong direction around the first knob. I charged around Knobs 3 and 2 and cut in between Knobs 2 and 1 for another interception. And there I was fooled again. The wandering caribou was now out in the flat a hundred yards watching me run crazily around. Finding that dull stuff, he started feeding and walking on up the mountain, not particularly concerned. At that moment I realized I had just as much chance of running into that bull caribou by going in the opposite direction as I did by following him. And I may have run into him again sometime for all I know, but how can you tell. Most of them look alike.

Anyway I started back down the little line of knobs, which actually were on the crest of a draw that led down to one of the main creeks in the drainage. Only they were back from the creek a half mile or so and were maybe 400 feet higher. Heavy tall brush grew up the slope from the creek, and by sneaking along at the crest I could scout the whole thing pretty well. This I was carrying off in style when I nearly ran into a moose lying in my path. Instantly I dropped to my knees so I could be out of sight and look things over better. Then I realized it was just a calf moose and he was asleep.

But, I told myself—someone had to—if a baby moose is there, nearby a papa moose with big antlers might be hiding too. So I tippytoed back the way I came, went out of sight over the crest, and sneaked back in beyond where the calf was dozing. Then all hell broke loose. The calf got up about 20 yards away and stood and looked at me, but below a big moose got up from a bed in a standing broad jump that took it almost out of sight instantly. All I saw was the back end of an adult moose that looked like it was trying to cut around me to get over the crest.

Running for all I was worth on the muskeg and brush, I circled back around a low rise to the next logical pass where the moose might come out. My feet were as light as feathers as I raced over the muskeg—about like running on a mattress. I had it made, too, until one of those light feet hooked something. I remember a rather spectacular arching trajectory through the air, and then I hit, left arm holding my bow away, right arm extended over my head. Instantly my right shoulder plowed down in the soft muskeg, wrenching my right arm back in a way it is not meant to go.

I remember crawling back into a standing position and doing a mental checklist of all my working parts. Nothing seemed too bad. I had a funny feeling in my right shoulder, though, rather like all the muscles in it had been stretched to the ripping point and then let snap back. Then I tried to lift it. The grating, crunching, and popping was unbelievable. I put it down, rubbed it for a moment, and raised it once more. Again it sounded like a rock crusher at work. It didn't hurt much just then, but I didn't need a fortune-teller to inform me trouble was coming. And to make matters

57

even more impossible, the moose never did come out the way I expected. He ran straight downhill, and as I was fitting my parts back together, I saw him run out in the open at the bottom—and he turned out to be a she anyway, a big cow. My first nonreason event!

I had a long walk back, and by now most of the day was used up so I went downhill to the creek which flowed into another creek that Buzby's camp was on. Along the way I took several shots at ptarmigan without hitting one, and to this day I am still amazed that I could pull the 55-pound-draw bow.

I got back to camp just in time for dinner, and by then my shoulder was aching steadily and getting worse. Fred had investigated several salt licks and although it seemed as if he wasn't hunting much, it was now obvious to me that setting up blinds near places the caribou and moose would frequent was the only practical way to hunt. He also learned that the main migration from summer range to winter range of the caribou had not come through, and that moose were not rutting and doing all the silly things that go with it yet.

The next morning after a pained erratic sleep, I found it was impossible to move my arm more than an inch away from my side. The pain was so intense that all the strength in my right shoulder was gone and the arm just hung uselessly at my side. That was a fine fix for a bowhunter to be in at the beginning of a hunt. All day long I spent heating sand on the wood stove in the tent Fred and I shared and then putting it in a plastic bag and packing it on my shoulder. That helped the pain and by the end of the day I could move my arm slightly. But I was still a long way from being able to hunt. I had two choices. I could fly out to Fairbanks to a doctor or try to luck it out on the chance it would get better.

I elected to stay on at Dry Creek. Even without hunting it was still one of the most beautiful places I have ever been. Even now I would rather be there with a shoulder that hurts like hell than in a hospital bed in Fairbanks with nurses jabbing me with painkillers.

Fred had much the same attitude. It was just being there that counted. For several days I just poked around camp and the nearby woods, something that most hunters never take time to do. And it was great. I saw ptarmigan and snowshoe rabbits, I found wolf skulls, and generally got a lot more out of the trip than I might have otherwise. Fred hunted a little and messed around with me a lot.

The Painful Moose

Each day I was working on getting my shoulder so I could use it again. I had some cortisone and that helped. I got my arm to the point where I could raise it about shoulder-high, but it still cracked and crunched a lot and had no strength. I had to get it back to something like full mobility quickly, and so I started taking a small rope and throwing it over a cross piece in the center of our cabin, and then by wrapping it around my right hand I would slowly draw the arm up by pulling down on the rope with my left hand. It was torture the first time or two, but after a while it did seem to help my injured shoulder.

After about a week of our two-week hunt I decided to try a short rabbit hunt with Fred. I could draw the bow back but not all the way, which is necessary for aiming and power. Needless to say I didn't hit a single rabbit, but at least I was hunting. Fred on the other hand was a real Indian at rabbit hunting and bagged several. I remember once he stopped as we were chasing rabbits through the willows and remarked that we were hunting rabbits at $150 a day per person, but it sure was fun. And it was.

Fred also liked to ride and took long tours of the surrounding mountains. On one of these afternoons he returned to camp with the casual information that he had just shot a bull moose. But that was a story unto itself no matter how he tended to make it seem a trifle. He had been riding his favorite horse and had come out on a promontory of one hill where he stopped to look things over. Across a small valley where a plateau crested before the terrain dropped down to the creek he saw two cow moose and a nice bull. It was midday and they were feeding in the willows just at the break of the plateau. Actually it was not far from where I had hurt my shoulder.

The bull obviously was interested in other things as well as willows, for he was raking every tall willow he came to with his antlers and in moose language this is as much as saying, "I'm pretty tough and anytime you two girls feel like getting on with propagating the species, I'm ready." They weren't ready, but he was bent on hanging around until they were. All this Fred understood.

After eating a while, the moose bedded down for a noonday nap, which gave Fred a chance to ride to the creek, tie up his horse, and sneak up the hillside below the moose as close as he dared. Below the willows at the crest of the hill was open low brush for about a hundred yards down to the last bit of cover, a clump of dead willows about the diameter of a

59

bushel basket. Fred managed to sneak to this cluster of willows, but he could go no farther, so he waited.

After an hour or so the cows began to stir, and soon they came out of the lower edge of the willows, heading for a natural salt lick along the creek more or less in Fred's direction. They passed within a few yards as they meandered down. But the bull didn't come, so Fred stayed.

Fred told me later he figured the bull would eventually discover the cows were gone and go after them. And sure enough after a while he rose from his bed, looked around, thrashed a few more willows, and started downhill, on the same trail the cows had used. Fred got ready.

Then just as the bull was about to pass he spied the clump of willows behind which Fred was hiding. Turning off the trail, he headed straight for them, obviously intent on working them over with his antlers. At 13 steps, Fred decided that was close enough and stood up. The bull stopped in surprise and that was enough time for Fred to shoot. The moose turned, went 50 yards in a few seconds and fell dead.

That night Joe returned with a good Dall sheep which he had earned by days of arduous stalking high up in the mountains, and the next afternoon, in contrast to his difficult sheep hunting, he spotted a moose on a hillside above camp, stalked it and shot it with a rifle, all within an hour or so.

Days now passed uneventfully with each of us hunting in his own way. I could now draw my bow completely, but painfully, and so I spent my time in blinds at natural salt licks. Caribou and moose came within scant yards of my hiding place, but not ones that I wanted. So I took pictures and waited. Nothing. We extended our hunt a week, knowing that as soon as the first cold weather came many animals would move through the valley.

Finally the next-to-the-last day arrived. We decided that on that day we would cross a high ridge and hunt in the next valley over from camp, perhaps five miles away but a difficult climb and walk in muskeg. That's where the caribou were. Hundreds of them were in the open flats of the valley. We scattered, each trying to find a way to get near the animals. Nothing I tried seemed to work. I was always in the wrong place and out in the open. Joe had gone down along the creek where a line of trees provided concealment behind which he could walk, and sure enough late in the day I heard him shoot. He was then a mile or two farther from camp than I was, and I remember wondering how he could take care of the meat and get the trophy back to camp. I wasn't even certain of his exact location, he was that far away.

Evening was coming and I had a long walk back across muskeg, which is difficult crossing even in the light. Mixed in with the low brush which drags at your legs are endless numbers of small potholes the size of a bathtub and smaller. These must be avoided, because although some are shallow, some are deep and filled with mud. It's frustrating in the daytime and a nightmare in the dark. Also there was always the climb back over the mountain to consider.

After waiting as long as I could and watching for anyone else, I finally gave up and started back. It was dark before I reached camp. Everyone was there but Joe.

We had a drink while we waited. Occasionally one of us would step outside the cabin to shine a light and yell. No answer. Would he stay out all night? We doubted it. Could he find his way in the dark through the mountains and in the muskeg? Probably, but it would be slow and very hard.

At last I decided to take a light and walk up as far as the top of the mountain where I could yell farther. Halfway up I heard Joe answer one of my yells, and shortly we met on the trail. Not only had he come almost all the way back in the dark, he was carrying the caribou head and cape on his back. It had to weigh 50 pounds. I would have been proud to carry it the rest of the way back for him, but he refused. That's the kind of man who will fly the space shuttle. Not a bad choice.

The final day of the hunt came and I still had bagged nothing besides rabbits and ptarmigan, but the caribou were coming. We had seen them, so I took a blind at the first salt lick they would come to in our valley. I got there early and hunched down waiting for the winter sun to warm me up. No caribou were in sight. I read a book and got cold.

Suddenly I heard a noise, and there passing right in front of the blind was a caribou, then another, and then dozens. As they saw the lick they began to run for it. Some nearly jumped over the blind in passing. It was exciting. Soon there must have been 50 or more right in front of me. Nothing I did seemed to make the slightest difference to them. But I couldn't see one I wanted to shoot.

And so it went all day—caribou around all the time but either out of range or nothing I wanted. At last one magnificent head came in the far end of the lick. He was at least 120 yards away. too far. But he was wandering around and might come closer. He was obviously hanging out with a smaller bull. Wherever one went the other followed. The range got down to 90 yards, then 80. I wanted no more than 45 yards. But now they had been in the lick quite awhile and were showing signs of leaving. Soon the smaller bull walked out in the grass going away on the far side. This was it, I knew. I stood up and estimated the angle. Not a caribou made an effort to run. Some looked at me casually. Finally I let go. It was hopeless from the start. A bow will shoot 80 yards and more, but who can aim at that distance? The arrow dug into the mud far short of the mark and my bull loped away.

For a long time no more animals came into the lick. Then late in the day a smallish bull with a few cows and calves came by. As the fate of hunters will have it, I easily shot the bull dead.

Back at camp we had an early dinner, and because I hated to quit I talked Joe and Fred into one last rabbit hunt along the runway of the landing strip. It was a pleasant place to hunt, not more than a couple of hundred yards from camp, and there were always plenty of snowshoes, which are excellent to eat. We bagged a few and laid them along the edge of the strip where they would be easy to find. I even shot a ptarmigan. But finally it was time to quit. Fred wanted to go back to the cabin, and so Joe and I offered to walk back the length of the strip to pick up a rabbit he had left there.

With all the rabbits collected, we started back, taking long shots down the runway, picking up our arrows and shooting again. It was just as we were picking up our rabbit arrows that we heard a grunt in the willows right beside us. Because I couldn't believe my ears, I asked what had to be the stupid question of the year.

"What was that?"

"A moose," Joe replied. "Shoot him."

Luckily I had left my big-game arrows in my bow quiver. Dropping my rabbit arrow, I switched to a broadhead and slipped to the edge of the willows. There broadside was a big bull moose looking at me. A barn couldn't have looked bigger, and I had been shooting rabbits at the same distance. But I just couldn't believe he was so close, and instead of aiming with the same sight I had been using on rabbits I chose one for greater distance and let go. As far as I know that arrow is still circling the earth because it passed high over the moose and was still on its way when I saw it last.

"Did you hit him?" Joe whispered.

"No."

Groan.

The moose now decided to move a little farther along, parallel to the runway, still in the willows, and went out of sight. I backtracked into the runway and ran ahead to cut him off, again vowing not to make the same mistake twice.

Again the moose and I met, same as before, only this time I had my aiming figured out. Again I shot for just back of the shoulder. The arrow flew perfectly. There was a loud "bonk." It had stuck just in the edge of his antler, which covered his shoulder as the moose turned his head to face me.

As he tore through the brush I could see the arrow firmly attached to the antler, not bothering him in the least.

Back to the runway I raced, and 50 yards ahead again. This time when the moose stepped out I made a perfect shot. He went slightly farther on ahead and I thought I saw him go down, but the willows were thick and I wasn't sure. All was silence. In the meanwhile I had lost track of Joe.

Then I heard a whisper—a loud whisper—and I thought Joe said, "Come fast."

So out of the willows I raced again to the end of the runway and around the corner where the willows ended. The moose was there all right, and seeing me was all he needed to rise up and start to move out fast. I drew and hit him again right where I was supposed to. The bull charged full speed straight for the creek, and to my surprise right in his path on the rocky bar was our astronaut. Just when it looked as if a collision was inevitable—and I could see headlines, ASTRONAUT LAUNCHED BY MOOSE —Joe crouched in a ball and the moose stormed past, one antler passing over Joe's head. Thirty yards more and the bull collapsed dead, the biggest of the trip. Joe had actually whispered to me, "Hold fast," I learned later as we recounted the chaotic event.

And so what makes you remember one hunt more than another? If you have to ask, you haven't had one yet. But you will. You will!

GYPSY

by Jerry Gibbs

A black dog came into our lives a while ago. She was a seal-shiny, big-footed pup, unable from the time she could walk to ignore the call of a nose that promised the best of life's wind-borne mysteries. She was a wanderer. Because of that, we named her Gypsy.

Gypsy was a Labrador retriever. Books and trainers acclaim the versatility of the breed, and versatility was what I thought I needed when we decided it was time to get a dog. Later I learned not to rely on textbook generalities. They sometimes lead to trouble, even tragedy. And I learned about something else you can't take literally: a dog owner's declaration that the heartache of losing a beloved animal is too much to face again. "No more dogs, not ever," he might say. Don't believe it. If you love dogs, you won't want to be without one, regardless of what may come. But let me tell you about Gypsy.

I had been a long time without a dog. My wife, Judy, and I had lived some time in suburban apartments, but when we had a couple of boys we needed a house. To me, the best thing about the increased space was that there was room for a dog. We were barely moved in when we found her.

We built a soft nest in a washtub for carrying the pup home from the breeder. She easily convinced our older son, Greg, then six, that other places were better. A knot near the tip of her tail gave the appendage the appearance of a windblown flag. That slightly canted tail beat merrily as she wormed herself from the tub onto Greg's lap. She was asleep in moments.

A dog becomes a physical part of your life immediately. Emotionally, it takes just a little longer.

You rarely remember the inconveniences of raising a pup. It's the way you remember kids growing up, the good parts stick. With a dog it's the

64

funny, crazy times, and the way the animal earns your admiration and respect if it's any good at all as a hunter.

Gypsy was a water dog. She was seven weeks old when we got her. A week later she traveled with us on a camping trip to Cape Hatteras, North Carolina. She was too young for water training; in fact I had yet to introduce her to any water deeper than her drinking pail. It didn't matter. She bounced down the beach, a coal-black India-rubber ball, then looked up and suddenly discovered the ocean. With her four feet planted defiantly in the sand, she eyed the wind-lashed surf, barked several times, and waded into the wash. Throughout the trip, she galloped in the shallows, chased herring gulls and sandpipers, and dug caverns in the sand. I started her formal training soon after we returned home.

The intensity and single-mindedness of a retriever bent on capturing a dummy or a bird is special, a beautiful thing. Gypsy was barely able to mouth the smallest training dummy I could find, but she managed with no coaxing. I remember how she grew into the dummies. My memory of her is like an elapsed-time-sequence film. I see her growing from bouncing puppy to sleek retrieving machine, her chest in an air-borne arc ending in that explosive, flat-out water entry unique to retrievers. Gypsy had spirit and desire; she needed only refining and control.

As Gypsy's training continued, one thing bothered me. Occasionally she broke from a retrieve to follow some intriguing scent. Other times, she seemed to hit a scent and to turn deaf to return commands, running through backyards and down suburban roads. I tried the usual remedies, from check cords to discipline. They seemed to work for a while. Friends experienced in dog training chalked up the dog's weakness either to my inept training or to some flaw in her makeup.

The problem did not appear consistently. Long stretches of perfect behavior tended to make us forget Gypsy's occasional lapses. Besides, she was an inseparable member of the family. There were hilarious times when Judy or I released Gypsy into the midst of our boys' softball games. The dog knew exactly what was going on. She charged into the field, seized the ball, and ran the bases several times before stopping. If she went after a just-hit ball, she frequently clipped the base runner, bowling him over for a certain out, then licked his face despite howls of protest.

Gypsy loved winter. She chased our boys' toboggans and usually leaped aboard just before the sled caromed off a mogul and sent her sailing through the air. She helped our younger boy, Jon, learn to cope with interference when he was trying to learn ice hockey. She played husky in a harness while towing provisions lashed on a sled to winter camp. But it was water that Gypsy loved most of all.

After she began to work heavily on water retrieves, Gypsy rarely allowed the boys to swim in peace. The dog would swim around them, grabbing T-shirts. Much to his annoyance, Jon was retireved more than once. As author James Michener once wrote, a Lab is "a kind of perpetual five-year-old, forever young, forever loving."

Gypsy was rarely content to rest. With typical retriever hardiness, she broke through thin ice to complete a retrieve. If I thought conditions were perhaps a bit dangerous and therefore threw nothing, she crashed in anyway, then clambered ashore like a bear, showering pinwheels of frigid water on spectators.

None of her breaking and running problems were apparent during water work. She quickly learned to retrieve among decoys without becoming entangled in their anchor cords. I was amazed at the speed with which she learned to make multiple retrieves, to take a line on hand signals, and even to check on command in the midst of one retrieve and head for another target. I shouldn't have been surprised, for the miracle of retrievers is their incredible memory and intelligence. On land, though, Gypsy's problem continued to recur periodically.

I began to hear of others whose dogs had similar problems. One fellow from Iowa had spent a considerable sum on professional training in hopes that his high-spirited Lab could be used for flushing pheasants, as so many are. The trainer had accomplished some things but made no guarantees. The dog's owner had several good days, but eventually the dog locked in on one bird that either was running or had left a scent too strong to resist. The big male Lab cannonballed through the cornfields out of sight. Eventually the owner brought him back with the whistle, but, from then on, the dog was totally unreliable as a controlled flusher. Another chap in Nebraska had the same experience. At heel, sometimes on a check thong, his Lab functioned as a retriever after pointing dogs locked in and the gunners brought the raucous cock pheasants down. I didn't like the sound of any of it and went back to preparing Gypsy for waterfowl hunting.

Gypsy's first birds were ducks—big orange-leg blacks and fat greenhead mallards from the salt marshes of southern New Jersey. Here, hip-deep black-gumbo muck awaits the returning hunter who has neglected to pull his boat up on the marsh at high tide. But the birds are there on the creeks or far back in the potholes where few hunters care to slog. We had some good days, that Gypsy dog and I, and I'll remember every one of them. Sometimes we lay flat on the far edges of marsh, away from other hunters, and waited for the birds to come. Flocks of little greenwing teal flashed in the low sun, making quick course changes as they came in. Bigger ducks would make one pass, then bore in straight. If we were lucky, they sat hard with the decoys I had packed on my back.

We had skies full of Canada and snow geese to watch, and silly grebes to laugh at as we motored back up the big creek. We savored the raspy cry of a startled great blue heron, and that special kind of tiredness that comes after a day of work that you truly love.

Once, during a rain, I explored a section of marsh where I had never been. It was a high marsh, the grasses taller than my head. Gypsy and I pushed far back, though the going was tough and became tougher. Small potholes pocked the marsh. From time to time, we put up a duck. So intriguing was this country that I forgot the reason for the height of the grasses—tide.

When I realized that water was deepening around my boots, I stepped on a small hummock, made a reconnaisance of our position, and began to worry. We had paralleled the side of the marsh from which the flood tide now came. I could not retrace my steps before the water would become too deep and I could not cut out of the marsh as I had planned. I had to move inland. I was tired, but there was no choice.

As we moved ahead, the marsh became softer. With each step I sank calf deep, then knee deep in muck. Rain came in sheets, smoking across the seemingly endless marsh, obliterating the grassy plain before us. I was as wet from perspiration as I would have been without my waterproof parka.

Ducks flushed from potholes in front of us, almost close enough to touch, but I had no time or interest for them. I had to will each step now. My breathing was ragged. Still the tide pressed from behind. I knelt a moment to rest. Gypsy must have understood the seriousness of the situation because she walked close to me. When I faltered, she bumped me with her solid 75 pounds. At first I was enraged; then I realized what she was doing.

We went on like that for what seemed hours before the footing gradually firmed. I staggered in the rain back to the camper, drank two quarts of water, stripped, and began to dry off. Gypsy curled on her pad, steaming, smelling like wet dog and looking at me with an expression that seemed to say, "Really, we weren't in all that much trouble." I was exhausted. I lay in my bunk wondering just how much she really had contributed to getting me back. Even after all of that, I could not accept the dog's faulty behavior on land.

I persisted in trying to work her in upland covers. At times she worked to perfection, quartering ahead, working field or woodland edge in classic form. Then she took interest in something and drifted away. There was no consistency.

I began working her at heel while walking up birds. She bolted very few times during this training. Unhappily, I realized this might be the only way I could trust her away from water. Not long afterward, we moved to northern Vermont.

Big lakes, freshwater swamps, and potholes promised new water-fowling opportunities. We lived in a cottage on a large lake. A decaying blind stood within an easy walk. From it Gypsy retrieved her first north-country black duck. Whistlers, buffleheads, geese, and mergansers used the big water. Greg was old enough to join me that first season. He held the dog while I broke the clear skim ice so we could set the decoys in the predawn darkness.

The second season the boy helped me construct a blind on the far side of the lake. We hauled lumber and drove corner stakes while Gypsy swam from shore to blind, explored the beach, and watched our work. She seemed more content to stay close than I had ever seen her. Maybe it was the newness of it all, maybe something else. Those warm, late-summer days of blind building and hauling out decoys are some of the finest in my memory. Greg and I watched as the dog swam and ran the beach.

The grouse cycle started up again in Vermont. Back in old, rough highland pastures and abandoned orchards, we flushed more birds than I had seen in a long time. In spring the drummers had thumped like old generators. The broods had come through that worrisome period, and now we were finding not only singles but coveys of young ruffed grouse yet to split up. The hunting was impossible to resist.

I made a couple of successful hunts alone, holding Gypsy by command at heel. Grouse hunting looked good, and it was time to start Greg on these wonderful birds. One afternoon we hunted near the house that we'd built far back on an old logging road. We walked down the road, then cut into the broken woodland. This was mostly thick cover, and any shooting would be fast. I gave the boy the left-handed position. If the going became too rough or too confusing, he could cut to the roadside to get his bearings. To be safe, we talked or whistled back and forth constantly as we moved ahead, revealing our positions.

Gypsy was at a tight heel, anxious for a shot bird and the retrieve. Shortly, two birds exploded in front of Greg. When I asked why he didn't shoot, he said he couldn't believe how fast they went. We laughed and moved ahead. Another bird rocketed off somewhere between us, closer to me, but too far to my left for a safe shot. I let it go. Greg had dropped a little behind, and while I told him to move up, a bird thundered through the trees off my right shoulder. Evidently it had been sitting in a tree, and it had let me pass as grouse sometimes do. The bird flew somewhat toward me, then made a 90-degree turn going away. I fired once and missed. As I began lowering the 20-gauge, another grouse burst from the ground in dense cover just ahead and slightly to the right. I wheeled quickly and locked on its low flight. As I began to pull the trigger, my brain screamed a warning to stop. Peripheral vision detected a black, blurred shape bolting at the bird, but the message was an instant too late. The primer was punched and the shot on its way before my responses caught up, and I pulled the barrels up in a hopeless attempt to correct. I remember the roar of my voice over the sound of the gun, then a scream of pain. The dog wheeled in circles as I ran to her and dropped to my knees. I cradled her in my arms, seeing where some of the shot had cut through the top of her back. I tried to console her, tried. . . .

Gypsy had stopped crying by the time Greg reached us. Her breathing was ragged, but she did not cry. Her head was on my arm. She watched me patiently, fully trusting me to make things well again. Through blurred eyes I saw that Greg had moved swiftly; no man could have reacted better in an emergency. Both guns were broken, the shells were shucked, and he asked whether I needed help to carry her out. I sent him to bring his mother with the truck. I worked my arms gently beneath the dog, lifted her, and stumbled to the road.

"She'll be all right, won't she?" Greg pleaded. I had nothing to tell him.

The scene of moments before ran over and over in my mind. Never cured of her tendency to break, Gypsy had bolted while I turned away to fire at the first bird. She must have nearly caught the second bird as it frantically beat through the thick, low cover. She had leaped after the escaping grouse into my line of fire.

"Let's hope no pellet struck the spinal column," the veterinarian said. "If it did—well, she could be paralyzed—or she just might not make it. I won't encourage you, or take away all hope."

While the doctor gave her several injections, she watched me quietly, patiently, and with trust. I put a hand beneath her head. She took one deep breath, then rested. I knew she would not live.

Gypsy died during the night. I buried her near a group of birches on a flat place overlooking the woods, the valley below, and the lake, where the duck blind went unused that season. If there is any kind of justice, I know where she is right now. There is a shore with an endless beach to run, a sky full of ducks, and a kid or two to throw sticks and swim with her. Hie on, Gypsy. There's nothing to stop you now.

Outdoor Life
December 1979

WOUNDED LION IN KENYA

by J. C. Rikhoff

O n the fourth night of our safari in Kenya's Masailand we sat with our two leopards propped up in front of the fire and celebrated. We shared a camaraderie that can only come when everything has gone for the best. My professional hunter, John Kingsley-Heath, and I had strung up three fresh baits the day before. My partner, Scott Healy and his hunter, Dave Ommanney, had hung another two. This evening Scotty and I both had knocked over leopards, which must be some sort of record for speed and efficiency in leopard hunting.

We had the best of everything and that happens rarely in anyone's life. We knew it and we were making the most of it. Tomorrow would be another day—perhaps the same as today or, by some fantastic chance, better, but more likely a little drab in comparison to the achievements of this fine day.

Then, as we sat with our drinks late into the night, we heard a distant cough. Silence fell upon the group as if by some signal. A grunting rumble rolled in from the night. It was a sound I had heard only once before, in Mozambique. Scotty, even though he had never heard the sound before, knew exactly what it ws.

"Yes, that's a lion—a big, hungry, male lion," Scotty said. "It's over there on that hill where the Masai boy said it would be." It was that simple. We got up from the fire, the excitement of our leopards swept away by the insistence of the impatient, grunting demand.

We had a lion in our district and it was only a mile away. Everything had changed. We now had a lion in our own backyard, and it was up to us to figure how to take the animal.

In our beds that night we listened to the lion over on its hill. The animal

71

was either very hungry, very passionate or very disgruntled because it kept up its steady grunting-coughing routine for as long as I could keep my eyes open. I went to sleep with its roar in my ears and its picture in my mind. The picture was sharply defined. The lion was big, with a heavy black mane. It was stone dead and I, gun in hand, stood over it in a Teddy Roosevelt stance.

At breakfast the next morning our leopards were almost forgotten. The talk was of lions. John Kingsley-Heath spoke in the quiet, final tone that I had grown to respect. "Listen, chaps," he said, "we should not pass up that poached giraffe that Scotty and Dave spotted over on the private farm outside the preserve." A lion had been working on one of the hindquarters. Scotty and Dave agreed that they would check the carcass.

"Jim and I will head for the lion's hill," John said, nodding toward me. "It probably killed last night on the plain and is sleeping its gluttony off not very far from the remains."

Breakfast was a hurried affair. We had other things on our minds. With Scott and Dave off in one direction, John and I loaded up the other Land Rover and made a straight line for the round hill where the lion had spent its noisy night. It was a short trip and in a very few minutes we were loading our rifles for a sneak up a path we had noted the day before.

I had brought only one rifle to Africa with me—my favorite Winchester Model 70 in .264 Winchester Magnum. But Kenya's law requires that a .375 or larger must be used on lion, so John had loaned me a well-stocked and slightly worn Model 70 in .375 H&H Magnum.

As I loaded the big rifle with 300-grain Silvertip ammunition I hoped that I would shoot well—or miss cleanly. A wounded lion is no nicked whitetail deer. Many consider a wounded lion to be the most dangerous animal on earth and the record would seem to bear this out. More hunters have been killed by wounded lions than by any other species in Africa. The year before a wounded lion had killed an American hunter in Angola shortly after he had made the mistake of shooting the big cat with a small .300 Magnum bullet.

John loaded his .470 double-gun, handed it to Kiebe, his senior gun bearer, and with an inquisitive glance at me, started walking up the hill. He had the lion figured for an area immediately on the crest. We would follow our winding path from the base of the hill, proceed around it toward the opposite side and would hope to come up on the animal before it either winded or heard us. From that moment on, its actions would decide what form the script would take. I slung the .375 over my shoulder and followed John. I kept thinking, This is really it—I am finally going after a lion and anything can happen.

I had spent a lot of time speculating on exactly what could happen. First, the lion could be gone and that would take care of the matter right away. Or, the animal could be there and I could kill it with one shot—and that would be fine for everybody, with the obvious exception of dead simba (Swahili for lion). Next, I could miss completely and the lion could take off in the other direction; we could consider this a draw—we don't get the lion but then the lion doesn't get any of us. Lastly, I could wound the lion. I didn't like to think about this at all, but it kept intruding into my thoughts. It was not a happy picture.

But none of these possibilities turned out. We crept along the trail for about 15 or 20 minutes. We were steadily climbing and the going was rough in spots, so that I began to find myself a little winded. Suddenly, as we neared the top and were coming around a corner, John stopped short and called me urgently. But all I had seen was a flash of yellow hurtling with unbelievable speed into the brush. I didn't even get the rifle to my shoulder.

On the way back to camp John outlined a plan. While he thought we had ruined our chances with our lion that morning, he felt that we should at least make a drive through the heavy cover the lion had disappeared into on the slope of the hill. There was a chance the lion had remained hidden there rather than cross the open plain for another patch of cover somewhere in the surrounding country. We would equip the camp personnel with pots and tin cans and send them across the cover. Scotty and I would be on stands.

Scott and Dave were having lunch when we drove up. They had had bad luck too. They had heard the lion coming to the dead giraffe. But the animal must have winded them before coming into the open. In any event, it had suspected all was not quite right and had never shown itself. They were still full of hope for the evening or following morning. In the meantime, they were enthusiastic about John's plans for the afternoon lion drive.

In a short time our mixed band of hunters was back at the hill. After a bit of planning and assignment of responsibilities, Scotty and I were taken to our stands by Dave. I was left by a tree about midway up the hill with instructions to climb it, get comfortable on a good-sized limb, keep quiet and wait.

Dave and Scotty took off and I felt very much alone. I got up the tree in very short order, but my position dismayed me somewhat. While there was quite a bit of space between the ground and my limb in front, there was very little between my sagging posterior and the sharply rising ground behind me.

John had taken the drivers to the opposite side of the brush. After another 10 minutes or so I suddenly heard the first tentative banging and rattling of pots and cans, and some of the most unenthusiastic shouting I've ever heard. The Africans, understandably, were not very keen about their job. The noise continued and then I made out the first figure carefully wending its way forward through the brush on the opposite flank of our hill. Soon a few more men drifted into view. Nothing seemed to be stirred by their noisemaking. If there were any lions in the vicinity, they were lying mighty low.

Then I heard a slight noise. Perhaps it was the rattle of a small rock as it rolled downhill. I saw or heard nothing for the next few moments but I knew that something was making its stealthy, quiet way toward my tree ahead of the beaters on the other side. I gripped my rifle and my limb tightly, checked my safety, placed it on half-safe, tentatively raised the Model 70 to my shoulder.

Another noise. And then I noted a movement in the brush a scant 20 yards directly in front of my perch. I brought the rifle up as the silent figure glided out of the brush and walked directly under my tree and I almost fell off the limb as the hyena lost itself in the brush behind me. It was the only animal the beaters put out that day.

We were now a discouraged crew. On the way back to camp John gently pointed out that our lion hunting days were probably over. We had had our chance, which is all any man can ask for, and now we would go back to hunting plains game in a nice leisurely fashion. Meanwhile, Scotty and Dave would go back to their giraffe carcass to wait out their lion. They had a good chance since that particular beast had not been rustled up as much as mine.

Dave and Scotty got up in the middle of the night and were off for their lion site long before dawn. John and I luxuriated in our cots until the decadent hour of six A.M., had a long lazy breakfast and decided to make an easy hunt on the plains in the early morning air about seven A.M. In short order we were casually rolling along in the Land Rover with Kiebe and Mohammed as companions. There was an early morning haze drifting up from the plain.

There was a grove of acacia and fever trees shielding a small water hole to the right of our intended path some 300 or 400 yards away. We were plotting a course between yesterday's lion hill and that water hole when John suddenly pulled to a halt. He remained silent as he continued to stare ahead. I looked forward and suddenly something—I know not what to this day—made me uneasy. I was aware that something was somehow wrong, but I could not put my finger on it. At the same time Kiebe murmured something in Swahili to John, who grunted what seemed to be an affirmative.

"Listen to those jackals over at the water hole," I remarked, "sounds like they're really feasting."

"Yes, yes, look a minute, Jim." John's quiet tones had an undercurrent of expectant excitement. "See those kongoni! They should be staring at the water hole or us, but they're not . . . they're looking up at the hill. Let's see . . . hell's bells, there are two lions!" He shoved the Land Rover into low, spun the steering wheel, drove in a wide circle. We were heading back behind the hill.

In no time flat John had the Rover revved up into second and then third. We were soon bouncing along the plain at a good 35 miles an hour, which is a lot faster than anyone should. I crawled back into the rear seat and got our big-bore rifles ready. Then—as we jostled and bounced along our way—I stuck my head and shoulders through the porthole in the top of the cab so I could keep the lions in sight. John wanted to know if they moved or showed any alarm at our movement.

Once we rounded the hill the lions were out of sight. Without a word, everyone but Mohammed jumped from the vehicle. With John in the lead, we took off at a fast pace for the top of the hill. I stayed right on John's heels.

"Look, you'll have about half a minute at best for your shot when we pop over that hill. The lion will be in that thick brush in a flash when it gets wind of us," John whispered as he lengthened his stride.

75

I nodded, a thousand thoughts and questions going through my head. And then we were at the top of the hill and John crouched down as he eased his body over the crest. I was a second behind him, but only a second. I looked down and there they were. I threw my rifle to my shoulder as the lioness popped her head up and the male jumped to its feet.

"Shoot—shoot quick! They've seen us!" There was a flash of yellow that sped through the telescopic sight. I swung the Model 70 like a shotgun and pulled the trigger as my sight swept through the lion's running shoulder. The crack of the rifle blurred my vision in the sight and I raised my head for a second just in time to see the lion spin its back quarters a bit. I hurriedly worked another cartridge into the chamber and tossed another bullet behind the lion as it disappeared into the brush, the lioness hard on its heels. The whole thing was over in less than 10 seconds.

"Oh, hell . . . you've missed. Well, that ties it, you'll never get another chance like that!" Kingsley-Heath said in quiet despair. "Two great chances . . . I guess lions just aren't your meat."

"No, no!" Kiebe was gesturing violently and with firm conviction. He had raised his left arm and repeatedly pointed with his right forefinger to the rib area directly below the armpit.

"Shot? Are you sure?" John turned to me, "Jim, Kiebe says that you hit. Did you? I didn't hear the bullet hit or see anything."

"I think I hit him the first time . . . his hind end seemed to spin around. It happened so fast I can't be sure, but I think so." Kiebe had run to where the lions had been sitting and was shouting and wildly gesturing. We ran forward. There was blood and bits of flesh on the ground.

"Oh, my lord, you've shot him in the ass," John sighed as if someone had just passed a hanging sentence with little hope of reprieve. He stood there shaking his head, silent for a moment or two, listening carefully for another minute and then turning to speak in a long, low conversation in Swahili with Kiebe, who had lost quite a bit of his previous enthusiasm. After a moment, he turned to me, gave me a careful glance, seemed to make up his mind about something, and motioned me to check my rifle and closely follow him. Kiebe brought up the rear.

We walked very slowly and quietly forward for a few paces and then stopped. John and Kiebe said nothing and I—in the blackest despair—

kept my mouth shut. Both of my companions seemed to be straining for some sixth sense that would keen their natural five to some sort of hint of what was ahead. Silence. No bird sang. No animal chattered. The wind was still. We went forward a few more paces. We were entering the first scattered bits of brush and bush that thickened a few yards ahead and concealed anything that might be lurking in the shadows.

We stopped, listened and then continued a bit farther. Again and again we stopped. Still nothing. Only an occasional bit of flesh on a bush or a crimson drop on the grass forced the reality of the situation onto us. We could not forget or pretend that it had never happened. And then John motioned us back.

We slowly walked backward, our faces and guns pointed forward into the hidden danger ahead. In a few more minutes we were back in the open and down the slope. Mohammed was waiting for us by the tree that had sheltered the lions for their sunbath another world before. He had brought the Land Rover up, expecting to load a lion. Instead he had found a mess—the classical case of the wounded lion in heavy brush with possible death for some.

When we got back to the vehicle, John sighed heavily, propped his rifle against the fender and lit a cigarette. I stood silent ashamed. Ashamed that I had put these decent, hardworking, honorable people in such a rotten mess. I knew that John had been badly mauled by a client's wounded lion in 1961 and had very nearly died. Kiebe saved his life but had been chewed up a bit as well. Both of them had a finely engraved memory of wounded lions.

Kiebe suddenly barked a short Swahili sentence and pointed downhill and across the plain below us. We followed his finger to the slowly moving Land Rover patiently making its way on a parallel path some miles distant. A lazy ribbon of dust rose behind the car for some distance. We ran forward shouting and waving our shirts. When it seemed that they would continue on without seeing us, the Rover suddenly veered in our direction and picked up speed. It was Scotty and Dave, of course, and in five minutes they pulled up beside us.

''What goes, chaps, got a lion or something?'' Dave said with a grin.

''Yes, a wounded lion—over there in that brush,'' John said.

''Good-bye,'' Dave said. But they got out of the car. Dave's grin was gone. He had been bitten by a wounded leopard a couple of years before.

77

As I hurriedly briefed Scotty on one side, Dave and John held a conference with their senior gun bearers. In a few moments they came over and told us to load up our rifles and take a stand on the top of the Land Rovers. We would be able to command the area below a small bluff they intended to climb for a view of the brush they thought hid the lion. They took a long swing around through the open, went over the rim of the ridge and approached the knoll from behind. We watched from below as they hunkered down to scan the brush below them.

They sat and sat and sat. Then they conferred and sat some more. And so it went for a good 20 minutes. Finally a decision was reached. The whole party got up and proceeded down on the opposite side—through the brush—from which they had climbed originally. In another 10 minutes they were back.

"We got a surprise," John said. "We thought he was down in that brush under that little knob. But when we took a long swing around and down through the brush on our way back, we cut his blood trail leading out over to that heavy brush farther along the side of the hill. We've got to follow him up right away before he runs across a native."

The two pros got out their double rifles—both .470's. Scott limbered up his .458 Model 70. Kiebe, Katheka and I all had .375 H&H Model 70 rifles. John outlined the ground rules. The name of the game was kill the lion as fast and as completely as possible. If you saw the lion, start shooting . . . you might not get many seconds to make up your mind. Dave led the way and John backed him up. Scotty covered the high ground. I covered the low ground below our path. Kiebe and Katheka covered our rear.

We would stalk a few yards and stop to listen. When we did, everyone would face outward to form the classic "British square." Safeties off. In no time at all we had picked up a patch of blood where the lion had lain down after its first escape. Spots here and there showed its retreat on a steady line to the left around the hill.

We went forward a few yards and stopped as before. Every sense was tense, expecting the worst. Curiously, I felt a strange excitement. We continued a few more yards and stopped, then a few more punctuated by another hesitation. And then suddenly John, who was immediately in front of me and slightly above to the left, raised his rifle and fired. All heads and rifles turned toward the spot where he had aimed. Nothing moved.

"I missed him," John said. "I just saw the top of his mane and took an estimate where his head was and shot. Couldn't take a chance. I saw him take off." He moved forward and held something up. His .470 bullet had clipped a bit of mane.

A shout from Kiebe drew our attention behind us. We turned to see Kiebe bending down over a dark patch 20 feet directly behind where Scott and I had stood.

When we ran down, we found a patch of darkening, already clotting blood.

"John, you shot at another lion!" Dave gasped and turned his rifle toward a bloody path leading away from the gore. "He must have laid doggo here through the whole thing . . . boy we're lucky he didn't take somebody when we all turned at John's shot. Two lions . . . just what we needed!"

"Let's get to it," John said. "He can't be far ahead and from the look of that blood he's hurt worse than we thought." Without another word, the white hunters started down the path of broken grass and occasional blood spore.

We had just got our party sorted out and in their customary position on the trail—with each guarding an approach to the group—when there was a low growl. Dave came skittering back toward me and a flash of yellow spurted out of the brush as two quick shots split the air. The lion turned and was gone again.

"Missed him, I think, but maybe not," Dave said. "Can't tell, but he won't be turned again. Come on, Jim, he's your lion. Scotty, keep your safety off too." He checked his partner with a glance and they were off. We hadn't gone 20 yards when that same growl filled my ears, heart, bowels and every inch of my frame. I forced my feet forward just as I saw Dave raise his rifle again. The lion was coming out of the grass. Dave shot. The lion jumped, the bullet tearing into its back.

"Get him, Jim!" I shot. The bullet bit into the upper shoulder, breaking the animal down. The lion savagely bit at the wound as I shot another time. The bullet hit the paw and entered the head. The animal raised its head, but the mane obscured a good shot. I shot again, tearing into its spine. The lion was turning and twisting, trying to get back at us. I shot again and the lion collapsed. I had finally found the brain. The lion quivered, shuddered in a last convulsion and relaxed into death. We watched the still form for a few tentative moments. Kiebe tossed a rock, then another. He poked a long stick at the lion's eyelid.

"He's dead," John said. "He ought to be—with all those holes in him."

"You said shoot till he didn't move and I shot," I answered.

"I'm not complaining, I'm not complaining!" John's face opened in a wide, happy grin. "Well, I must say I'm glad this ended this way." Kiebe was examining the lion's chest and muttering to himself.

"What's that?" John asked. "Jim hit him in the ribs with the first shot after all?" Kiebe was acting very smug. His estimation of my original shot was right. My shot had entered directly below and behind the shoulder. But due to my elevated position on the top of the hill, the bullet had angled down to come out of the bottom of the lion's body instead of coursing through the lungs to the other side and out.

"I take back all those things I've said and the many more I've thought," John said. "That was either the best or the luckiest damn shot you've ever made in your life!"

"Lucky. I didn't even know I'd hit him for sure, but I'm glad I didn't make a botch of it with a shot in his rear."

"That would have been a dead lion in a couple more hours," Dave added.

The mention of time brought me back to reality. We had not been thinking about hours and minutes. I looked at my watch. It was 11 o'clock. I had shot the lion at about seven-thirty. This had been a hair-raising way to spend a sunny morning in Africa.

THE LEOPARD

by Jack O'Connor

The leopard is one of the handsomest of the great cats and in historic times it has certainly been the most widely distributed. With black rosettes on a golden body, the leopard makes such uniformly colored cats as the lion and the cougar seem drab by comparison. Some even consider the leopard more beautiful than the great tiger.

In recent times no other large cat has had anything like the enormous range of the leopard, and no other cat has clung to its range so tenaciously. There are leopards in the frozen subarctic forests of Siberia, in the bamboo and reed beds of China, over a large part of central Asia, in the Caucasus Mountains, in Asia Minor, over most of Africa, all of India, in Java, Sumatra, on the Malay Peninsula, and on the island of Ceylon.

The leopard is still found over most of this vast range. But the range of the lion is constantly shrinking, and as game is killed off and jungle is cut down, the tiger is found in fewer and fewer places. Yet the cunning and furtive leopard manages to maintain its numbers remarkably well. Kill off the deer and wild pig on which the leopard preys, and cut down the jungle which shelters it, and the leopard will find a home in a little rocky hill next door to a village and live on scrubby chickens, village goats and dogs. Keep the goats locked up and the leopard will turn cattle killer.

The leopard is a gleaming, golden animal. In tropical areas its hair is short; in cold climates the pelage grows long in winter. In moist, dark forests, the coats of the leopards are darker—almost an orange. Melanism is not uncommon among the leopards of those areas, and now and then a black leopard turns up. These are often seen in zoos and are generally called black panthers, (in India leopards are more often called panthers than leopards). These handsome creatures do not belong to a separate race. Instead, a black leopard will show up in a litter of ordinary ones, just as a female black bear may have one black cub and one brown one.

In desert areas, leopards tend to be lighter in color, just as they are darker when they live in heavy forest. In 1958, when I was hunting in the southern part of the Sahara desert and in brush country that borders it, my companion, Elgin Gates, shot a very large and heavy leopard that was a pale buff, the lightest in color I have ever seen. The desert cheetahs we saw on that trip were even lighter in color, much lighter than the cheetahs of the high grasslands of East Africa.

As compared to the lion and the tiger, the leopard is not a large animal. The big male leopard shot by Gates in Chad had then the second largest skull ever recorded and as leopards go it was an enormous animal. I helped measure the creature and it went eight feet, two inches between pegs, the proper way to measure all cats. In the then current edition of Rowland Ward's *Records of Big Game*, the record leopard (before skinning) is listed as nine feet, seven inches. I no more believe that record than I would believe the record of a man 15 feet tall. The notion of a leopard measuring between pegs the same as the largest lion is simply preposterous.

In fact, I cannot think of any more worthless piece of information for a record book than the length of an animal before skinning. Hunters will exaggerate just as handily as fishermen, and once an animal is skinned there is no way either to prove or to disprove his statements. Some of the "length before skinning" data on lions in the record book are equally preposterous. As is the case with American bears, the only measurements not open to chicanery are those of the skull.

Be that as it may, the usual safari leopard measures between pegs from five feet four inches to seven feet in length, and weighs from 60 to 125 or 130 pounds.

A. A. Dunbar Brander, author of *The Wild Animals of Central India*, says the leopards that hang around villages picking up an occasional chicken or dog are much smaller and lighter than those that live in the jungle and devour deer and wild boar. The big jungle leopards, he writes, measure from seven feet two inches to seven feet nine inches. What he calls a "fair average specimen" measured seven feet five inches between pegs and weighed 152 pounds. This sounds like a pretty big leopard to me. I haven't weighed many leopards but I have weighed dozens of deer and can usually guess an animal's weight fairly well. I don't think I have ever seen a leopard that would weigh much over 150 pounds. One I shot in 1959 in Tanzania probably measured about seven feet eight inches, as the hide made into a rug is now exactly eight feet long. This was a larger but not extraordinary male, solid and chunky, but I doubt if it weighed 150 pounds. I have heard of 185-pound leopards but they must be rare.

For its size the leopard is enormously strong. In East Africa, where there are many hyenas and where a pack of these strong-jawed scavengers will run a leopard off its kill, the spotted cat habitually hangs its kill in a tree, wedging the head into a fork made by two branches. It is not uncommon to see antelope and large zebra colts weighing twice as much as a large leopard hung up in a tree. One observer reports seeing a young giraffe that would weigh twice as much as the heaviest leopard neatly strung up.

I have never heard of a man-eating leopard in Africa, probably because wild game is plentiful and there is little incentive for the handsome cats to gnaw on human beings. In India, man-eaters are common and some of the most cunning and destructive of all man-eaters have been leopards. A leopard finally shot by the famous Colonel Jim Corbett, author of *Man Eaters of India*, killed and ate 125 people between the time it started its grisly career in 1918 until it was finally shot in 1926. This deadly creature was a light-colored leopard with short, brittle hair. It measured between pegs seven feet six inches, and seven feet ten inches over curves. A rug-mounted hide of this sort would measure over 8 feet.

In India the leopard is a remorseless hunter of the monkeys, which are sacred to the Hindus and which are called langurs. The monkeys hate and fear leopards and scream at them whenever they are in sight. Every inhabitant of the jungle hates the leopard. The spotted deer (chital) bark at them and so do the little hog deer. When the large sambar see a tiger or a leopard they make a sound called "belling." It is possible to follow the progress of a tiger or a leopard through the jungle by listening to the racket made by the jungle folk. Corbett says that leopards are not difficult to stalk, since the leopard has no very keen sense of smell and since monkeys, deer and birds keep the hunter informed as to the cat's location.

In Africa, leopards are exceedingly fond of baboon meat, and the baboons hate them for it. On a couple of occasions I have seen leopards because baboons were making a racket. Baboons are courageous creatures and when the odds are on their side they do not hesitate to gang up on a leopard—and generally the leopard takes off while still in one piece.

All of the creatures of the jungle and the veldt are afraid of leopards and never fail to watch one when it is in sight. I have seen lions stroll through herds of feeding game. Individual animals would move off a little way to give the lions room, but otherwise they paid little attention to the great cats.

But when a leopard is in sight, everything watches it. Once in northeast Tanzania, Syd Downey, famous Kenya professional hunter, my wife, Eleanor, and I were scouting some new territory when we saw a herd of about 30 topis all gazing fixedly in one direction. We turned our attention in that direction and there, lit by the rays of the rising sun, was a gorgeous gold-and-black leopard standing against the dark-red stone toward the top of one of the little rocky hills called kopjes in Africa. I have never seen a more lovely sight. It was so perfectly staged that it seemed theatrical.

A leopard will prey on anything it can overpower, even creatures several times as large as it is. When I was hunting tigers in India, leopards killed two of our tiger baits, half-grown water buffalos that must have been three to five times as heavy as the leopard. In both India and Africa, leopards simply love domestic dogs, and many a beloved pet has been stolen by a leopard right out from under its master's nose. Mickey and Monique Micheletti, who outfitted me in the Chad in 1958, had a charming little mongrel bitch who used to awaken me during the night by sticking her cold little nose in my hand to be petted. A leopard came right into the Micheletti yard on the outskirts of Fort Archambault and killed her.

In the wild parts of Africa, the leopard certainly has its place in the balance of nature. Wherever leopards are trapped out for their handsome hides, the baboons and warthogs increase, destroy the crops in the native shambas, and often bring the tribesmen to the point of starvation. Along the Save River in Mozambique, where my wife and I hunted in 1962, the natives had just about exterminated both lions and leopards by building thorn fences around the waterholes and then putting heavy wire snares in the gaps so animals coming to water would be caught. Since a predator has to have water in order to digest meat, lions and leopards were more easily caught than the grass-eating antelope. Now the country has a surplus of baboons and simply swarms with warthogs and the odd-looking wildebeests. There is also a great surplus of impalas, animals about the size of whitetail deer and favorite leopard prey.

In the mountains of the Middle East, where it gets very cold and heavy snows often lie for weeks, the leopards prey on wild sheep, ibex, roe deer, their young on wild boar and Caspian red deer. They also pick up domestic sheep and goats, colts, village dogs. I have never gone out in Iran deliberately to hunt leopards, but in hunting sheep and ibex I have seen a surprising amount of leopard sign.

In 1959 I actually saw a leopard there. An Iranian nobleman named Yar Mohammed Shadloo and I had seen three handsome urial rams on a ridge across a wide draw. There was absolutely no way to stalk them, so the only thing we could do was to lie low and hope the rams would feed over to the other side of the ridge.

Presently they did so. My friend and I gave them time to settle down and also to come back for a peek over the ridge to make sure they weren't being followed, a wise but annoying precaution wild sheep often take. Then, fully expecting to find the rams as soon as we topped the ridge, we crossed the draw. But no rams did we see. Instead, we saw the signs that all three had left suddenly and in a hurry. Then we saw why. About 200 yards away and below us was the head of a juniper-filled draw and slipping through it we saw the gold-and-black body of a fine leopard. Yar Mohammed thought it would be worthwhile for him to go around and come into the draw from below on the chance that the leopard might still be there and emerge. But we never saw that handsome cat again.

The Uralian country on the border of Iran and Russia looks exactly like the rolling, juniper-covered hills and brakes of Wyoming, Colorado, Utah, New Mexico and Arizona. And like this country in the western United States, these Iranian mountains can get very cold with deep snow and driving, frigid winds. I had always thought of the leopard as an exotic, tropical animal, and seeing one in country just like our West gave me a feeling of overwhelming strangeness. It was as odd as if I had bumped into a giraffe when I was hunting pheasants in an Idaho stubblefield. . . .

Ask any experienced African hunter which he considers the most dangerous African animal and he will answer right out of his own experience. If he has had a close one with a lion, the lion gets the vote. If he had been run over and hurt by a buffalo or tossed by an elephant, these are the creatures he nominates. Enough people have had close ones with leopards to hold them in great respect.

As a fellow with a tender regard for my own hide, I seldom take chances with dangerous game and try never to shoot except when I know precisely where the bullet is going to land. As a consequence, I have on five African safaris been charged only once and that was by a buffalo. I have, however, read everything I could find on dangerous game and I have talked to many white hunters who have had experience which cannot be duplicated in these days of less game and smaller bags. My own notion is that the lion is by far the most dangerous of the African animals, but the leopard if it were as large and as powerful as the lion would be much more dangerous.

A good big male lion will weigh around 400 pounds; an exceptional one may go 500. As we have seen, it takes a big leopard to weigh 150, and some weigh less than 100. A big lion, therefore, is around three times heavier than a big leopard and is, of course, enormously stronger. Anyone mauled by a lion is much more apt to stay mauled than if he had been worked over by a leopard. There are two reasons for this. First is the greater strength of the lion; second is the lion's greater tendency to stay with a victim. The lion that mauled my white-hunter friend John Kingsley-Heath so badly a few years ago stayed right with him and was oblivious of other people. On the other hand the leopard will leap from person to person, inflicting painful but not necessarily deadly wounds.

Powerful men have actually killed leopards (generally wounded) with their bare hands. A famous case was that of Carl Ackley, the taxidermist and sculptor who collected and mounted many of the animals in the Hall of African Mammals at the American Museum of Natural History in New York.

The leopard, a small female, sprang on Ackley, chewing and scratching him painfully. He grappled with it, kept its teeth away from his throat, managed to get it down, and crushed the life out of it with one knee by driving the ribs through its lungs.

I have been told that wounded leopards are even more apt to stand their ground and fight than lions. They are very fast, they are tricky, and unlike lions they do not reveal their presence by growling before they charge. Suddenly there is a snarling ball of black-and-yellow fury and all hell breaks loose.

One white hunter who was rather messily chewed was following a leopard wounded by a client. When the leopard charged, the client turned to run and got in the hunter's way so he was unable to shoot. The leopard knocked the hunter down and his rifle flew from his hands. The leopard then bounced from white hunter to gun bearer, then back to white hunter, biting and clawing each. The second gun bearer ran the client down, took his rifle away from him, and returned to kill the leopard.

This white hunter was mauled quite severely. He had to go to a hospital, where he spent weeks in recovering. He did not, however, lose his nerve. Not long after he went back to work again, another client gut-shot a leopard and it was the white hunter's painful duty to follow it into a kopje where it had taken refuge in a crack between two great boulders. The white hunter followed up the wounded cat, and killed it with buckshot from a shotgun when it charged. Safaris out for leopards always carry shotguns for just such emergencies, incidentally, as a speeding leopard is much easier to hit with a shotgun than with a rifle.

A leopard story I'll never forget concerned the famous Bwana Cottar, an Oklahoman who moved to Kenya prior to World War I and made his living as a professional hunter and an ivory hunter. Cottar was rough and tough, a crack shot, and a powerful giant of a man. He had many close calls with animals and was mauled by leopards several times. He always said that somewhere in the bush there was a leopard who was going to kill him, but actually he was finally killed by a rhino.

A leopard mauling had left Cottar's left arm so stiff and crooked that it was almost useless for hunting and he had to do his shooting one-handed. Then one day he and a white hunter of my acquaintance went into some brush to knock off a leopard that had been wounded by a Kenya farmer. Cottar took the charge, but because of his handicap of a bad arm he missed his shot. The leopard mauled him briefly and very painfully, then bounced off of him to maul a gunbearer for a few seconds before it got away into another heavy patch of brush.

The sun was going down then and a storm was coming up. The other white hunter felt that it would be the better part of wisdom to leave the leopard alone for the night. It would probably stiffen up and might even die. No matter what it did, it would probably stay in that patch of heavy brush.

So the party, temporarily defeated, retreated to the farmhouse, which was not far away. Cottar's painful wounds were washed, disinfected and dressed, and Cottar began drinking whiskey to ease his pain. After dinner he was suffering so that he could not lie down and rest. Instead, the maimed and wounded old white hunter walked up and down on the veranda while the wind blew and the rain fell, taking an occasional shot of pain killer, and cursing every leopard that had ever lived.

As he drank and cursed he gradually worked himself up into such a rage that he could no longer stand it. He picked up a shotgun, hung a barn lantern on his crooked arm, and rushed out into the stormy night to settle accounts with the leopard. The wounded cat was still in its patch of brush, still angry, and still full of bitter and defiant courage. Cottar induced it to charge and that time he didn't miss. He returned in triumph carrying his shotgun in one hand and the limp and rain-bedraggled leopard over his shoulder.

"By God," he told the other white hunter and the farmer when he awakened them. "I feel better already now that I have settled scores with the blighter. A few more drinks and I'll be able to sleep!"

The first time I went on safari in Africa, I didn't buy a leopard license because it cost $75 and an official told me that I stood but one chance in 10 of seeing a leopard. This struck me as being pretty poor odds for my 75 bucks. Actually I must have seen a dozen or more leopards, several of which I could have shot. I saw my first leopard within a half hour after leaving camp the first morning we hunted. One of the gun bearers whispered, "Chui," the Swahili word for leopard, and I saw the beautiful gold-and-black cat bounding across the fragrant grass for some brush.

Another time I had made a hike of about a mile just at dawn to take a look at a zebra a companion and his white hunter had put up as a lion bait. At that time my companion had shot a lion but I was still looking for one. When my white hunter and I got to the "hide" (the spot behind some bushes where the bait could be observed) a magnificent leopard was feeding on the bait and only about 80 yards away. I wished, of course, that I had bought a license but I had not and there was nothing I could do about it. Then two lionesses and three cubs showed up. They told the leopard what they thought of spotted cats in general and of it in particular

88

and it had some appropriate remarks to make about lions. However, as the two lady lions moved in the leopard moved off.

In 1959, the first time I ever went all out to shoot a leopard, my wife, Eleanor, Syd Downey, and I went out the first afternoon to put up some leopard baits. Eleanor shot a zebra, her first head of African game. We cut it in half and hung the pieces in two trees about a mile apart. The next afternoon, in the second of the two trees, we saw a nice big male leopard lying on a limb above the dangling bait. At the foot of the tree was a hungry male lion. Since it wouldn't be sporting to shoot a leopard that was helpless and marooned by a lion, we passed the leopard up and led the lion away from the bait tree with a freshly shot Grant's gazelle. But we never did get another leopard on that bait as a pride of lions insisted on hanging around and kept their smaller cousins away. We finally cut the bait down and let the lions have it.

Old lions do not climb much; they are too heavy. But the leopard is as much at home in trees as on the ground, and it can sleep in a tree with every evidence of sound and satisfactory slumber, quiet except for its long and writhing tail, which tells the quality of its dreams. Unlike most other animals, the leopard comes down a tree head first. Try that sometime when you don't have anything else to do.

In India, the shikaris (hunting parties) do not hang dead baits for leopards as they do in Africa. Instead, they stake out a bleating goat or a lonesome, howling dog, then either hide on a pile of rocks or in the brush or on a platform called a machan in a tree. They then wait for a leopard to come for a free meal. In Iran, so far as I know, sitting up with a "calling" goat is the only method of leopard hunting ever used.

East Africa has the finest leopard hunters in the world. What I know about baiting for leopards I learned from a master—Syd Downey. Syd selects his bait trees with care. He likes to find a tree near a rocky kopje, where leopards like to den up. If the kopje is in good leopard country and near open water it is almost certain to contain a leopard. He likes to have the tree in such a spot that the prevailing wind will blow in a direction so that human scent from the waiting hunter will not blow past the leopard on the route it is apt to follow. A leopard, incidentally, will seldom approach through a large open area. Instead it will come to a bait tree from the nearest brush. If it can find one it prefers a route along a line of bushes. A leopard is as silent as a shadow. One moment the tree is empty and nothing is moving except some vultures in a nearby tree and some buzzing bees on the bait. The next moment, there is the leopard, alert, beautiful, and terrible.

When Syd and I were hunting leopards, our "hide" by the tree where I finally shot mine was a pile of stones about 50 yards from the bait. We could squat behind them, and then when the leopard finally came, all I had to do was to stand up, put my left hand on the rock, rest the fore end of the .375 against my hand, steady the crosswires in the scope against Old Chui, and gently squeeze the trigger. The leopard was quartering away from me and fell from the tree as inert as a bag of flour and never moved.

In more unsophisticated parts of Africa, leopards are generally shot simply when someone blunders into one, and the art of baiting is not understood. In Angola I saw some baits a Portuguese white hunter had hung. Nothing had been shot on them—and small wonder! They were out in the open—both distant from water and from any place where a leopard would lie up. There was no concealed approach so a leopard would feel happy about sneaking up and looking the bait over unobserved. And the baits were so hung that the leopard would have no comfortable spot from which to feed. Finally, there was no way for the hunters to stalk the baits and no place within 100 yards for them to hide.

In another area in Portuguese Africa, no white hunter had ever been able to bait a leopard and had no notion how it was done. A veteran East African white hunter came in, hung three baits, and shot three leopards off them in two days.

Brought to a bait either live or dead, a leopard usually affords a very easy shot and there is little excuse for missing or wounding one. However, there are several things to contend with. For one thing, the hunter must be still and remain quiet as the leopard has wonderful ears and eyes. For another, the hunter must keep his shirt on and not move into a position to shoot until the leopard is eating or looking in another direction. The hunter must also fight buck fever, a malady that is apt to attack almost anyone the first time he gets a good look at a wild leopard. Also, the leopard has an annoying habit of showing up when it is almost dark.

I shot my only leopard with a .275 Magnum, but I doubt a .375 kills leopard one bit deader than a rifle of a much lighter caliber. A skilled and experienced white hunter I know swears by a .243 Winchester with

100-grain bullets. Another has shot several with a .270 and 130-grain bullets and has never had a miscue. Yet another prefers a .30/06 with 180-grain soft-point bullets. Whatever the caliber used, the rifle should be equipped with a scope. My idea of the best scope for leopard shooting in poor light is about 2½ or 3X with a coarse crosswire reticle. With such a scope, the shot can be well placed, even when it is too dark to see the intersection of the crosswires.

The leopard is a frail creature with delicate bones. It isn't hard to kill when hit right with a bullet that expands quickly against light resistance. But hit wrong, a leopard can be one of the most dangerous and vindictive animals in the world.

Outdoor Life
August 1964

THE WILDERNESS HUNTER THEODORE ROOSEVELT

by Theodore Roosevelt

A s regards strenuous, vigorous work, and pleasurable excitement of the chase the bighorn alone stands higher. But the bighorn, grand beast of the chase though he be, is surpassed in size, both of body and of horns, by certain of the giant sheep of Central Asia; whereas the wapiti is not only the most stately and beautiful of American game—far more so than the bison and the moose, his only rivals in size—but is also the noblest of the stag kind throughout the world. Whoever kills him has killed the chief of his race; for he stands far above his brethren of Asia and Europe.

—Theodore Roosevelt, 1893

IN THE BITTERROOT MOUNTAINS

I spent a week in vain effort to kill a moose. Then as we had no meat, we determined to try for elk. We were camped with a wagon, as high among the foothills as we could go, but hours' walk from the range of game, for it was still early in the season, and they had not yet come down from the upper slopes. Accordingly we made a practice of leaving the wagon for days at a time to hunt, only to return to get a night's rest in the tent preparatory for a fresh start. On these trips we carried neither blankets nor packs, as the walking was difficult and we had much ground to cover. Each merely put on his jacket with a loaf of frying pan bread and a paper of salt stuffed into the pockets. We were cumbered with nothing save our rifles and cartridges.

We left camp at sunrise, walking uphill through a rather open growth of small pines and spruces, the traveling being easy. Then we came to the edge of a deep valley a couple of miles across. Into this we scrambled down a steep slide, where the forest had grown up amongst immense boulder masses. Going was difficult: Great rocks, dead timber, slippery pine needles, and loose gravel entailed caution at every step, while we had to guard our rifles carefully against the consequences of a slip. It was not much better at the bottom, which was covered by a tangled mass of swampy forest. Through this we hunted carefully but with no success, in spite of our toil. For the only tracks we saw were those of moose. Finally in the afternoon we left the valley and began to climb a steep gorge, down which a mountain torrent roared and foamed in a succession of cataracts.

Three hours' hard climbing brought us to another valley, but of an entirely different character. It was several miles long but less than a mile broad. Save at the mouth it was walled in completely by chains of high rock peaks, their summits snow-capped; the forest extended a short distance up their sides. The bottom of the valley was in places covered by open woodland, everywhere by marshy meadows dotted with dense groves of spruce.

Hardly had we entered this valley before we caught a glimpse of a yearling elk walking rapidly along a game path. We followed as quickly as we could without making a noise but after the first glimpse never saw it again. It is astonishing how fast an elk travels with its ground-covering walk. We went up the valley and saw abundant fresh elk sign. Two or three bands made the valley their headquarters. Among them were some large bulls, which had been trying their horns not only on the quaking asp and willow but also on one another, though the rut had barely begun. By one pool they scooped out a kind of wallow or bare spot in the grass. The place smelt strongly of urine.

By the time the sun set we were sure the elk were toward the head of the valley. We utilized the short twilight in arranging our sleeping place, choosing a thick grove of spruce beside a small mountain tarn at the foot of a great cliff. We were chiefly influenced in our choice by the abundance of dead timber of a size easy to handle—the fuel question being all-important on such a trip where one has to lie without bedding and keep up a fire with no axe to cut wood.

We dragged enough logs to feed the fire throughout the night, then drank our fill at the icy pool and ate a few mouthfuls of bread. As dark came on we sat silently gazing into the flickering blaze, the owls muttering and hooting. Clearing the ground of stones, we lay down beside the fire, pulled our hats over our ears and went to sleep. Of course our slumbers were fitful and broken, for every hour or two the fire got low and had to be replenished. We wakened shivering out of each spell of restless sleep to find the logs smouldering. We were alternately scorched and frozen.

As the first faint streak of light appeared in the dark sky my companion touched me lightly on the arm. We felt numbed by the cold air. At once we sprang up, stretched our arms, examined our rifles, swallowed a mouthful of bread and walked off through the gloomy forest. At first we could scarcely see our way, but it grew rapidly lighter. The gray mist wavered over the wet pools. Morning voices of wilderness began to break the deathlike stillness. After we had walked a couple of miles our hands reddened in the sun rays.

Then, as we trod noiselessly over the dense moss and on the pine needles under the scattered trees, we heard a sharp clang ahead. We knew this meant game of some sort . . . and stealing cautiously ahead soon saw the cause. One hundred twenty-five yards from us in a glade were two bull elk engaged in deadly combat. Two other elk were looking on. It was a splendid sight. The great beasts faced each other with lowered horns, the manes that covered their thick necks and the hair on their shoulders bristling and erect. They charged furiously, the crash of meeting antlers resounding through the valley. The shock threw them both on their haunches; with locked horns and glaring eyes they strove against each other, getting their hind legs well under them, straining every muscle in their huge bodies and squealing savagely. They were evenly matched in weight, strength and courage, and push as they might neither got the upper hand. First one yielded a few inches, then the other. They swayed to and fro in their struggles, smashing the bushes and ploughing the soil.

Finally they separated and stood apart, their sides heaving and columns of steam rising from their nostrils through the frosty air of the brightening morning. Again they rushed together with a crash and each strove mightily to overthrow the other. But the branching antlers caught every vicious lunge and thrust. This set-to was stopped rather curiously. One of the onlooking elk was a yearling while the other was a bit older. The younger was evidently much excited by this battle and now he began to walk toward the two combatants nodding his head and whistling a queer noise. They dared not leave their flanks uncovered to his assault. And as he approached they promptly separated. In a moment one spun around and jumped at his old adversary, seeking to stab the unprotected flank. But the latter was just as quick and caught the onrush with his horns. They closed furiously as ever but the most either could do was to inflict punches on the neck and shoulders of his foe. Again the peace-maker approached, nodding, whistling, threatening, and again they separated.

This was repeated twice more and I began to be afraid lest the breeze which was light and puffy should give them my wind. So resting my rifle on my knee I fired twice, putting a bullet behind the shoulder of one combatant. It was a deadly shot, but, as so often with wapiti, the animal at that moment did not show any sign of being hit. In a moment he fell.

We ran to him, caring for the hide and horns and making a fire over which to have breakfast. We roasted some elk loin and I never ate anything that tasted better.

For all his noble looks the wapiti is a very unamiable beast, who behaves with brutal ferocity to the weak and shows abject terror of the strong. According to his powers, he is guilty of rape, robbery and even murder. And heard at a distance, the call of the wapiti is one of the grandest and most beautiful sounds in nature. This is especially true when several rivals are answering one another on some frosty moonlit night in the mountains. The wild melody rings from chasm to chasm under the giant pine, sustained and modulated with challenge and proud anger.

The next day we walked long and hard and during the night I slept the heavy sleep of the weary. Early in the morning just as the east began to grow gray I awakened and soon sounds caused me to sit up and throw off my cap. Bull elk were challenging among the mountains. I soon left with my rifle. The air was very cold and rang with the challenge of wapiti, their incessant calling peeling down through the woods. First one challenged then another answered. Two herds were approaching one another from opposite sides of the valley. Master bulls were roaring defiance as they mustered their harems.

I walked stealthily up the valley until I felt that I was between the two herds and stood motionless under a pine. The ground was open and nearby ran a little brook with a strangled murmur as the ice along its edges skimmed its breath. What little wind there was breathed in my face and kept me from discovery. I made up my mind from the sound of the challenging that the bull on my right was advancing toward a rival on my left, who answered every call. The former approached so that I could hear him crack the branches and beat the bushes with his horns. I slipped through the trees so as to meet him when he came out of the woodland.

Day broke and crimson gleams played across the mountains and I soon heard the wapiti not 50 yards from me. I cocked my rifle and stood motionless. In a moment the belt of spruces before me swayed open and the lordly bull stepped out. He bore his massive antlers aloft. He sniffed the air and stamped the ground as he walked. As I drew a bead the motion caught his eye and his warlike self-confidence changed to alarm. My bullet smote through his shoulder blades, he plunged wildly forward and fell full length.

Nothing can be finer than a wapiti's carriage when excited or alarmed. He seems the embodiment of strength and stately grace. My guide and I caped the wapiti, cut some meat and then clambered back to camp. It lacked an hour of nightfall and we had a hard climb out of the canyon. There was not a vestige of a path and the climbing was laborious . . . at one or two points not entirely without danger. Personally I was nearly done when we reached the top.

At Two Ocean Pass

The next year I returned with my hunting partner to the Shoshone Mountains in northwestern Wyoming . . . and there is no more beautiful game country in the United States. It is a parkland where glades break the forest and high mountain pastures dot the country. It is open compared to the woodlands farther north. The peaks show a striking boldness in their lofty outlines. We had a pack train and took a complete outfit. In itself packing is both an art and a mystery, and a skillful professional packer, versed in the intricacies of the hitch, packs with a speed which no nonprofessional can hope to rival. Unless a man can pack, it is not possible to make a really hard hunt in the mountains alone or only with a single companion. The mere fair-weather hunter who trusts entirely to the exertions of others and does nothing more than walk or ride under favorable circumstances and shoot at what someone else shows him is a hunter in name only. It is often well to be with some old mountain hunter

who is usually a first-rate hand at finding game an
if wounded. With such a companion one not on
learns many things by observation instead of by [

We traveled and hunted on the eastern edge oɪ ᴜ ᵤ
and mountainous, wherein rise the headwaters of the mighty ᴜ...
River. Most of the distance we followed elk trails. It is heartbreaking
work to drive a pack train through thick timber and over mountains
where there is either a dim trail or none. The animals have a perverse
faculty for choosing the wrong turn at critical moments and they are
continuously scraping under branches or squeezing between tree trunks
to the jeopardy or destruction of their burdens. After having laboriously
been driven up a steep incline, the foolish creatures turn and run to the
bottom so that the work has to be done over again. Yet one cannot but
admire their toughness and the way they pick their way along sheer
mountain sides and among boulders and over fallen logs.

Our way was rough and we had to stop every hour to fix the packs.
And it was no easy task to get the horses across the bogs. Riding a pack
train becomes irritating unless one is held up by the hope of game country
ahead and delight in exploration of the unknown. Buoyed by such a hope
there is pleasure in the experience. After several days we approached the
threshold of our hunting grounds.

The next day gusts of rain blew in my face as I started to ride at the
head of the train. Suddenly the call of a bull elk came down through the
wet woodland and was answered by a rival. We slipped off our horses.
The elk was traveling slowly upwind, challenging every two minutes,
doubtless excited about the fact of his rival on the next mountain. We
followed, being guided by the incessant calling. It was exciting as the
challenge grew nearer. Each call made our veins thrill. Soon I saw the
tips of the horns through the timber and stepped to get a better shot.
Seeing us, but not making out what we were, and full of fierce and
insolent excitement, the bull stepped toward us with a stately and
swinging gait. His 12-tined antlers tossed aloft. I fired into his chest. A
second bullet was not needed.

The dead elk fell among evergreens. The huge shapely body was set
on legs that are strong as steel rods, yet slender, clean and smooth. We
bore off the head and packed it back to the horses.

The next day opened with fog and rain. A stormy morning is a trial to the temper. Nevertheless we started off, down a ravine, up a mountain, onto a plateau. As day drew to an end the storm lulled and we had at least made it to country dotted with well-beaten elk trails. We managed to make it to a forest with good shelter and grass and pitched camp. Next morning brought only occasional rain squalls but we managed to climb the mountains and hunt. We came to a small gorge where we saw some small elk and by the second evening the storm broke and we were comfortable again in camp. The next day dawned clear and cold. As we came up through a deep narrow ravine onto a plateau we heard the call of a bull elk. We headed toward the bugle but the slight wind turned and brought him our scent. He went fast, traveling faster than we did but soon we heard another sonorous challenge to our left. It came from a ridge crest at the edge of the woods. We stumbled up the mountain but in a minute met an outlying spike bull evidently kept on the outskirts of the herd by the master bull. He stood, then we started to move and suddenly we came into view of two cows. We tried to slip out of sight. And were moderately successful. Suddenly I saw the tips of another pair of mighty antlers and 30 yards beyond stood a huge bull. I fired a bullet into his shoulder and he raced off. With my fourth shot I broke his neck. An elk often hesitates in the first moments of surprise and fright and does not really get under way for two or three hundred yards. Once started, he can go several miles, even when wounded. The hunter, after the first shot, should therefore run forward as fast as he can and fire at the quarry until it is dropped. In this way many animals that would otherwise be lost are obtained. But be careful to aim carefully with each shot as if it were the last. No possible rapidity of fire can atone for carelessness of aim with the first shot.

This elk was a giant. And here we stood in the home of homes of all elk: a mountain wilderness, forest broken by park and glade, by bare hillside and barren land and far to the south the daring beauty of the Tetons shot into the sky. Too sheer for the snow to rest on their sides, it filled the rents in their flanks and lay deep between the towering pinnacles of the dark rock. In a hunting trip the days of long monotony of getting to the hunting ground and the days of unrequited toil after it has been reached always far outnumber the red-letter days of success. But it is these times that test the hunter. In the long run common sense and perseverance avail more than any other qualities. The man who does not give up but hunts steadily and resolutely through spells of bad luck is the man who wins success in the end. I was at the end of my hunt.

To me hunting elk in the mountains when they are calling is one of the most attractive of sports, not only because of the size and stately beauty of the quarry and grand nature of the trophy, but because of the magnificence of the scenery and the stirring, manly exciting nature of the chase itself. It yields more vigorous enjoyment than does lurking stealthily through the grand but gloomy monotony of the marshy woodland where dwells the moose. The climbing among the steep forest-clad and glade-strewn mountains is just difficult enough thoroughly to test soundness in wind and limb while without the heartbreaking fatigue of white-goat climbing.

The actual grapple with an angry grizzly is of course far more full of strong eager pleasure, but bear hunting is the most uncertain and usually the least productive. I repeat, whoever kills the elk has killed the chief of his race . . . for he stands far above his brethren of Asia and Europe.

G.P. Putnam's Sons, 1893

BIRD DOGS NEVER DIE

by Charles B. Martin, Sr.

The dark sky seemed to mirror my troubled soul that long-ago November day. Leaden clouds hung heavy as I slowly deepened and widened a grave. Each spadeful of dank, musty earth brought me closer to a moment I faced with mounting dread. The time had come to bury old Crip, an English setter that meant the world to me.

Only someone who has loved a pet can know the bond that exists between a boy and his dog. In this case that bond was especially strong. I was a hunter, and Crip was one of the finest bird dogs that ever lived. What's more, he was one of the final, tangible links that bound us to the memory of my Uncle Luther. Crip was the last dog Luther had owned.

As I paused a moment in my digging, my mind was flooded with nostalgia for those long-gone days when Luther, Dad, Crip, and I hunted mountain grouse and meadow-dwelling bobwhite quail. I recalled the reason we used the nickname Crip instead of his real name, Spot. A car had run him down when he was just a pup, breaking many bones and dooming him to hobble through life on three legs.

This handicap was physical only. There was nothing crippled about his noble spirit or his burning desire to hunt. His inability to range as wide as healthy dogs seemed to intensify his desire to find any bird nearby. I'd seen him put many of the county's finest dogs to shame when it came to pointing birds. He was exceptionally good at finding quail and holding his point until his hunter would flush the birds. Nobody who hunted with old Crip could remember a time when he flushed a quail.

While tossing the last bits of clay from the grave, I was crushed with the realization that I would never hunt again with my uncle and old Crip. Luther had traded his double-barrel shotgun and hunting clothes for an M1 rifle and the olive drab of a World War II infantry soldier. Leaving behind his lovely young wife and baby daughter, he had marched out of

100

our valley never to return. Less than a month after his departure we had read and reread the tear-stained telegram that told us Luther wasn't coming home. A white cross in a Belgian cemetery marks his place for eternity.

I remembered well what he had said to me when he left home: "Take good care of Crip and take him hunting every chance you get."

So the years had flown and Crip had grown old and the guns of hatred had long since ceased. Their rumble faded, and the significant sounds of war could be heard—the silent but somehow deafening sounds of sorrow and mourning. How long till men shall learn that the way to peace is not through war?

With the grave completed, I walked to the barn where Crip was lying on his bed of hay. I picked up a rifle I had left leaning against a manger and softly called his name. He wagged his tail feebly and lifted his pain-racked body. I couldn't bear to look at the sores that were robbing him of life. We had tried every medical means we could find in an attempt to heal them, but all were to no avail. The only merciful thing we could do was to put him out of his misery.

My dad and aunt had discussed having him put to sleep by a veterinarian, but I couldn't tolerate the idea because I didn't want Crip to die in unfamiliar surroundings. Instead, I determined to end his suffering myself and decided the best way to do that would be to let him think we were going hunting again. Soon we headed toward his grave.

As Crip followed me through the woods he knew so well, he made a valiant effort to hunt. Neither the weakness of his legs nor the pain he bore could dim his enthusiasm for guns and hunting. His was the most indomitable spirit I had ever known.

When we reached the mound of freshly dug clay, I kneeled and cradled his head in my lap. No longer was I the teenager who had volunteered with false bravado to do this thing. I was now a heartsick boy whose tears fell on that noble head in my arms.

A few minutes later those arms trembled as I slowly raised the gun. "Dear God," I prayed, "if I'm ever to make a perfect shot, please let it be this." And then old Crip was gone.

I had chosen his final resting place carefully. It was along a trail, up near a meadow we had hunted many times. It was a place where we had often paused to admire the grandeur of the hazy Blue Ridge Mountains stretching from horizon to horizon. I alone know of the place where old Crip turned again toward home. But I realized that the location of a grave is unimportant. The place to bury a dog is in its master's heart. Buried there, it never really dies.

That's where I keep the memory of old Crip. Sometimes when the mood is right, I hear his footsteps on the pathways of my mind. He still returns to me in dreams though the winds above his grave have been blowing for 30 years. When frosty nights have splashed the forest canopy with red and gold, the memory of old Crip still walks beside me.

The ability to remember and to relive the past is one of the greatest gifts bestowed on man.

Through it we can transcend time and even death. It also complements the deep human desire to be remembered. I hope someone I love will pause to think of me when I too have vanished in that labyrinth of ended days.

Outdoor Life
December 1981

BROWN BEAR—1962

by Fred Bear

Here are the day-by-day notes that Fred Bear wrote in his notebook in 1962, when he traveled with his bow to Alaska to hunt brown bear. The challenge proved one of the most dangerous of his career. Try to imagine driving an arrow into a giant brown bear at 20 feet! This is Fred Bear's amazing story.

FRIDAY, April 27—Aboard the *Valiant Maid*. Bob Munger, my hunting companion; Ed Bilderback, skipper; Harley King, guide; Dan Korea, cook. Left Cordova, Alaska, at 11:00 A.M. today. Went into Sheep Bay to check on bears. No sign anywhere. Will sleep here tonight.

SATURDAY, April 28—Came over past Montague Island and tied up at the cannery dock at Port Ashton. It rained this morning, but cleared into a fine day. Am concerned about the heavy snow still here. Most snow they have had in 20 years. The bears will sleep late this spring.

SUNDAY, April 29—Dropped anchor this evening in Nuka Bay after an eight-hour run from Port Ashton. Thought this might be a good place for black bear. We saw a coyote and some whales but no bear. Too much snow here too. We are early for bears. Heading for Afognak Island hoping it will be warmer there.

MONDAY, April 30—The weather was bad last evening. We dropped anchor for the night in Chugach Bay with its small coves and arms. Not so much snow here. Black bears in this area. We saw one in an open place on the side of the mountain. Went ashore and made a stalk, but the wind crossed us up. Took the skiff about five miles downshore and located another bear on a small beach, but he wandered off into the woods. When we saw a third bear on a beach nearby, we were almost within range when the wind changed and he made off.

Later, on another beach, we located more bears and circled through

103

the woods until we were close. One of them came off the beach and bedded down about 20 yards from us. I shot some film of two on the beach. Later the one who had bedded down joined the others. They are digging kelp buried in the gravel. Bob shot an arrow at one and they scampered off into the woods. We scattered and sneaked after them through the spruce, trying to get within range. One had crossed a small frozen pond and I crossed after him. About halfway over I got an opening and shot the bear at about 25 yards. It was a lung shot and I kept after him. With my eyes on the bear, not looking where I was going, I walked into thin ice, and broke through to hips. I found my bear a hundred yards away.

We saw a total of six bears today.

TUESDAY, May 1—We're anchored near an abandoned cannery in Graham Bay—too rough to cross to Barren Islands. Got here about 10:00 P.M. and immediately saw two black bears on the side of the mountain. We decided that Ed should show us how to do it this time. He started off with his bow and arrow. Grass very dry and noisy. The bear heard him and he got only a running shot. We did not see it again.

Did some scrounging around the cannery and an abandoned sawmill. Getting back to the *Valiant Maid* we found her listing badly. There had been a minus tide and she was on bottom. Tide came back in and we are afloat again.

WEDNESDAY, May 2—Made the first half of the run to Afognak. Threw anchor in a bay off an island this morning and got in the skiff to go seal hunting. We got a few nice skins. This country is covered with brant, yellowlegs, honkers, sandhill cranes, swans, all kinds of ducks, cormorants and gulls and terns by the millions. The wind is blowing a gale. Hope it calms down so we can move on to brown bear country. Wonderful weather all the time except for the wind.

THURSDAY, May 3—The wind is even stronger today. We went ashore to hunt marmots. Ed shot one and I saw a parka squirrel. Back at the boat by 12:00 o'clock and departed for Shuyak Island. This is off the tip of Afognak, a short run of about three hours. It was not too rough. We plan to do our brown bear hunting here and on Afognak. It is doubtful if we will get to the Peninsula.

After dropping anchor we got in the skiff and went bear hunting, checking the beaches for tracks. Found some and later saw two bears, about a mile ahead, coming toward us. Perched on a high point overhanging the beach we watched for them to come nearer, but after about 10 minutes they had not come in sight. Our time was short as Harley had the skiff with orders to come up the shore an hour after we left. It was time for him now and we were afraid he would flush the bears. We decided to move toward where we had last seen them. There was a small gully behind the beach and coming down off the point, I was suddenly faced with two bears, looking at me from about 20 yards away. I guess I felt relief when they ran off into the spruce and we saw no more of them.

Getting back to the boat we had a great dinner at 8:30 P.M. This is the nicest bay we have anchored in. Not a breeze stirring. Ducks are quacking and geese are honking. The low island is almost covered with spruce. We think the bears will have to come out to the beach for food. They, both the blacks and brownies, like to dig among the logs for kelp buried by the storms.

FRIDAY, May 4—Dropped anchor in Seal Bay on Afognak. Saw a bear near shore from the *Valiant Maid*, but he saw us and made off over the mountain. We hunted all the bays in the area and at 8:00 P.M. saw two bears on a grassy hillside, but they also saw us.

We went after them. Ed and Bob went one way and Harley and I another. We climbed up beside a big spruce thicket and stood there about 10 minutes. A bear cracked some brush near us, but we did not see him. Had to leave then because of darkness. We saw two foxes and two otters and caught six king crabs in our trap. One crab measured 48 inches across.

SATURDAY, May 5—No bears today. There do not seem to be too many in this area. Perhaps they are not out of hibernation yet. Saw seven foxes though. All color variations from grays through reds to blue to silver. Some were very beautiful. We ate three king crabs tonight, keeping the others alive hung from a cord in the ocean. Weather still holding fine. Sunny and not too cold.

SUNDAY, May 6—Continuing our search today we went down along the east side of Afognak to Isut Bay and saw a lone bear about three miles away in the hills but did not try for him.

I stalked and photographed a fox today. He looked like a cross between a red and gray. These foxes are the largest I have ever seen. They live by beachcombing at low tide—starfish, mussels, sand fleas, and other oddities.

We had a three-hour run back this evening and got here at seven-thirty. Going ashore we found that a bear had been combing the beach while we were gone. We plan to stay here now and hunt the area tomorrow.

Weather is beautiful. The reason we stay on at Afognak is that this definitely is a late spring. Afognak, being low country, is warm and we reason that the bears should be out here earlier. Kodiak Island is higher and has more snow. Two years ago, with an earlier spring, many bears were out there at this time. Had planned this hunt for the Alaska Peninsula, but that is closed for hunting this year from Puale Bay south. There is only a short strip of open hunting area north of the National Katmei Monument Park. Hardly worth the hazardous trip across. Plan to put a seal carcass out for bait today to see if we can create some action. Saw a herd of about 40 Afognak elk and got pictures. Filmed whales and a sea lion eating a fish. Going into a cannery tomorrow for supplies.

MONDAY, May 7—Shot a sea lion this morning and a seal for bear bait. Placed them on different beaches and built a blind near each. A good way to photograph eagles and foxes also. We needed water and ran into Port Williams where we also stocked up on meat and groceries. We met a hunter from Flint, Michigan, and got some bear information from him. He said there was good bear hunting farther down the west side of Afognak. We decided to check it out and made a run into Big Bay. Took the skiff and ran over to a likely beach. As we rose to look over the bank above the beach, there was a bear just beyond, among the logs on the high-tide mark. We tried a stalk but the wind was wrong and he made off into the dense spruce. Checked several bays afoot and found many bear signs. This seems like the spot we have been looking for. As a matter of fact, it looks almost too good.

TUESDAY, May 8—Went hunting afoot this morning. I got busy photographing some eagles and had to track Bob and Ed down. Finally found them and Bob had a big brownie dead on the beach. He shot him with a .375, but I did not hear the shot. Measurements will not be available until the head and feet are skinned. He has a monstrous head and should measure up well. There was another bear with the one Bob shot. Ed and I spent an hour looking for him, but no luck. Ed packed Bob's bearskin and headed back to the skiff. We weighed it when we got to the boat; 175 pounds. After a snack we went foot hunting again. Cut across land to some beaches. Back from the hunt at 8:00 P.M. I'm tired.

WEDNESDAY, May 9—Went to look at the bear and seal carcasses to see if any bears were there. Cruised some beaches and came upon a medium-sized bear. Took some pictures of him and then decided to maneuver through the brush and try to get a shot at him with a blunt for pictures. The bear was about 30 yards out on the beach from us. As we were just about to come out of the spruce, somebody cracked a twig. The bear stood on his hind legs for a full 30 seconds. Bob had the camera and Ed was in front of me. I took the camera and started to run film as he made for the spruce to our right. He was huffing and puffing and I got some pictures of him before he was gone and I was out of film.

Another beautiful day. Ran 400 feet of film. About two o'clock we left the area to scout the country north of us. Plan to give this place a rest and then come back if we don't get a bear before that. Dropped anchor at 4:00 P.M. and went scouting afoot and by skiff. Found some tracks that look promising.

THURSDAY, May 10—Took the skiff and went out cruising the ocean-side this morning. Saw one bear, but he heard the motor and ran off when we were half a mile away. Got back in at 8:00 P.M. Found two rubber crab-pot floats. This makes seven we have found on the beaches as well as a good supply of half-inch nylon rope. We do a lot of beachcombing when looking for bears.

This country has a very comprehensive bird population and we spend a lot of time trying to identify them. The most unique. I believe, is the parrot duck. It has an orange, parrotlike beak, a black body, and black-and-white head. The harlequin duck is spendid, too, as are several variations of cormorant and the noisy, orange-billed oyster catchers. Land otters seem to the be only animals besides the bears.

Went out again at 6:00 P.M. Back at 10:00. Rained all day today, not hard, but steady. Located a bear at 8:30. He came toward us grubbing along the beach. We were hidden in the edge of the spruce. At 17 yards he turned broadside and I started my draw. He saw me out of the corner of his eye and made off. I got a bouncing-away shot at 40 yards. I was not too disappointed since he was rather small. We are well wet down tonight. Having the last two king crabs for dinner.

FRIDAY, May 11, 6:00 A.M.—On our way back to the big bay we left a few days ago. Almost all tracks are headed south and that is easy to hunt on foot. We are leaving at this hour because we need high tide to get the big boat out of the bay. Rained all night and is still coming down. Fog settling in now.

I learned a lesson yesterday in my encounter with the brownie. I thought he would stare at me at least long enough for me to complete my draw, but the first slow movement and he was gone in a flash. He was 40 yards away before I could get the shot off, bounding like a rubber ball over the sharp rocks.

Those smaller bears move like lightning. He ran into Bob and Harley who were waiting up the beach, turned and came straight back past the place we had first seen him.

The bears are not eating grass. Those we have seen are eating sand fleas. These fleas are one half to three quarters of an inch long and look like a small shrimp. They live in about a foot of beach gravel. The bears lick fleas up so greedily that they swallow gravel along with them. The stomach of Bob's bear had a handful of rocks in it.

Last night we tried to eat all of the two king crabs but could not do it. Dan plans to make a crab omelet for breakfast with the leftovers.

We are constantly amazed at the bird life. Almost every day there are new ones. Yesterday it was the beautiful eider duck. Among the logs on the beaches we saw a wren that Ed's Alaskan bird book says is the Aleutian wren. It is the only bird here with a melodious song the book says, but I have not heard it utter a note.

The rain has stopped and the fog is clearing. Five P.M. Hunted the beaches on foot in the area where Bob shot his bear. One fresh track and that was all. Back at the boat at 2:00 P.M. and finished up the crab. Went out again an hour ago and rain started coming down in earnest. Decided to abandon this area and go to the east side of Afognak.

On our way now. May stop at the cannery at Port Williams for fuel and supplies. I believe this is the first day we have not seen at least one bear. We feel that we have this area well polluted with man scent and should move on to fresh territory.

9:15 P.M.—Sitting in the galley. Dan and Ed are playing cribbage. It is getting dark and fog is settling in the bay. We are anchored near the mouth of a creek in Perenosa Bay. Bob and Harley went up the creek to see if they could catch some rainbow trout. Ed and I will go after them in a few minutes with the skiff. Saw a fox on the beach as we dropped anchor.

SATURDAY, May 12—Back at the bay where we placed seal bait. We had the seals wired to logs. Bears had broken the wire and carried them off. In late afternoon Ed and I were hunting beaches afoot and saw a bear. We hid in the edge of the spruce and waited as he slowly fed toward us. The wind was not exactly right, however, and he became suspicious and swerved off.

I photographed a silver, or cross, fox this evening and also a seal this afternoon. Start hunting at daylight in the morning.

SUNDAY, May 13—Went in to Tonki Bay with the big boat this morning. Located two bears on a beach. Got into the skiff, went ashore, and started the stalk. Almost overran them as they walked part way up the steep, grassy mountain that rose from the beach. Ed and I climbed to get above and ahead of them. Up to this point we had seen only a back or a patch of fur. We were carefully approaching the crest of a ridge when I saw a bear's head look over about 20 feet above us. At the same time I heard a snarl below me and there was a brownie prancing on his front feet and not liking the intrusion at all. I realized that it was a sow and the one above us a two-year-old. Fortunately the cub ran off and the sow was satisfied by his escape and also disappeared over the ridge.

Saw two more brownies on a hillside about two miles inland. Wind was wrong. May try for them in the morning. Caught some Dolly Varden trout for dinner. Clouding over and wind starting to blow.

MONDAY, May 14—A strong wind came up during the night, blowing directly into the bay where we were anchored. Pulled anchor in early morning and had a rough trip to the little harbor where we are anchored now. Ed pulled in alongside a small crab-fishing boat that was in here for the same reason—weather.

We planned to be on our way to Kodiak now to catch the early-morning plane, but weather will dictate the time. It has been raining hard all night. Got four king crabs from the fishermen and had a fine meal.

Guess I will have to call this hunt a blank. I have been within 30 yards of four bears. One of them 15 feet. Something always seemed to go wrong. None of them were monsters. Saw a great many Afognak elk yesterday. Some of them down close to the beach. Ed stalked some and shot blunts at them. Have picked up many shed horns.

10:30 P.M.—Still confined to our little harbor. Still raining hard, although the wind has let up somewhat. If it does not get worse we will make a run for Kodiak early in the morning. A lazy day. Have everything packed. Wrote cards, took a nap, and ate the day out.

TUESDAY, May 15, 9:00 P.M.—Up at 3:00 A.M. this morning. Weather better so we pulled anchor and headed for Kodiak. Got here at 9:00 A.M. and tied up at the dock. We all had showers in a barbershop. Did some shopping.

I called home to see if I was needed and got orders to stay until I got a bear. Ed will give me a few days bear hunting in between seal hunts and I have good hopes of getting a brownie. Bob left at 5:30 tonight for home.

We will be here tomorrow for some repairs on the boat. May leave in the afternoon—if not, on Thursday morning.

THURSDAY, May 17—Left the city of Kodiak at 4:00 P.M. heading northeast on the outside of Marmot Island. Ten thousand seals were reported here, but they turned out to be 5,000 sea lions. Several beaches are covered solid with them.

Am sitting topside in a bright sun. Not a cloud in the sky. There is a slight breeze blowing and some rather heavy swells running. At 8:30 we are rounding the north tip of Marmot to the mainland of Afognak to search the shores for bear. We will hunt north of where we were last Monday.

1:00 P.M.—Checked a whale that had washed up on the outside beach of Marmot Island. Apparently it went ashore last winter. Got some handsome ivory teeth from the jaw and pondered over the scrimshaw work done by becalmed sailors at sea in days gone by.

9:00 P.M.—Anchored in Seal Bay, really a part of Tonki Bay. The weather was closing in with an offshore wind and cloudy sky. Bow in hand, I walked the beach for a while. On the open beach ahead a dark object was identified as a bear. Our plan was to circle through the spruce and come out on the beach where the bear was.

He was about 200 yards away, digging sand fleas and not greatly concerned about anything else since he rarely looked up. It was not possible to make the approach through the spruce as a cliff broke off between us. However, some large rocks furnished cover for the first hundred yards, and a few smaller ones from there on.

Ed had forgotten his .375 backing gun but had his .22 Hornet seal gun. Harley had nothing. I had my bow and a .44 Magnum. The question was, who was backing whom, and with what?

We took our hip boots off and made the stalk in stocking feet. There was a small rock near the bear that hid his head from us when it was down after the sand fleas. Almost no cover between us otherwise. Fortunately he was busy pawing among the kelp. Only once did he look up. We happened to be motionless at that time and he went right back to his meal.

We finally reached a point 30 yards from him that seemed to be the spot for action. Between us was noisy, loose gravel. The bear was broadside, but facing me slightly. His front leg was slightly back covering part of his chest. One more move and he would be in position for my favorite rib-lung shot.

The move turned out to be a look to scan the beach and there we were. Brownie ran off with much woofing and did not show up again.

FRIDAY, May 18, 3:00 P.M.—Stopped at Port Williams and deposited some mail. Anchored in Big Bay now. Ed is changing oil and filters.

8:00 P.M.—Just came back from hunting the beaches that were so productive a week ago. Not any tracks since we left here. Disappointing and no need to spend any more time here. Plan to leave for the Alaska Peninsula at 3:00 A.M. tomorrow. Got some T-bone steaks and some Dungeness crabs at the cannery at Port Williams.

SATURDAY, May 19, 7:00 P.M.—Made a start for the Peninsula at 2:30 this morning. A southwestern wind made it impossible. Came back to Big Bay and are anchored peacefully here in the sun. Boating, like flying, is unpredictable. Plans can be made, but it is not always possible to follow them through.

9:00 P.M.—After the wind eased up we left Big Bay, came south, and went along the west side of Afognak to Paramanof Bay. Anchored in a small bay out of the wind about 200 yards off a small beach.

We were having coffee and cookies before leaving for a hunt in the skiff when I looked out the galley window to see a bear walking across the beach. He went into some alders that came down along one side of a creek. We rowed over, made a stalk, but the wind was wrong and he sneaked over the mountain through a draw. He was not a big bear.

We did some miles in the skiff. Examined beaches and found but few tracks. Went into a bay that drains an inland lake. Saw Dungeness crabs on the bottom in water five to eight feet deep. Speared a dozen with the long-handled spring gaff. Plan to go up this creek at daylight in the morning. There could be bears in the meadows surrounding this lake.

SUNDAY, May 20, 5:00 P.M.—Up at 6:00 A.M. Hunted with the skiff until 2:30, but did not see a bear. Went around Ban Island and dug some littleneck clams. Saw and photographed two foxes. These are not good beaches for bear. No kelp. There seems to be no waterfowl either.

Left Paramanof Bay and just got in here to Malina Bay. Saw a single bear and a sow and cub high on the mountain as we came in. They made off as soon as they saw the boat. Planned to go ashore and hike in to Afognak Lake. Just got our gear on when the rain started. Decided to steam the clams instead.

Flowers are beginning to bloom and the brown hillsides are dappled with light green.

9:30 P.M.—Ate a mess of clams and then hiked over the rise toward Lake Afognak. Did not get to the lake, but looked over a little country. Very little bear sign, but quite a lot of elk activity, although we did not see any. Took the skiff and hunted down toward the end of the bay. Bad wind came up and we turned back. Finished up the littleneck clams. Very delicious. Cloudy all day and cold. Rain off and on. Tops of the hills have been in the clouds all day.

MONDAY, May 21, 8:00 A.M.—Rain and strong wind all night. Everybody slept in. Our generator quit working several days ago, delaying our move to the Peninsula. Voltage has dropped and we are now lifting anchor to run around the corner to a cannery in Raspberry Straits. Rain has let up but the wind is still blowing. Everything lashed down for the trip, although we will be on the lee side of the blow.

Ed climbed a cliff along a beach yesterday and was amusing himself rolling rocks down on the beach. Harley and I were on the beach appraising the results when the larger ones fell on logs. A big rock weighing five or six tons perched precariously near the edge was finally toppled over and came down thundering with ear-splitting pandemonium as it crashed into the logs. Ed later told us of his efforts in dislodging this big rock. He put his feet on the rock and his shoulder against the bank and "gave it everything I had." He felt it move slightly and then "gave it a little bit more" and down it came. He didn't explain where "the little bit more" came from.

These rocks are hard on arrows. I have gone through two dozen blunts on this trip and have just six broadheads left. My bow is holding up well and so is the eight-arrow quiver. This has been a rugged test for it.

112

Yesterday we found a skiff pulled up on shore beside a Fish and Wildlife shack. Bear hunters had been there. We found a freshly killed bear skull, a fox carcass, and a skinned seal. This is the first evidence of humans we have seen on this hunt. Not even an old tin can or the remains of a campsite. Found a wrecked fishing boat on the beach in Malina Bay.

3:00 P.M.—Tied up at a cannery having their electrician repair the generator. A short in the brush holder. It was a good idea to take it out of the boat. It definitely needed a cleaning job if nothing else. Raining and still blowing. Very cooperative people at the cannery. I left my films there for them to run tonight. They will forward them to Kodiak for me. Left the cannery at 6:00 P.M. and dropped anchor here in a small bay. Hiked through a valley up a creek, but no bear signs. Plan to leave here at 3:00 A.M. in the morning.

TUESDAY, May 22, 6:00 A.M.—Heard Ed start the engine at 4:00 A.M. Got up at five when the boat started to roll. We are headed for the Alaska Peninsula. We were wrong in believing it is closed to hunting. I did not know last night if we would go this way or to Kodiak. If to Kodiak, I would admit defeat and go back home. Dan has not been feeling well (the cook) and would like to get off the boat, but Ed is about as bullheaded as I am and he is the boss and we are heading for the Peninsula.

This surely stretches out this hunt and were it not for needing pictures I could have taken Dan's side and we probably would be heading for Kodiak. If I can get pictures of taking a bear, this will make the finest film in our company library and I am pushing my luck to this end. Still overcast.

10:00 P.M.—Just got back from hunting with the skiff. Got here to Alinchak Bay at 9:30. Saw a sow and two cubs on the beach. Would have stopped for pictures, but it was raining. It has been raining almost all day. Chilly, too. There is snow on the hills. Saw no bears from the skiff.

WEDNESDAY, May 23—On our way with the *Maid* southwest. Not enough bear sign here. Going back to where we saw the bears coming in. It is still heavily clouded over and some fog, but no rain.

9:00 P.M.—Ran into Puale Bay early this morning. This is where I killed the big brownie two years ago. Hunted by skiff and found the tracks of a medium-sized bear in a mud flat. It was fairly fresh as the tide had been out only a few hours. Failed to find him, however. Cooked up a mulligan and planned to hunt bears between four and dark.

113

Had an hour of sunshine this morning, but later we had rain and at four o'clock the wind started blowing the raindrops horizontally and we could not go out. Two crab boats came in here out of the storm and one anchored beside us. I took a nap, drank a lot of coffee, and dried my gear. Everything is wet down.

Keeping camera, gear, and feathers dry is a serious problem. Cameras are carried in my backpack, which is not entirely waterproof. Have a heavy rubber pouch that I chuck the whole business in and tie it tight. Have to keep a plastic bag over the feathers of my arrows, even in fair weather, to protect them from spray.

THURSDAY, May 24—Did a skiff hunt for four hours, but saw nothing. Had a lunch about 2:00 P.M. and then went bear hunting again. Got back at 8:00 P.M. Saw quite a few tracks, but no bears.

Our eating habits are very irregular. Governed by the tide and weather and not so much by the hour. Low tide is about the middle of the day now. Had a few hours of sunshine this morning and then rain again.

FRIDAY, May 25—This was the big day. The sun was shining early and kept on shining all day. It was a good day for bears, seals, king crabs, and pictures. This was perhaps the most thrilling day of my hunting career, and not without some humor too.

Our hunting day did not start early. The crab pot was lifted first to yield three fine king crabs. One average size and two monsters. Next we took the skiff into Bear Bay, a rocky, shallow site with a short beach about 300 yards long. As we rounded the point and the beach came into view, a fine bear chose this time to walk out of the alders into sight on the sand.

We were a good half mile away. The engine was quickly shut off while we studied the bear throught glasses. He busied himself pawing and eating in the sand and kelp while Ed slowly and quietly rowed toward the rocky shore about 200 yards beyond the edge of the beach. If we could make this without being seen, we would be hidden by a small point that came between us and the bear.

Harley watched the bear with glasses to alert Ed to stop rowing when the bear looked our way. It was touch and go. Brownie would paw and eat and lie down intermittently. The warm sunshine on his heavy winter fur doubtless brought out sleepy dreams of great summer days ahead gorging on spawning salmon.

Before we reached shore he waded out into the ocean, rolled over on his back, and, with his head and four feet sticking out, enjoyed the luxury of a saltwater bath. The tide was out. The narrow rocky shore met the thick alders at the high-tide line.The mountain started up steeply from there.

While rowing across the bay I had shot some 16mm film of the bear. On shore Harley was to pinch-hit as photographer. I reasoned that he could cover our stalk from a point some distance from us and would need the telephoto lens. As it turned out, the 25mm would have been proper. Mounted underneath the movie camera lens, I have a 35mm sequence camera operated by a push button on the fore part of the gunstock mount. This camera, a Robot Royal, will expose 24 pictures on one wind at the press of the button. In this way with one operator, both still pictures and moviews can be taken. The 50mm lens covers the same area as the 25mm movie.

Leaving the skiff, we made our way toward a point that would afford a view of the beach and the bear. Ed and I ahead and Harley with his .270 and the cameras about 25 yards behind. When we were some 50 yards from the skiff we saw the bear's blond ears coming toward us. The wind was right. We motioned Harley to squat and be still. Ahead of us, there was a heaven-sent big rock about four by four feet. Hunkering down we made our way to it. This was the only cover on this entire shore and we were lucky that it was placed so conveniently.

We both knelt down in the shadow of the rock, Ed a bit to my left and I on one knee with the arrow on the string. We kept our heads down, sure that he would pass on the ocean side, and waited in great anticipation (not to say, apprehension) for the appearance of this alder king.

He was a good-sized bear. We had concluded that while watching him, through glasses, crossing the bay. Up to now, however, our only close look at him had been his ears and there seemed to be quite a space between them.

All kinds of thoughts go through one's mind in suspense-filled moments like this. Would he bolt like the one did two weeks ago when he saw me slowly start to draw the arrow or would I have only a frontal shot when he saw us and stared in amazement? We had to stop about 10 feet from the rock because of some sticks that lay ahead. He would see us before he was even with the rock.

I was determined to place the razorhead through the ribs close up to the shoulder. This would be a clean kill. There could be no excuses. I worried about the three strands of my bowstring that had chafed off on sharp barnacles as I got out of the skiff. Would it hold for this one shot?

We waited. Finally, he was in sight. Twenty-five feet away and coming closer. He turned toward us and looked us over, standing still. We remained as motionless and quiet as stumps and did not register in the bear's consciousness. We could almost see his mind working—"Odd pieces of driftwood came in on the last tide. . . ." (Stationary objects are not considered harmful by the animal kingdom.) He turned broadside and walked to pass us. The 65-pound Kodiak bow came back with the ease of a toy. He did not notice the movement. The razorhead sank to the feathers near the front leg. The impact was considerable and as he roared and exploded down the shore straight toward Harley, we wondered what the outcome would be.

Harley, however, endowed with the tradition of good showmanship, stood his ground operating the camera until the bear began to fill the viewer and it seemed prudent to abandon the camera for the rifle. Cameras are delicate instruments and should be put down carefully. But life is precious. The open shore, between the steep alder-covered bank and the water, measured a scant 20 feet and Harley's position was squarely in the middle of it. The bear's direction of travel was also right down the middle.

In some alarm we saw Harley, legs and arms flailing the air, cameras in one hand, rifle in the other, trying to scurry up the slope to leave the open shore to the bear. Ed yelled in his booming voice, "Take pictures. I'm covering you."

At any rate, the bear passed him at full speed. A short way beyond it tried to climb into the alders, but could not make it and rolled back down the slope near the skiff. He was dead in less than a minute after he was hit. The arrow nicked a rib close to the front leg, passed through a lung, cut a heavy artery near the liver, went through the diaphragm, and just through the skin near the back ribs on the far side.

We took pictures and left him to go back to the *Valiant Maid* for a bite to eat. It was high tide when we got back and his feet were in the water. With ropes slung under him we were able to roll him into the skiff and winch him aboard for skinning on the aft deck.

With the carcass intact he tipped the scales at 810 pounds. The skin squared nine feet and the length and width of the skull measured 27 inches. Ed paced the distance of the shot at 20 feet. The bear ran 90 yards from where he was hit.

It has been a very busy day, a very exciting one, and gratifying. A bear at 20 feet looks big when one is down on his knees looking up. Again it was proved that an arrow in the right spot will do the job quickly and humanely, regardless of the size of the animal. This was a day when everything worked out just right. The sun was out all day and the bear did his part in coming to us. Actually, it would have been a difficult stalk if he had remained on the open beach.

It takes breaks like this to be successful with either the bow or gun, except that with a bow the circumstances have to be more refined and the timing exact. This makes the fifth bear that we have been within 30 yards of. The other four times something went wrong. The range handicap of the bow is great, but the thrills of getting close to your target make up for it. A good-sized, bow-legged brownie strutting toward one at 25 feet is a thrill well worth the time and effort. It's a great privilege to match wits with a noble animal such as this that nature has so ably equipped to take care of itself.

SATURDAY, May 26—This was an easy day. Fleshing the bear skin. Cleaning the skull. Cleaning up in general. There was time to make a summary of brown bear hunting:

They have only two enemies. Man and larger brown bears. As a result, small bears are jittery and alert, always expecting a larger bear to pounce upon them. The big ones are easier to stalk, having more self-confidence and an admirable cockiness that commands respect.

Fred Bear's Field Notes
Doubleday, 1976

THE LAST STAND
OF A WILY JAGUAR

by Frank C. Hibben

T he growls and the roar of the dog pack were far ahead. I clawed at the mangrove roots around me; it was impossible to crawl under the things, or climb over them. There was the sound of splashing above the barking of the dogs and I knew the hounds were fighting the cat in the water. One hound barked shrilly. That would be Drifter. Drifter's voice was blotted out as though a giant hand had closed on his throat. The jaguar had him. Drifter was our last good hound. If the jaguar killed him. . . .

We should not have been in that part of the swamp, and we should not have been after that particular jaguar. We knew this old spotted cat, or at least we knew him by reputation and we had heard about the place where he lived. Both the jaguar and the lost swamp were impossible. But we tried it anyway.

Dale Lee, who had located the Agua Bravo swamps a few years ago, is one of the two remaining of the five Lee brothers who have been, during their lives, the outstanding hound and cat men in North America. During their careers they have probably accounted for more lions and more jaguars than even such famous oldsters as Ben Lilly. But of the five, only Clell and Dale remain and only Dale still goes after jaguar.

"It'll kill a man, and it certainly kills hounds," Dale often drawls in his slow manner, "but I kinda like it."

This is to say that when Dale said he had found a jaguar swamp which was crawling with the spotted cats, he knew what he was talking about. The swamp which Dale had located is in the state of Nyarit on the west coast of Mexico. Along this shoreline, south of the city of Mazatlan, the Agua Bravo swamp stretches for 150 miles. Through the middle of this

118

long strip, the Rio Bravo itself, a sluggish tidewater creek, cuts diagonally ıorthwest to the sea. Dale had found jaguar tracks where the cats came down out of the mountains, crossed the Pan American Highway and moved into the swamp. He found other tracks where the jaguars moved back into the mountains. As a matter of fact, the big spotted cats seemed to love the place in spite of the fact that there were few deer or any other ordinary jaguar feed in the Bravo area.

During the last few years, Dale has taken some dozens of American sportsmen into the area and has caught many jaguars there. Dale hauled some flat-bottomed duck boats into the head of the Bravo where the ground is fairly solid. In a clearing near a side creek he established a base camp. From this base camp, Dale took his parties by boat down the many winding creeks into the heart of the Bravo swamps. It's real hunting, as any mosquito-bitten survivor of these junkets can testify. Dale fits each of his customers with a pair of basketball sneakers and tells them not to try to keep dry. This last advice is really unnecessary either in the boat or out of it, a jaguar hunter is never dry from the time he starts with Dale to the time he comes back to the base camp.

As it would be almost impossible to stagger through the mangrove-edged creeks looking for a jaguar track, Dale has worked out a system for locating the cats. During the mating season, jaguars roar very much like an African lion. As a matter of fact, both male and female jaguars sometimes roar on any occasion.

Dale had rigged up a large gourd, cut open at one end, and covered with a sheet of rawhide like an Indian drum. Attached to the drum head is a thong rubbed with resin. By pulling the thong between his thumb and forefinger with a quick jerky motion, Dale can make a grunting roar which sounds more like a jaguar than another jaguar. Dale has been so successful with this "bromadura," or roarer, that on several occasions he has called jaguars up within a few feet. At one time, in the Bravo swamps, when Dale and his brother Clell were hunting in a native dugout canoe, a jaguar answered the call so enthusiastically that the cat swam out and threatened to climb into the canoe with them. They beat him off with a wooden paddle. On another occasion, when Dale was sitting on an island roaring with his gourd, a jaguar swam to the island and walked up to within 20 feet in the moonlight. As the sportsman who was with him at that time had gone back to camp, Dale did not shoot the jaguar.

By calling jaguars during the night, Dale is able to locate one of the cats so that he can put the hounds on a fresh track at daylight. If a jaguar keeps answering and the client stays with him, it is an almost foolproof system. That is, it is a system for anyone fool enough to want a jaguar that badly. Chasing jaguars in the Bravo swamps is worse on dogs than on men. During all of these hunts, jaguars have accounted for some 20 of Dale's hounds. It is always the best dogs that get killed. On one previous hunt, while crossing an open place of the Agua Bravo in a high wind, one of the boats capsized and drowned a whole boatload of dogs.

Tom Bolack and I had been hunting with Dale before. We were bitten by mosquitoes and chewed by gnats, and we spent about 10 uncomfortable nights floating around in Dale's boat calling jaguars back in the swamps. We caught one jaguar, too, not far from the base camp, but that in itself wasn't the thrill. The most exciting episode of that hunt was a single night as we floated on the edge of the main Bravo and Dale stroked his bromadura with the "oum, OUM, OUM" of the jaguar call. Over across the water to the west, out of the darkness, a throaty voice answered, "Oum, oum, OUM, OUM!" The hair on the back of my neck prickled as the coughing roar floated down on the night wind. Tom Bolack, who had been sleeping facedown over a boat seat like a bag of wet rice, straightened up. Even Dale stiffened. "That will be Old Bravo himself," Dale whispered. "I'd know that voice anywhere."

Again Dale jerked the thong of the bromadura. Over across the water, the jaguar answered again. Then there was silence, with the occasional splash of a snook in the water or cry of night bird.

Tom and I were all for trying for Old Bravo the next morning at daylight. But Dale explained to us that his two Mexican guides, Felix and Pascacio, had told him that between the Bravo and the sea were some 10 miles of the worst mangrove thickets in all of Mexico. "Old Bravo has never been out of that place, and we've never been in it, but if you guys want to. . . ."

Tom and I lasted about 30 minutes on the west side of the Bravo. In that time, we penetrated about 100 yards. Pascacio and Felix had understated the situation. Unfortunately, in a patch of mud between two mangrove clumps, we saw a jaguar track. It was twice as big as any mountain lion imprint I had ever seen. Even Dale was impressed. "That'll be Old Bravo," Dale commented. "His feet are as big as his roar."

Tom is not one to give up just because of a few miles of mangrove thickets that no human being can get through. So recently we outfitted another expedition. We told Dale that we would be down a few days before Easter and persuaded a friends of ours, Bill Cutter of Albuquerque, to fly us down in his plane. We could have taken the commercial plane to Mazatlan, but we wanted to look the ground over.

As we circled low over the swamp in Cutter's plane, Bill was groaning. "Never saw such an awful-looking bunch of nothing in my life," he commented. But Tom and I were jubilant. Below us, between the Bravo and the ocean beach, there were mangrove thickets all right, but there were also several large open flats. These were lagoons, or pools of water, during the wet season. Now, in the spring, they were already beginning to dry. Wide areas of mud appeared with lines of solid mangroves in between. On the mud and in the shallow water were tens of thousands of ducks, herons, and other water birds that rose in clouds at the sound of the airplane engine. As we clipped the tops of the mangroves with a swinging dive we could see jaguar tracks leading across one mud flat.

Dale met us at Tepic, some 60 miles away, where we could land the plane. Bill Cutter, after one look at our jaguar swamps, decided that he didn't want a jaguar as badly as he had thought. Bolack and I outlined the situation to Dale. From the air we had found a small clearing at the head of one of the side creeks which looked like a good camping place.

It was, if you consider sitting on a wet sponge comfortable. The spot was about 25 miles from Dale's base camp by boat. It took two days to make the trip twice, poling and pulling the boats by hand, to haul in drinking water, extra gasoline, and set up a camp. We got some very fine snook and sea bass from some Mexican fishermen and made ourselves comfortable in a soggy sort of way.

On the first night, Dale tried his jaguar call. There was no answer. The second night it was the same. No throaty roar came to us out of the darkness. This was discouraging. Perhaps Old Bravo had left the swamp, or he may have died of old age.

The next morning, with Pascacio and Felix wielding machetes, we began to cut a trail due west from our camp. In four hours of cutting, we progressed about half a mile. Then the dark tangle of mangroves ahead lightened and we broke out into the first open flat. On the mud ahead of us was a line of jaguar tracks. The imprints were big, even for a jaguar.

In the mud we could see where the toes were turned out and flattened. "It's Old Fallen Arches himself," Tom said.

Dale nodded. The tracks were fresh. We followed where Old Bravo had crossed the mud flat and had caught a bird roosting in the shallow water. White feathers marked the place where the jaguar had killed and eaten an egret.

We decided not to try for him that first morning until we had cut a trail through the more difficult bands of mangroves between the next mud flats. In that tangle of roots, a jaguar would come to bay and kill every dog we had unless we could arrive on the spot very quickly.

In two days of machete work, Felix Pascacio and Tom Bolack had cut a fairly creditable trail west from our camp through four big mud flats almost to the ocean beach. Tom insisted on doing some of the machete work himself. The only thing that discouraged him was a lamentable occasion when his swinging blade cleaved a termite nest high in the forks of a mangrove tree. With our machete trail through the very heart of the Lost Swamp, we would be able to get at Old Bravo no matter where he went. And through the open flats we could double back in almost any direction.

There were other lesser jaguars, too, judging by the tracks. Dale was worried about his shortage of good dogs. He had lost so many of his best hounds that he only had 11 left and only four of these were top-notch trailers. But Tom and I didn't share his pessimism. We were in a jubilant mood as we tried the jaguar call on the third night.

We had followed our cut trail to the first big open flat in the Lost Swamp. We sat down in the mud. Dale opened the special moisture-proof box in which he kept his bromadura. He balanced it on his knee and gave the long throaty cry of a lovesick jaguar. Far away, out of the darkness, came the answer. Tom and I sat bolt upright. Again Dale called. After five minutes of silence, the jaguar answered. Felix and Pascacio shook their heads. Tom and I knew what they meant. That call was behind us, over in the direction of the Agua Bravo on the other side of camp. All of our machete cutting had been for nothing. But there was no help for it.

With Felix and Pascacio still shaking their heads, we splashed back to camp, got in the boat, and paddled silently across the tidewater creek. In the darkness we picked our way through the mangrove clumps to another open flat perhaps a mile east of camp. Here Dale took out the bromadura and called again. Almost immediately the jaguar answered, "Oum, oum, oum!" The throaty roar was just across the flat. The mangrove leaves behind our backs almost vibrated with the noise.

Dale was whispering with Felix and Pascacio in Spanish. "No bueno —no bueno," they were saying. Tom and I gripped our rifles tightly. So Old Bravo had moved out of his usual haunts! This was going to be thrilling. Already we could hear the soft splashing of cautious feet in the shallow water.

Dale stroked his jaguar call once again. The answer was terrifyingly close. The jaguar was moving toward us. Roseate spoonbills and roosting egrets darted up from the water as the jaguar trotted closer. The splashing was very near now. In the darkness I could see something darker. I nudged Tom. We both raised our rifles. The dark shadow darted from side to side. It stopped. It ran toward us again, moving jerkily.

Jaguars don't jerk. Another swiftly moving form joined the first, and then another. Tom and I lowered our rifles.

"Como estan, senores?" said a voice out of the darkness. Three dogs ran up to us. Three men followed. One of the men carried a gourd similar to that which Dale still held. "Ah, it is the famous tigrero himself," said the leading man in Spanish as he recognized Dale. "We also have come to try for the old cat who lives in the swamp by the sea."

As we paddled back to camp, Dale said apologetically, "Sorry I taught those natives how to call jaguars." Dale added reflectively, "I offered a reward for news of the old jaguar. But I never dreamed those birds would come way out here in the middle of the night."

We didn't catch Old Bravo at night, and he never answered a call in the seven nights that we tried. We gave the three local enthusiasts a few pesos and persuaded them to pole their dugout canoe the 30 or 40 miles back to their village so that we would have no more competition in the swamp. Two or three lesser jaguars did answer our call, but from different directions and with different voices. We wanted no small fry on this hunt. We were after Old Fallen Arches, as Tom insisted on calling him because of his flat, splayed-out feet.

As Old Bravo wouldn't answer the mating call, we decided to go into the Lost Swamp and track him down. We had cut some additional machete trails between various lagoons so that we could move through the swamp in any direction with fair speed. Our job was made a lot more difficult not only because Old Bravo wouldn't answer, but because Dale insisted on keeping his two best hounds on leash, for if his two remaining reliable trailers got killed, we were finished.

In three days of circling in the Lost Swamp, we had found a lot of places where Old Bravo had been but not the place where he was. There was no doubt that the old jaguar was feeding on birds and turtles and little else. As the shallow water in the flats dried, he caught the snook and mullet that were trapped there. But all of this activity was several days old. Perhaps Old Bravo had detected something sour in our nightly calling. Perhaps, also, he knew some corners of the Lost Swamp that we had not yet found.

On our fourth day of hunting, just at daylight, we ran into him. We didn't find him. He found us. Dale had turned old Drifter loose as a strike dog. There seemed little likelihood that we were going to find fresh tracks anyway. Drifter and Old Bravo met nose to nose in the machete trail. We heard the jaguar growl first. Drifter snarled. There was a flurry of sound. Drifter gave the squealing bark of a dog looking at game. Two hounds that Pascacio held darted forward and jerked Pascacio face down in the mud. Dale was already running ahead.

As we rounded the corner in the trail, the jaguar, with Drifter close behind, jumped into the mangroves. We couldn't see them but we could hear them and they were close. Dale quickly unnecked two of the younger dogs.

"This will warm up the chase a bit, but I'll keep these others—"

Dale's words were drowned in a roar of barking and splashing. All the loose dogs had got to the jaguar and were fighting.

The sound of the hounds quickly moved away. The jaguar was running again, running and fighting. The hounds which we still held on short leashes tried to drag us into the mangrove roots. But no man could get through that awful stuff without cutting a trail. Tom and I made a quick decision—he and Dale would go ahead to the next open flat and go down that one to get ahead of the chase. I would go back to the last opening we had crossed and parallel the fight from that side. Either way the chase turned, we'd have him.

As Felix and I ran along the mud we crossed a line of fresh tracks.

There was no mistaking those big splayed-out imprints. It was Old Bravo all right. He had walked from here not 10 minutes before when he bumped into Drifter on the trail.

Old Bravo knew his own swamp better than we did. He never crossed one of the open flats where dogs and men would have had the advantage but stayed in the mangroves and in the water. A mile from where Drifter had jumped him, he climbed a tree.

Tom and I got to the tree together, both badly winded. The old jaguar was about 15 feet above our heads on a dead mangrove. All of the dogs were below. This was too easy. I took a quick picture. When Tom had quieted his breathing, he raised his .30/30 rifle. Now that we were face to face with Old Bravo, I was almost disappointed. As he turned to snarl at us, I saw that most of his teeth were gone. No wonder he had been eating birds and turtles.

His frame was big, but he was not fat. His paws were enormous where they clutched the dead mangrove which was none too big to support his weight.

"Kill him dead, Tom," Dale whispered. At that instant the mangrove branch broke. Even the jaguar was surprised. The dogs scattered. Old Bravo landed on his feet. Tom still stood there with his .30/30 pointed at the sky.

The big cat was up and away. Before the startled hounds could move, the jaguar had jumped in a long leap into the mangroves and was gone. It was seconds before Dale could drag two of the dogs to the place and shove their noses into the hot scent. None of the hounds had seen him go.

"If we ever get up to him again, don't stand around fooling with that camera," Dale snarled as we started off.

We had only been at the tree a few seconds. Not only that, but it was Tom's jaguar. Both Tom and I were pretty abashed at missing our chance. It might be our only chance.

I directed Tom back the way I had come to the open flat. If he ran along the edge of the mangroves a few hundred yards, he could get ahead of the chase. "When you see him, shoot him," I yelled above the roar of the dogs.

With Felix and two spare dogs on a leash, I doubled back through the mangroves to our machete trail. From there I could hit an open-water lagoon through which I could wade for a mile or so. If Old Bravo turned to the westward again, we'd have him between us. With the two fresh dogs that we dragged along, Old Bravo could not get away.

He didn't either. Felix and I splashed through a screen of mangroves and there he was. The jaguar had doubled back and come to bay in the water. Felix let go of the two hounds. Even necked together, they cut off the jaguar but did not close in. Behind came the other dogs. Another dog, and then another reached the shallow water. Old Bravo was surrounded.

He fought well. No dog dared come too close. If they did, they were dead. The jaguar may have been old and his teeth broken, but he could move like lightning. Water was his home. The hounds were out of their element. Dale had said not to fiddle with the camera but I did anyway. I snapped a picture, and then another. In the finder I saw a hound lunge. It was Pluto. Old Bravo whirled so fast that I couldn't follow the motion.

He caught the hound by the side of the face. I heard Tom and Dale crash through the last fringe of mangroves. Now they were in the water with the fighting dogs and the jaguar. Another dog jumped in front. Dale was yelling to hold the hound back or they'd all be killed. Muddy water, wet dogs and Old Bravo were a swirling mass of paws and claws.

Tom reversed his carbine and struck downward with the stock at the jaguar's head. Bravo's grip broke. A piece of flesh ripped away from the dog's muzzle. If Old Bravo had been a year younger, he'd have killed the hound at the first bite.

Tom fired quickly without sighting. Old Bravo sank beneath the murky water. Blood welled up with the mud. The hounds closed in. It was finished. In another minute, the old male jaguar of Lost Swamp was a sodden carcass being chewed and mouthed by the dogs.

"He's a big-footed old jaguar for the size of his teeth," Dale commented as we examined the beautiful spotted body that hung from a tree near our camp.

"His teeth may be broken, and he may be old," Tom replied, "but I wouldn't trade him for any other jaguar in all of Mexico. I'm going to have him mounted whole just as we saw him in that water back there."

BUFFALO

by John Taylor

The African buffalo is the biggest, heaviest, and most massively boned of all buffalo. He's a magnificent fellow. Next to elephant hunting I prefer the hunting of buffalo to that of any other species of big game. I know that except for elephant I've shot many more buffalo than any other animal. But although I deprecate those men who allow the thought of buffalo to scare them, I do not suggest you should become contemptuous of them. Far from it! The African buffalo can hit back and hit hard. What I do say is, don't let all the tales you hear about the African buffalo start your imagination working overtime, so that you get all steamed up and are scared stiff before you ever see your first buffalo. I've met a number of men who have done just that. They were so frightened that they completely lost their heads when they got their chance for a shot. They seemed to have the notion that a buffalo will attack the instant he sees you, even though you haven't fired or in any way interfered with him. There are others who believe that a buffalo will invariably whip around and charge the moment he feels the lead if you don't kill him stone-dead with your first shot. I'm not making any dogmatic statements but I have never experienced such a charge in all the years I've been hunting buffalo—and I've killed close to twelve hundred of them. It's possible that you might experience such a charge; I can only say that I never have, and give it as my belief, based on personal experience that such an instantaneous charge would be definitely exceptional—unique. I am, of course, referring to an unwounded buffalo. The situation is entirely different if you are following up or have encountered a buff that has been recently wounded either by yourself or someone else. But then, we all know that wounded buff can be horribly dangerous. He's quite a different proposition.

The buffalo gained his reputation for savage vitality and fiendish

127

vindictiveness in the days of black powder and lead bullets. It is practically impossible to stop a charging buffalo with certainty with anything much smaller than an eight-bore or a very heavily loaded 10-bore. The animals can, of course, be killed with much less powerful weapons—the trouble arises when the hunter only wounds and has to follow up. Time and again a man would fire, drop the charging beast, and, thinking he was dead, lean his rifle up against a convenient tree or even against the "dead" buff while he sits himself down for a rest and a smoke. And the next thing the hunter knows the buff has come to life and is savaging him to death. It has happened on innumerable occasions, the lead bullet coming up against the mighty boss of the horns, where they meet in the center of the forehead, and failing to penetrate. If one hunter has been killed that way, scores have; but although the African buffalo is a magnificent antagonist he would never have won his deadly reputation had those old-timers been armed with modern rifles and bullets. All the same, you must not despise him. Men who permit familiarity with any species of dangerous game to make them contemptuous are themselves deserving of a real hunter's contempt.

I knew a Dutchman* who professed a scorn of buffalo. "Why they're only cows," he would say. "They're easy." Yet a buffalo killed him. There was another, also a Dutchman, who sneered at lion (though he admitted he was afraid of elephant). He caught a lion in the ribs with his Mauser one day and then strolled carelessly into the long grass to finish him off. But he didn't get a chance to fire again. The lion ripped him open. He had in the same way stated that lion were only cats and were easy. There was another, an Englishman who reckoned it was bunk to class rhino as dangerous game; but a rhino finally impaled him on a 22-inch horn, which gave him several very unpleasant hours before he died. Then there was another Englishman, one of those know-it-alls, who had shot two or three elephant—lone bulls—and gave it out that there was nothing to elephant hunting, that those professionals who spoke and wrote of the dangers of their profession were merely putting it on so that the uninitiated might be persuaded they were braver fellows than they really were. He was killed by an elephant next time he went out. One could go on like this almost indefinitely. As I have said, the

---

*Throughout the African continent "Dutchman" refers to a South African of Dutch descent. A visitor or settler from Holland is called a Hollander.—"John Taylor"

hunter who allows himself to become contemptuous or think slightingly of any particular species will inevitably became careless when hunting, and that is likely to have but one result. Don't let the thought of an animal frighten you before you leave camp; but being cautious is different from being either frightened or contemptuous.

An unwounded buffalo is unlikely to attack, but once wounded he can be infernally dangerous in thick cover—and, like any wounded beast, he will make for cover if there's any around. It's a never-ending source of amazement to me how little cover is necessary to conceal entirely some big beast like an elephant or buffalo which has decided to ambush you. The inexperienced man naturally pictures the animal standing behind the thickest clump of bush in sight and so passes over with the most cursory glance, if that, some light, smaller bit of cover on the opposite side of the trail. Yet often as not it's there that the animal is waiting. His very bulk is his best camouflage—that, and the fact that he will be standing absolutely motionless. I once looked clean through a tuskless elephant bull when he was ambushing me behind a sapling no thicker than my wrist, scarcely forty paces away and no other cover about. Had he not commenced to swing out his ears, in all probability I should have walked right into him. You can do exactly the same thing with buffalo. And since a wounded buff will usually be found standing within 20 to 30 yards of his spoor, on one or the other side of it, and if he sees you coming and decides to attack will have sufficient cunning to wait until you have actually passed before charging, you will find it disconcerting to have to swing around for a quick shot in an unexpected direction. (Buffalo are well known for this tactic.) Moreover, you are usually accompanied by native followers, and since the charge may be directed toward them there is all the greater possibility of confusion. The men's agility will usually enable them to get clear without much difficulty, but fear of accidentally shooting someone may make it necessary for the hunter to hold his fire until the charging buff is very close. It has even been known for one of the men inadvertently to bump the hunter and knock him off balance just as he was about to fire. It might be asked, "Then why in hell go wandering around with a gang of spare men?" The answer is that when you are hunting dangerous game, and especially when following up a wounded animal, trackers are not only desirable but, in my considered opinion, essential. It's their job to keep their eyes

129

on the spoor and follow it while the hunter's eyes are constantly roving ahead and around for the first glimpse of the quarry. Remember, far more often than not, it will be but a glimpse you'll get before the charge—if that. Eyes that have been glued to the spoor will inevitably become tired far sooner than if they have just been roving ahead at their own level. Moreover, the quick and hasty glance thrown ahead won't always be sufficient, and you may easily overlook the animal that is standing there waiting for you to come a mite closer. Another thing: If you have more than one rifle with you, you will naturally want someone to carry it for you; and since it's the height of folly to load yourself down with water bottles, spare ammunition, and various other odds and ends in addition to handgun and knife, you will also be wanting someone to carry those things. In addition, if you are hunting for camp meat you should have at least one other fellow to act as guide to the butchers later—if you haven't brought the butchers themselves, that is. Naturally, when following a wounded beast you will tell your followers to keep well to the rear, all except your gun bearer and trackers; but if the chase has been a long one, or the bush very thick, the lads will naturally close up both for moral support, if you're following a dangerous beast and so as not to lose you. They may be very much closer than you suppose.

There have been men who boast they go out entirely alone to hunt dangerous game. In my opinion that's nothing to boast about—quite the contrary. I consider it the act of a fool.

I'm thinking right now of a fellow I knew, a South African Dutchman, who went out alone after buffalo one day although his men begged him not to. He wounded a bull with his Mauser and followed him into very dense bush. The buffalo was waiting not ten yards within the fringe of the bush. The hunter, with his eye glued to the animal's tracks, actually passed the buff, as his spoor clearly showed, and failed to see it. The bull then charged from a range of less than 10 paces. It would seem that the charge came from the hunter's right rear, so that he would have had to turn around to face it. He wasn't quick enough, didn't get a chance to fire his rifle at all, and was trampled and savaged to death.

Back in camp his men had heard the shot and then, as hour followed hour with no sign of their boss, began to get worried. Finally they decided they had better go out themselves to see if they could pick up any sign. They went in the direction from which the sound of the shot had come, finally reaching a spot where a herd of buffalo had been. They then scouted around until they found the place where the herd had stampeded, and then where one big bull had left the herd and gone off on his own—showing that he had probably been wounded. Proof positive came when they found blood and saw that he had made for the thick bush. They very cautiously entered the bush and there for the first time struck the spoor of shod feet on the sandy soil: obviously those of their boss. They found him in a pool of his own blood, with his unfired rifle beside him. The tracks told the whole story. There was no sign of the wounded bull; he must have wandered away into the depths of the forest.

I must admit that I often go out unaccompanied to shoot a buck for camp meat. But the shot is fired well within earshot of the camp and my men know that there will be meat and start out right away toward where they heard my rifle. They know me well enough by now to realize that I don't waste ammo taking chancy shots. Having killed, I just sit down for a smoke until I figure my men are within earshot of my whistle. Then I blow a blast or two on it to give them the exact position. When they arrive I leave them to bring in the meat, and return to camp alone. I thoroughly enjoy these lone hunts because when natives are along inevitably much of the actual hunting is left to them. When you are out alone you have only yourself and your own bushcraft to rely upon.

Here are some general rules. When following up wounded and potentially dangerous animals you must on no account hurry. Move slowly and carefully, rifle ready for instant use, eyes searching out every bit and scrap of likely and unlikely cover. Don't bother about the spoor—that's your tracker's job, and he'll make a very much better job of it if he knows that he can rely upon you to spot any movement ahead. It doesn't have to be a movement of your quarry: The movements of monkeys and birds can sometimes tell you where he is if you are walking with your eyes and ears open; you may spot some other animal, such as a small buck, looking fixedly at one spot. It's more than probable, then, that he's watching the beast you're following.

If you're careful you will usually spot your wounded buffalo in time to get a shot before he comes—that is, unless the grass is very long or the bush very dense. In the more open types of scrub he may spot you coming and clear off himself without giving you a shot. He has halted to ease his wound, just as any other wounded beast will do—stopping doesn't always mean a charge or ambush. In the thicker bush and long grass he may not have deliberately waited for you, it may have just happened that he was unable to see you coming until you were right on him. In such circumstances a charge is almost a certainty.

The answer to all this, of course, is: Don't wound. Take care to kill or cripple with your first shot and you have nothing to worry about. Despite all the buffalo I've hunted and shot, I can honestly state that I've very, very seldom been charged. And of those charges practically all were made by buffalo which had been wounded by someone else. Since there is no telling when you also may meet a buff which somebody else has wounded a day or two previously, it obviously behooves you to be carrying your rifle, and a rifle with a decent punch. You may spend the rest of life wandering around the bushveld without ever bumping into a buff wounded by someone else—but you may also do so the first day you go out. I know many men who have spent a lifetime in the bush without stumbling across a buff wounded like that, yet I have encountered three or four myself. I would certainly have been killed on at least two of the occasions, and at the best badly mauled on the others, if I hadn't been carrying a powerful double rifle at the ready. The attacks were so unexpected and came from such close quarters that I would never have succeeded in getting a magazine rifle into action in time. I'll tell you of just one to make my point clear.

There had been a Dutchman wounding a lot of buffalo in one district. The authorities had sent for me to try and kill them off because they had been responsible for a number of deaths, women and children and elderly men who accidentally encountered them when out collecting wild fruit and firewood. Having undertaken the job, I advised the powers to chase that fellow out of the district because he was a menace. They had done this—he had left the previous year. During the ensuing months I hunted down and slew all wounded buffalo in the district that hadn't been pulled down by the big buffalo-killing lion that follow the herds. I'd done a good job and knew it. There was no other hunter in the area, and I myself hadn't wounded and lost a buffalo for many years. Accordingly, I had no reason under the sun to suspect that there was a wounded buffalo anywhere in the whole district on this day in question. Still, I'm a hunter of considerable experience and it is my pride to live as I consider such should live—that is, I never become careless, never omit reasonable precautions, never act contrary to established practices which my long experience has proved wise and sound. And so, when making my way through a wide patch of long grass to where I knew I'd find a herd of buffalo, I was carrying a powerful double rifle. My gun bearer, who was breaking trail through the grass, carried my second rifle in front of me.

For no discernible reason I suddenly began to feel uneasy. I tapped my gun bearer on the shoulder and signed to him that I would take the lead. I didn't even speak—I knew this feeling so well that I felt in a moment or so, if I advanced, I would run into very real danger. As I have said before, you must never attempt to weigh inner urges like this against your very limited powers of objective reasoning: You must, without hesitation, accept and act upon them. That is what I did. As I always do when I do not expect to be wanting it immediately, I had been carrying my rifle muzzle foremost on my shoulder. I now reversed it so that I could get it into action with the minimum delay if and when it was needed. I advanced through the grass, slowly enough to be always collected and balanced. And I had gone scarcely 10 paces more when there came a rush through the grass close beside me. As the barrels of the rifle came down into my left hand my right thumb shoved forward the safety. It was then time to fire, there was no time to get the butt inside my forearm, pressed against my side. Had I been carrying the rifle wrong way round I would almost certainly have been unable to get it into action sufficiently quickly. I had no reason to suppose there was wounded buff anywhere around, but as it transpired this one had been wounded the previous day, or rather night, by a native armed with an old muzzle-loader. As well as I can recall, I fired that shot from a range of less than three feet.

"Oh, you fool! You triple-distilled bladder-headed fool! Don't you know by this time that a buff does not lift his head to look at you, but only his nose? And you call yourself a hunter!"

That outburst was occasioned by a piece of momentary forgetfulness on my part before I had acquired the experience I now have. I was hunting for meat for my men and encountered a troop of 25 or 30 buffalo. I let drive at the big leading bull, placing a hard-nose bullet immediately under the great boss of his horns where they meet in the center of his head—always a most tempting shot. He dropped instantly, and I presumed I had blown his brains out of the back of his head. I turned my

133

back on him to see if I couldn't get a shot as the animals stampeded in a semicircle past me, and was about to fire when there was a yell from one of my followers. I swung around, saw my bull on his feet, shaking his head to clear it, and dropped him again with a bullet in the neck just as he started a rush.

This brings up a point you would do well to remember if you ever try your hand at African buffalo. All buffalo carry their heads low, and when they want to look at you they don't lift their heads like other animals (except hogs): They only lift their noses. This means that the face is practically horizontal, and if you try to slip your bullet in under the boss of the horns, which is so tempting, your bullet may pass over the brain and out the back of the head. It will knock the bull out but won't necessarily kill him. You should take an imaginary line between his eyes and place your bullet just below it. Then when you examine your kill you will find that your bullet has actually entered the upper part of the nose and not the forehead.

Let me tell you now about the hunting down of the Maiembi man-killer. He was the last of the wounded buffalo left around by that Dutchman. I have always thought that the hunting down of this beast was one of the most difficult and dangerous jobs I have ever undertaken. The brute had taken up his residence in an impossible patch of impenetrable bush that extended over many acres. He only came out at night to water and feed close around the outskirts of the bush. There were four other big old bulls that lived in there and they had without doubt been wounded in previous years by other near-hunters; but they had long recovered from their wounds, their tempers had cooled off, and they were now quite innocuous. They lived together in a bachelor party—the brute I wanted was still solitary. It is true that if he were now left alone he might become as harmless as the other four, because nobody ever attempted to enter this patch of bush (he'd done all his killing before taking up residence in here); but since the bush abutted on lands near the kraal I didn't consider it fair to the villagers to take a chance on his good behavior. If any of them were late down at the river, which ran along the far side of their fields, they might easily bump into the killer on their way back up. The bull's spoor showed that he came out nightly, crossed the field, and made his way down to the water. He then fed along the river's edge where there was young grass, returning later to the bush for the day.

Buffalo

I mooched around the edge of the bush looking for an opening, but there was none. The greater part of the growth which comprised the patch was fairly free of leaf for about two or two and a half feet from the ground, but from there up it closed like a curtain behind anything entering. The big buffalo could brush through this, but no man could. And although the greater part of the growth was free of leaf for some distance from the ground, there was other vegetation growing among it which carried leaf and small twigs right down to the ground. Crawling in there to try to hunt any unwounded buffalo would have been difficult but not particularly dangerous, provided you took the greatest care to kill outright. To go in after a wounded man-killer could only be considered as a last alternative if all else failed.

It seemed that my best bet was to try for him by night when he came out. Had there been a moon all might have been well; but just then there was no moon. I clamped a flashlight on the barrels of my rifle. Unfortunately, the cells were nearly worn out, so I sent runners off to try to get me some fresh ones. In the meantime I determined to see what I could do with what I had—and bitterly regretted it afterward.

I went out about an hour after dark, knowing that buffalo must have their water and in a hot district like this would come out of the bush as soon as they felt it safe to do so. I strolled slowly along toward the river, swinging the beam of my flashlight around in all directions. For a considerable time I saw nothing and was drifting slowly back toward camp with the intention of waiting awhile and then trying again (so as to save my batteries as much as possible) when I picked up a very large eye in the ray of light thrown by my torch. I halted and stared at it. It was unlike anything I'd ever seen. As an eye it looked like a buffalo's, but it was only about five inches off the ground. Morever, when it moved it did so with a curious undulating gait: like a rabbit feeding, and hopping along a bit farther to halt and nibble again. I decided it must be a rabbit, though it had the biggest eye I'd ever seen in a rabbit. Still, what else could it be?

I watched it steadily. The light wasn't strong enough to show up the animal's body even though that was only about 20 yards away; it showed just the eye. And then another eye appeared, rather more than a foot from the first one but on the same level. That must be another rabbit. If the two eyes had been a decent height above the ground I would now have said that it was a buffalo looking straight toward me, but who ever heard of a buffalo with his head so low that his eyes were only five inches off the ground. One eye disappeared and the other continued to move along now, parallel with my own route, but with that strange undulating movement. I strolled along more or less level with it but it gradually got ahead of me. That didn't matter. It was a buffalo I wanted, not a rabbit.

And then suddenly and most unexpectedly the eye soared up until it was about four feet from the ground and immediately in front of me. It was now about 25 yards away and just on the edge of the bush. For the first time I realized it was my buffalo. The brute had been coming back from the river along an old hippo path which had been worn some three and a half feet deep there. It was this that had caused the eye to seem only a few inches above the ground, and the roughness of the track accounted for the undulating movement that had deceived me into thinking it a rabbit. It was only now, when the bull scrambled out of the hippo track, that my weak batteries dimly showed up horns and body. I took a despairing shot as the buffalo disappeared into the bush. I heard the thump of the bullet but knew I'd hit him too far back because his head and shoulders were already concealed in the bush. I don't normally shoot unless I'm sure of killing or crippling. But this wasn't a harmless unwounded beast; it was a man-killer which had already been wounded by someone else. As I looked at it, wounding him again could not make him any more vindictive than he had already shown himself to be, while my heavy soft-nose bullet, even though badly placed, would certainly not improve his health or strength. This is perfectly legitimate practice in the case of a man-killer, though naturally I wouldn't resort to it if I could avoid it. However, what I failed to realize was that my firing like that would inevitably put him on the alert in the future. He had never previously been shot at by night, and up to now hadn't associated the bright light of the flashlight with danger. I could have walked right up to him had I only realized in time that it was my quarry I was watching. In the future things would be different. It wouldn't be possible to stroll around and expect to get an easy shot. The instant the bull saw the beam of the flashlight he would make a beeline for safety—or would charge. Moreover, an additional reason, if it were needed, for him to associate danger with light was the fact that he must have got a whiff of my wind just before he received my bullet: That was probably why he had climbed out of the hippo track and made for the bush.

A careful examination of his spoor next morning showed that he habitually left his sanctuary at the same place, crossed the field, made his way down to the water, which was low at this season, and then after feeding for a while made use of the deep hippo track to get back to the bush. Standing in the field about 15 yards from the buffalo's tracks and about the same distance from the fringe of the bush there was a good-sized tree which the owner of the field hadn't bothered to fell. I decided to squat at the foot of this, on the river side, and hope for a shot when the bull came out that night. Accordingly, just before dark I took up my position. I had been sitting there only a short half hour when my quarry appeared. But it was a pitch-dark night and against the black background of the dense bush I was unable to see him until he was broadside on to me and silhouetted faintly against the horizon.

Unfortunately my flashlight had not been designed for sitting up like this or it would have had a switch which could have been turned on with the rifle and held ready for instant use. My light had only the ordinary side, which meant that after switching it on I had to return my left hand to the forearm of the heavy rifle in order to raise it to my shoulder. And that took too long in the circumstances. I had hoped the bull would stand for just a moment gazing at the light—that short moment would have been sufficient—but he now knew well just what the light portended. He didn't give me a chance. The instant the light sprang out he whipped around and was all out for his sanctuary. My dim light was not enough to show me his outline for a shot before he was gone.

I got up in disgust and returned to camp.

The following night I tried sitting in the same place without a light— my batteries were practically finished anyway—but except for a visit from a lion, which, I think, got an even greater shock than I did when he came around my tree from the opposite side and found me within a few feet of him, nothing happened.

My runners returned a day or so later to tell me there were no flashlight batteries to be had. So that was that.

Well then, there seemed no alternative but to try to make my way into that impossible patch of bush by day. Having wounded the bull myself now, I felt it incumbent upon me to kill him. I didn't fancy the notion of that bush, but there was nothing else to be done. I wasn't a wealthy sportsman who could stick around indefinitely: I wasn't being paid for this work (if I had been I would probably have waited until there was a moon and tried ambushing the bull). As it was, I had to kill the brute as soon as possible so as to be free to push along to where I could make my modest living.

Accordingly, the morning after my runners had returned I went out to reconnoiter again. I decided to wait until close to midday as I guessed the bull would be lying down then—and he must be lying down or it would be impossible for me to kill him. I decided it would be best to enter the bush where he was in the habit of coming out. There was probably some tiny clearing around the foot of a tree or under some bush which would give him shade during the hot hours. It would be my job to snake up along his spoor and hope to spot him before he spotted me. The one and only advantage I would have would be that he wouldn't expect to be hunted in there and so might not be on the alert. But it would call for very careful stalking, because if he became the least bit suspicious he would instantly scramble to his feet and then I would be helpless. The bush would completely cover all his vitals and I would see nothing but his feet and lower legs. If he sighted or winded me coming and decided to charge he could trample me underfoot without the slightest difficulty and I wouldn't be able to do anything. My only hope was to take him unaware when he was lying down so that I could see him under the bush. It wasn't a pleasant prospect to dwell on. It was best to think of something else until the time came to get on with it. So I returned to camp and picked up a miniature rifle with which to stalk spur-winged geese down by the lake shore.

By 11 o'clock I was back again with as many geese as my men and I could eat. I drank the pot of tea my cook had waiting for me. Then, taking my heavy rifle, I commenced what I still consider—as I say— probably the most dangerous stalk of my career. I would much rather have stalked a wounded lion under such conditions than a buffalo, because a lion's vitals would have been vulnerable whether he was standing or not. However, it was no use wishing; thinking about it would only make me more scared than I already was. Oh, I was frightened all right—make no mistake about that! I'd had enough experience to know just how dangerous a proposition it was, and how quixotically foolish I was to attempt it.

I reached the place where the bull habitually emerged from the bush. My men tried to dissuade me from entering, as they already had before. They also realized that their arguments weren't worth the candle.

My courageous gun bearer looked hurt when I insisted he remain outside with the others. But, as I explained to him, he would be unable to help me if things went wrong, and if the buffalo chose to come for him when we were both down on our bellies, I wouldn't be able to help him. I told the men they were on no account to enter the bush. If they heard a shot, or heard the bull bellowing, they were to wait at least an hour before doing anything. If I hadn't returned by then, they could come and look for me—and scrape me off the ground if they could be bothered to (but I said that last sentence to myself).

As I got down to start the crawl I grinned at my men, thinking to cheer them, but nary a grin responded. Instead they gave me that blank dead-pan look that only the African can produce. They knew I wasn't acting with my usual modicum of common sense, and they didn't like it. As I have said before, the African does not applaud those who take needless risks, stupid unnecessary risks; he looks upon it as plain damned foolishness. In which, of course, he's perfectly right. Far from sneering at me for being scared, if I had turned back now at the last moment they would have been greatly relieved. But I was determined to go ahead.

It wasn't possible to proceed even on hands and knees; I had to lie right down and literally snake along by means of elbows and toes. My greatest difficulty, and a serious and most important one, was to make sure that the muzzles of my rifle didn't pick up sand or other dirt. It was easy enough to keep on the spoor because the bull had used the same track a number of times. I would edge forward perhaps two or three times my own length and then pause for a careful reconnaissance in all directions; then on again for another short distance. The ground was a light sandy loam coverd with thick compost—the annual grass fires never entered here. There were no stones or pebbles and remarkably few dry twigs or dead sticks to bother about. The result was that I was able to move in absolute silence just so long as I was careful—and I was very careful!

I cannot give you any estimate of the distance I crawled or the time it took me. At first it was ghastly: sheer hard labor mixed with fright. But as I kept going and became more accustomed to the mode of progress and realized how quietly I was getting along, my spirits rose and I found myself tingling with excitement. My fear gradually departed and I became more optimistic of success. I came to realize more fully what I had learned long before: that anticipation of possible dangers is always

139

worse than the actual danger itself. I had scared myself beforehand by thinking of all the unpleasant things that might happen; but now that I was actually on the job I found it was becoming the most thrilling I had ever experienced. It was difficult and dangerous, yes—it would be foolish to forget the danger—but I knew now that when I eventually placed my bullet where it would do the most good I would derive greater satisfaction from that one shot than from any I had ever fired before.

My greatest danger lay in the possibility that the bull was lying downwind of me. However, there was nothing I could do about that, so it was best not to worry about it. At long last I came to a tall tree with a tiny clearing around its base. It was plain to see that it was used by buffalo from time to time, possibly by that party of four to which I've referred. There was nothing there now but droppings. Still, I welcomed the site because it gave me a chance to stand up and have a bit of a rest. Moreover, it suggested that there must be other similar places where these bulls lay. I gave myself a full 10 minutes' rest here and a smoke. I could see no harm in the latter, because if my quarry were lying downwind of me and could smell the tobacco, well, he could smell me also and that would have more effect on him than all the smoke in Africa.

Then on again. The god of hunters must have been on my side that day. When I think back over all the impossible places in which I might have encountered the wounded bull, and then remember just where I did find him, I have much cause to be grateful.

I was continuing to advance in exactly the same manner as that in which I'd started. It was, I suppose, some 15 or 20 minutes after leaving that little clearing under the tree that I found I was approaching another similar little clear patch with a tall tree in the center of it. And there was something else there also, something blacker and more solid than bush. Some of it was concealed by the tree trunk and some of it extended out to the right of the tree. It might have been an anthill, of course, or the trunk of a long-dead tree—but I had a feeling that it was my quarry. I could see it only indistinctly as yet and would have to go several lengths farther forward to be certain; but I had no real doubt as to what it was. And it certainly wasn't the quartet: The clearing was so small that they would have been lying all around the tree, easily discernible.

I snaked forward twice my own length; and again. Then I slowly took hold of my rifle with both hands and slid forward the safety catch.

Buffalo

The bull was lying down asleep with his nose on the ground like an old cow taking her ease in a meadow. His hindquarters were concealed by the tree, but the rest of his body was broadside on to me with the head turned away. I could have shot him then and there from where I lay, and I sometimes wonder why I didn't. But apart from the fact that I don't like shooting from the prone position if I can possibly avoid it, there was also the fact that if anything went wrong I'd be at a grave disadvantage. I had, of course, expected to be compelled to fire while prone, but it seemed to me now that it was worth making a major effort to get a bit farther forward so I could at least kneel, and possibly stand upright. So I very carefully inched forward until I was clear of the bush and in the tiny clearing along with the bull. I was now within three and a half steps of him (measured later). And still he slept.

I slowly got myself into a kneeling position, one knee down and the other up, raised my rifle and drove a heavy bullet into the bull's shoulder. He rolled over on his side without a murmur or a kick, dead as a kippered herring.

Far from allowing familiarity with dangerous game to breed contempt, I find that the greater my experience the greater my respect. I don't mean by this that I'm growing more frightened; quite the contrary. I used to be scared stiff in my early days, whereas nowadays I'm not—provided I have a decent rifle in my hands and equally reliable ammunition for it. What I mean is that the more I see of wild animals and the punishment they can take, the more I realize their potentialities for mischief when wounded and vengeful. My nervousness in days gone by was due to an overactive imagination's playing upon inexperience. There are many others who suffer from the same defect. Provided they realize it in time and have the courage to admit it there will probably be no harm done. The trouble is that so few of them will admit they're scared. They don't or won't realize that there is nothing to be ashamed of in being frightened—it's perfectly natural, and there must be something wrong with the man who can honestly say he has never been afraid when first facing death, whether from bullets, bombs, or a wounded elephant, buffalo, or lion.

Pondoro: Last of the Ivory Hunters
Simon & Schuster, 1955

SO THE POSSUM'S
A PUSHOVER?

by Joel F. Webber

With the possible exception of shooting tin cans off a back fence, no sport offers less thrills than possum hunting. Perhaps it's the "occupational hazards" that appeal to the gambling instinct.

Let me elucidate:

In my boyhood days, when I used to visit my uncle's farm in the Missouri Ozarks, the nickname "Stinky" probably hadn't been invented. But it is a safe bet that its inventor must have had someone like my cousin, Tom Blake, in mind. (The name, of course, is a phony—Tom isn't.) In short, we kids referred to him solely as "skunk-bait." This unfortunate but apt title resulted from his numerous brushes with the little beasties with B.O., from which he always emerged second best.

Notwithstanding his almost weird affinity for the striped woods pussy, Tom got to be, as the years passed, about the best possum hunter I have ever known. It seemed a foregone conclusion that when he started out with his dog, Pansy, you could start peeling sweet potatoes. The possum was guaranteed by Pansy. At least that's the word that seeped through to me in Chicago, where I now lived.

The district known as Spring Creek, where my uncle's farm was located, must have been the marsupial equivalent of Chicago's famous Gold Coast, or Park Avenue in New York. Our possums could look down their snouts at their less sleek brethren on the other nearby ridges. Miles of tangled grapevines loaded with bunches of juicy blue grapes, lush fields of corn aching to be raided, occasional watermelon patches, and countless birds' nests filled with succulent eggs. Could any true gourmet of the possum clan ask for more?

Often I have watched these peculiar-looking animals at their daily chores, but none is more amusing than the female with young, carrying them as they clutch precariously on her long fur or ratlike tail. Poking here, sniffing there, nothing escapes her black, beady eyes—a half-frozen persimmon, a bitter acorn, or a nice, plump fledgling.

In all Spring Creek, it seemed, these clever rascals had no mortal enemies except Tom and Pansy. At that, when it came to putting the blitz on a possum, Tom was merely an auxiliary. Pansy was a one-dog panzer division.

To identify her breed would be like asking a blind man to describe one of those fancy patchwork quilts the womenfolk like to whip up. Indubitably, she was all mutt, but she did manifest strange traits and characteristics of the bull terrier and the Airedale. And a few years before I crossed paths with this amazing pup, she had lost an eye in an encounter with a raccoon so large that its pelt covered the surface of one of those old-fashioned stove zincs. Tom said it was quite a battle up to the time Pansy clamped her strong white teeth over the animal's windpipe.

He bragged so much about the exploits of this alleged wonder dog that I decided to call his bluff once and for all. It was agreed that we would go possum hunting the first night the season opened. We shook hands over our agreement, and I returned to Chicago to bite my nails until the opening day.

Three months later I received a wire from Tom: "Pansy is expecting you down here a week from Thursday."

My reply was: "Tell her she won't be disappointed."

The big night arrived in a blaze of autumnal glory. A huge orange-colored moon hung low upon the horizon, and there was just a faint hint of frost in the air. The corn shocks were like endless rows of Indian tepees, and there was the pungent smell of wood smoke, frying "fat back" and steaming coffee. McCutcheon's famous cartoon, "Injun Summer," had come to life!

About nine o'clock in the evening, we started out. I carried an electric lantern and an ax. Tom fetched along his single-barrel shotgun. Pansy furnished the hunt party her usual irrepressible personality.

We walked down through the cow lot, climbed the rail fence, and started out over the ridge leading to Dry Fork. Pansy had been liberated as soon as we passed the cow lot and she lit out over the hills ki-yi-ing in high girlish glee—after nothing in particular. Her infallible success

formula was to enthusiastically whip the tar out of whatever she attacked
—and then investigate.

Tom and I followed her at what seemed a snail's pace, but it was all
that we could do just to keep within range of the sound of her voice.
Suddenly, I heard her barking furiously. I suggested to Tom that she
might have jumped a rabbit: He replied that he had long ago broken her of
that habit.

No, indeed! The mutt had somethin'. This yammering had a real
significance.

Puffing and blowing from exertion, we reached Pansy's side. She was
doing a war dance around a log about 20 feet long.

"Funny place fer a possum to hang out," commented Tom. Pansy
cocked her one good eye at him as if to say, "What's so funny about
it?" and went on with her harrying.

"You stand down at the lower end of the log and I'll cut a pole and
shove it inside," suggested Tom. "We'll poke it out in the open."

Handing over the ax I took up my strategic position to await the
emerging of our prey.

Tom's activities with the pole stirred up ominous scratchings within
the log. I brought up the light to have a better look at whatever had taken
cover there.

Just as I got the beam properly focused on the end of the log, out
marched three skunks—Mama—Papa—and Junior, all quite annoyed
indeed. They took one look at me, as if to say, "Well, Bud, you asked
for it," and raised their tails in unison. They must have been saving it up
for three months, and I got it all. If you have never been thoroughly
sprayed by three skunks at the same time, brother, you've missed
something! Especially when your partner is apoplectic with mirth. Then
you really know what the defendant in a murder trial means when he
says, " . . . I don't remember, Judge. Everything went black."

Fortunately, if you're the recipient of one of these blasts, your personal awareness of your condition passes within a few minutes. You no
longer smell it. But polite society may find it necessary to ostracize you
for a few days.

Now, ordinary dogs are either blinded by this acrid spray or have their
tender nasal membranes so inflamed by it that they roll on the ground in
anguish. But not our little Pansy! This wildflower went after the skunks
and dispatched them in one-two-three order.

So far, so good! Three pelts—not prime ones, but good enough to underwrite the cost of a bottle of Ozark croup medicine, and some smoking tobacco, "store made."

On we went to the next farm. There was a haystack that Pansy insisted upon inspecting. It turned out that she knew her haystacks, for, emerging from inside a dead horse nearby was a nice, sleek possum, licking his chops and spoiling for a fight. Many people imagine that these animals will invariably go into a trance, "play possum," but such is not the case. If a full-grown opossum does not resort to flight, it will often fight to the last gasp. And that is exactly what this one did. Its sharp teeth lashed out at Pansy's feet and forequarters. Warily the dog sidestepped, and attempted to circle her prey.

Like a wild pig, the boar possum can feint and slash in the manner of a lightweight pugilist. Every time Pansy attempted to dash in and settle the affray, Mr. Opposum was there to greet her with a mouthful of teeth. Finally, Tom took a hand in the matter, and belted the animal over the head with the blunt side of the ax. Poor Pansy! She acted as if someone had stolen her favorite buried bone. She looked at Tom with her one good eye. "And I thought you were a pal!" she seemed to chide.

Momentarily the vision of possum and sweet potatoes vanished from my mind.

"Never can tell where you'll find a possum," remarked Tom philosophically, "and sometimes they don't seem to be a bit choosy about their eatin' habits."

This possum vied with the skunks as far as aroma was concerned, but Pansy wasn't fazed a bit.

By now it was almost 11 o'clock, so Tom and I built a fire and ate some sandwiches of fatback and cornbread. (Something which no possum hunter should ever neglect to carry with him.)

Far off over the hills we heard the yapping of hounds chasing rabbits. Tom broke open the shotgun, removed the shell, and placed the muzzle to his lips. I've heard fox hunters blow their hunting horns down in Virginia, but if you want to hear the kind of hunt music that sends the blood coursing through your veins, there's nothing like a shotgun barrel blown upon by an artist like my cousin Tom. I tell you, the concert stage is really missing an artistic performance!

Pansy looked at him appreciatively and then threw back her head to render a vocal accompaniment. It was superb! Also, somewhat jarring to the nerves. The mutt could howl in undiscovered sharps and flats.

Then all was silent while the pack over the hill recovered their equilibrium. They barked back their tributes and (probably scenting me) veered off to investigate more fruitful and less odorous territory. Their cries died away in the distance.

"Probably the Flett boys," sagely commented Tom.

"Probably," I replied, and let it go at that.

We leaned back against a long-abandoned rail fence and filled our pipes with home-cured native leaf. While the stuff is pretty strong, most mountaineers smoke it—only dudes use the scented, blended tobacco that comes in fancy cans. My uncle Melvin made his own "eatin' " tobacco by boring a good-size hole in a sugar maple. Then he'd ram in a wad of native leaf, follow this with licorice, and alternate until the hole was nearly filled. Only then did he plug it up. The sap—coursing through the tree for a year—made chewing tobacco that you could almost eat at the opera.

Like most mountaineers, Tom was hardly ever without a quid of tobacco in his mouth. Most of the time he resembled a giant chipmunk. I've even seen him eat a dish of ice cream without first removing his cud! He merely shoved it up in the northeast corner of his puss and proceeded with the business at hand.

Tom rarely smoked except upon such occasions as this. When he relaxed with Lady Nicotine, it was with a homemade corncob pipe. The curling smoke put him in a reminiscent mood.

"I'll never forget," he began, "the time I nearly stopped chewin'. I wuz about twelve years old and Pappy had given me an old muzzle-loadin' shotgun fer a birthday present. The first thing I did was try it out. I had another dog, then, and he had a squirrel treed in a pin oak in the backyard. So I loaded the gun and started out to blast Mr. Squirrel to glory. I bit off a good-size mouthful of twist and pulled back both barrels. I took aim and pulled the trigger. Well, Pappy had fergot to tell me that that gun had hair triggers; when the first barrel went off, the other one did too. I got that quid of tobacco kicked right down my throat!

"Fer two days runnin' I thought I was goin' to die—then I was afraid I wouldn't. Maw said I turned at least four shades of green—none of 'em very purty ones!"

By now, Pansy's insatiable curiosity had overwhelmed her again, and she had strayed off. Soon we heard her bark—it sounded as if she might be a quarter mile away. Stamping out the fire, we started off to join forces, but just as we got under way, I tripped over a piece of grapevine and fell flat upon what my wife laughingly calls my handsome face, smashing the lantern lens and extinguishing the bulb.

Tom has a fine command of language and can easily put a mule skinner to shame. He traced my antecedents way back, and cussed me out in every civilized language, including the Scandinavian.

I finally managed to coax the lantern alight again, but that took time, and when we finally arrived, Pansy paid us little heed. She kept her muzzle pointed up the trunk of a pin oak and carried on a one-sided conversation with her unseen quarry.

"Looks like you'll have to shinny up the tree," opined Tom. "I'd do it myself, but my leg's been stiff ever since that there copperhead stung me last summer." In the Ozarks snakes don't bite, they "sting."

"O.K., chum," I agreed, "give me a boost."

I put down the lantern and started up the tree. Whether the snake bite had really bothered Tom I'll never know, but you need but climb a pin oak to discover you've been roped in. The branches grow in almost impossibly crazy angles, including downward. I was in ribbons before I even got started up the tree.

"Here, take the lantern along," advised my Judas cousin. "You'll want to take a look at the critter before you shake 'im down."

Onward and upward I struggled, the branches contesting bitterly every inch. Added to these discomforts was the awkward lantern, bail slung over my elbow, banging a bruising tattoo against my side.

I must have climbed nearly 75 feet when I became aware of a bit of grayfish fur about as large as a medium-sized snowball. It was a tiny possum perched in the topmost branches. Lots of folks claim that animals can laugh and smile the same as humans, and I'll swear that critter slipped me the most sarcastic grin I've ever seen!

There I was, torn between two ghoulish desires: one to slay in cold blood Tom and that werewolf, Pansy, and the other to take that little possum apart bone by bone to see what made it tick.

I inched my way up the trunk of the tree to where the bole was slender enough to rock to and fro. Leaning my weight against it, I started to give Br'er Possum a ride. He just took a firmer grip and leered at me. But I was too mad now to give up easily. Breaking off a small branch, I prodded my victim until he became giddy and lost his grip. Down he went and I heard Pansy clamp down on him, and Tom kicking her off.

The descent was as tedious and painful as the climb had been. Then I regained the ground, Tom was snickering.

"I knew he was a small 'un. They allus climb the tallest tree in the county!"

Sage advice, indeed! And well timed!

As if to bear witness to Tom's woodlore, the next possum we caught was in a hazel thicket, not much more than seven feet from the ground. We shook him out in jig time, and the big faker laid on his back, feet up in the air, as if he had been dead for weeks. Pansy tried nipping at him, hoping to get a fight. It was no use; just like trying to argue with a cigar-store Indian. So Tom whacked him over the neck with the ax handle, and we started homeward. The latest addition to our night's bag weighed about eight pounds.

You see what I mean by "occupational hazards"? Well, they weren't over yet.

The first thing that happened when we arrived home was that I had to strip naked in the backyard while Tom—who was as pure-smelling as an Easter lily—went into the house to fetch me a fresh suit of overalls. Just try putting on a September morn act when the frost is beginning to turn the grass white—you'll get the idea.

Next: My clothing was buried in the ground for three days. That beats the dry cleaners all hollow. And if you don't forget where you've buried them, they'll be perfectly respectable duds again.

When I was finally admitted to the house, Tom went about his work of skinning and stretching the pelts. Ordinarily this work would be done outside, but there was a compromise, and he was permitted to do it on the back porch instead. Meanwhile, I washed up and tried to read the newspapers before the fireplace. Before long I experienced a peculiar itching sensation on my hands and face. But aside from some vigorous scratching, I paid no attention to it.

The next morning I woke up looking like a leper. The campfire Tom and I had made contained some poison-ivy vines and I'd been well smoked! I spent the next ten days in retirement plastered up with sugar-of-lead ointment.

So the Possum's a Pushover?

Well, when I finally got around again, my shins were still black and blue. I must have had enough hide peeled off them to half sole the boots of six men.

That's what I mean by the occupational hazards of possum hunting. I always return from a hunt in worse condition than the possums, but somehow I heal up in time for the next trip. And my cherubic countenance—dripping possum grease—may not be something pretty to see, but it bears testimony to my love of the sport.

O.K.! Have it your way. I'm nuts about possum hunting and I admit it!

Outdoor Life
May 1942

BROWN FURY
OF THE MOUNTAINS

by Ben East

T he roar of a wounded grizzly bear is nicely designed to try the courage of a man. It's half snarl and half bellow, and it's full of blood and fangs and murderous rage. And when it comes at close range, when the bear rears up beside a windfall 30 feet away and starts for you, and you realize that no force at your command can keep him from reaching you, fangs and claws and blood and all—well, somewhere in the world there may be a more soul-shaking sound, but just offhand it would be pretty difficult to name it.

If you have any doubts that the roar of a bear under those conditions has the power to turn your blood to water, you might take a jaunt out Jasper Park way, in Alberta, and have a chat with Harry Phillips.

Harry, you see, is in what most folks would consider a position of undisputed authority. He not only knows what a wounded grizzly sounds like at the start of his charge. He knows what follows. He knows the feel of teeth and claws, and the smell of a bear's breath when he's been feeding on carrion for a month.

Not that the knowledge in itself is especially novel. Plenty of men have acquired it in the long history of encounters between grizzlies and hunters. But most of them paid with their lives for knowing. And of the ones who didn't, I doubt whether any had a closer call than Harry. He came about as near to glory, at the hands of an infuriated bear, as it's possible to come and live to tell the story.

Phillips was one of a party of six camped on the north fork of the Burland River, in the Athabasca Forest Reserve, two days by pack train beyond the north boundary of Jasper National Park, four days out the town of Jasper.

150

The hunters were A. W. Buck and Fred Robinson, sportsmen from Saint Louis. Phillips and Herschel Neighbor were guiding, both unarmed. The game regulations of Alberta do not permit licensed guides to carry firearms while handling hunters. A cook and wrangler filled out the party.

The time was late September. Snow came in the night, the first of the year. A wet fall of about eight inches, and the men rolled out of their bags in the morning to find the trees freighted. Buck, with plenty of experience in mountain hunting, called off his plans for the day.

Robinson, less seasoned, was restless to stir out. He voted to have a try for sheep. There was likely country about three miles from camp. Snow means good sheep hunting, makes it easy to spot tracks and animals alike.

Buck was reluctant to have any of the party go out. The horses would have tough going and there'd be danger of a bad fall, no matter how surefooted the animals might be. But his partner was eager for the sheep hunt. Buck didn't want to crimp anybody's fun. He gave in, and Robinson started off, with Harry Phillips guiding.

Halfway to the sheep country the two made a find. They stumbled onto the carcass of a big caribou, apparently killed by hunters earlier in the fall. It was picked all but clean, and the signs showed plainly that a grizzly had done the picking. Most exciting of all, the fresh tracks of the bear led away from the caribou on the new snow.

Robinson was ready to quit sheep hunting then and there. It was grizzly he wanted, and he was all for taking the track, but Harry talked him out of it. "That bear's probably ten miles away from here by now," the guide explained.

But the bighorn range yielded nothing, and in the early afternoon the two men rode back to the caribou bones. Robinson still wanted to try for the bear, and Harry gave in. "The tracks are going toward camp," he agreed. "We'll follow him for a while, anyway."

They tied the horses and took the grizzly's trail afoot. The hunt was surprisingly short. They had traveled no more than a quarter hour when a big, yellow-brown bear reared up in the brush ahead of them.

He sat erect on his haunches, his forepaws hanging down, his great head swinging from side to side as he tested the wind for definite news of the danger that was following him. Robinson smashed a shot at him and the bear went down on all fours and ran.

151

When the men came up on the track they found the grizzly was dragging a shattered front foot. The hunt began to take on a slightly different tone from that point. Both men knew the price of carelessness, for it's the trick of a wounded grizzly to double back on his track and ambush his pursuers. Phillips knew, too, the added chance he took by carrying no rifle.

They followed the bear around the side of the mountain, and finally Harry called a brief halt.

"We're getting pretty far away from the horses," he explained. "I'll go back and bring 'em up. You can follow the bear, but take it easy and be careful. Remember, a crippled silvertip is bad medicine at close quarters!"

He turned back; and Robinson went on alone, working slowly. For a second time, then, the grizzly showed himself, moving through brush on the mountain ahead.

Robinson placed his shot in the body. It knocked the bear down, sent him sliding and rolling down the slope 50 feet or more. He gathered himself up and was out of sight before Fred could shoot again. From that point on the track showed heavy bleeding. It developed later that the slug from Robinson's .35-caliber, slide-action rifle had struck high in the hip and ripped into the abdomen of the grizzly, breaking no bones but inflicting a wound from which the animal would have died finally of hemorrhage.

Robinson trailed slowly after that to give Phillips a chance to overtake him. A half mile farther along, he came to the edge of a thick windfall, stopped for a minute, and something in motion along the far edge of the windfall caught his eye.

It was the head of the grizzly.

The bear was walking along the side of the log jam, carrying his head high. Robinson could see the big, broad skull plainly. There was a chance for a head shot. Robinson weighed the odds in his mind. He recalled bear talk he had heard the previous autumn in the Jackson Hole country. A veteran guide had warned that a wounded grizzly is likely to charge if overtaken in an open spot, where he can come downhill, or across clear ground. There's not much chance he'll try it uphill or through tangles.

This was decidedly not open ground. All the same, the bear was uncomfortably close. Robinson decided to wait for a better chance. He backed away from the windfall, picked an open spot, and waited for the guide to return.

Phillips came up within a few minutes. Robinson told him what had happened, said he believed the bear was badly hurt and was trying to locate them by scent. The rest of the hunt, the two men agreed, was going to call for plenty of caution to avert disaster.

They moved carefully around the windfall, picked up the tracks of the grizzly leading away from the other side, called another halt for several minutes while they discussed the situation. When they took up the trail again, it was with both men well on the uphill side of the tracks, Robinson above Phillips. The guide repeated his warning that the bear might watch his back track, lying in wait for them. The atmosphere of the hunt was growing decidedly electric.

"I'll stay down where I can see the tracks—you stay where you can see me," Harry instructed. Within 50 yards they came to a second windfall that blocked their way, and made it necessary for both men to swing down onto the beat trail to go around the jam. They arrived together where the lower tip of the windfall ended in a thick clump of young spruce, growing out of the mountainside at an angle. The branches grew clear to the ground.

Phillips started to go around the thick tangle. Robinson, unwilling to let the unarmed guide take the lead, scrambled up beside him, turned half sidewise to force his way between the branches and Harry. And just ahead of them, not more than 30 feet away, the roar of an enraged bear exploded like a bomb of sound!

Thirty miles an hour is probably a conservative estimate of the speed of a charging grizzly. Forty might not be too high. Pace off 30 feet on your front lawn, imagine 700 pounds of bear covering it at 40 miles an hour, and you'll have the picture.

Robinson shot from his side, with the stock of the rifle still tucked under his arm, with no time to bring it up.

The soft-nosed, copper-jacketed bullet of the .35 rifle weighs 200 grains. It leaves the muzzle at a velocity of 2,180 feet per second. At 20 feet it delivers a jabbing, jolting, paralyzing wallop of better than 2,000 foot-pounds. That's enough to lift a ton more than one foot off the ground.

The grizzly absorbed that blow and never flinched. Robinson didn't even know his shot had hit the bear.

Later he learned that the slug had struck the bridge of the grizzly's nose two or three inches below the crossline of the eyes, mushroomed according to formula, gone literally down the bear's throat, and expended the rest of its momentum in the chest. Four inches higher on the target would have dropped the grizzly stone-dead in his tracks.

The bear came on without faltering, snarling and snapping from side to side like a mad dog. He did not rear up but struck as a bull strikes, charging into the men full tilt. It was Phillips he had seen and was after, but the men were standing only a couple of feet apart and he smashed into both of them. His shoulder or the side of his body hit Robinson and sent him sprawling back, clear of the spruce clump. The hunter landed, by no means gently, in a sitting position 10 or a dozen feet away. Through the rest of the fracas he escaped all attention from the bear. It was Phillips the grizzly was determined to finish off.

When Robinson regained his feet, the bear and Harry had slid eight or 10 yards down the side of the mountain. The grizzly was standing over the man, tearing at him, and in the back of Robinson's mind Phillips's one unearthly yell was still ringing. That one scream was all he heard from Harry. In fact it was all Harry had been capable of, but if Fred Robinson lives to be a very old man he stands little chance of ever forgetting it.

More than one big-game hunter, speculating on the sensations of a man mauled to death by one of the large carnivores, has voiced the belief that a merciful coma sets in at the outset of the attack. That the nerve shock serves as a powerful drug, a sedative that dulls the senses to pain and fear alike, making the death an easy one. Maybe so. Or maybe the breath was knocked out of Harry Phillips when he went down under the impact of the bear's charge. Anyway, all he was able to recall afterwards was hazy thought, to the effect that maybe the bear would leave him for dead if he did not move.

Robinson scrambled to his feet with that one scream loud in his ears, and looked around for his rifle to finish the affair.

The rifle was gone.

It had flown out of Fred's hands when the bear knocked him down. In the tangle of fallen timber and rock and spruce, with half a foot of snow on the ground, the chances were all against finding the rifle soon. And unless it was found very soon it wouldn't do any good.

What Robinson did next he didn't talk about for quite some time. He had been home weeks before he finally sketched in this part of the story to Buck, and then it was with the apologetic remark that he didn't expect or want anybody to believe him.

There was Phillips and the grizzly, 20 or 30 feet away down the side of the mountain, with the bear tearing at the man. There was only one thing to do, and Robinson did it by instinct, not by reason. He reached back and unsnapped the leather loop around the handle of his hunting knife. Something in the back of his mind told him that if he ran down and stuck the knife into the bear's side the grizzly would turn his attention from Harry. And he didn't take time to figure what would happen to either of them, after that.

"I didn't do it because of bravery," he told Buck afterward, scoffing at his own solution. "I did it because I had to do something."

He started down for the bear, freeing the knife as he went. But before he had it clear of the sheath the picture changed again.

Running those few paces down the slope toward the bear, Fred saw his rifle. The grizzly was standing on it. On the barrel, with one hind foot. The stock was sticking out from under the foot at a crazy angle.

The rifle looked all right. In fact it looked a great deal better than that. Fred didn't wait to see whether it had been damaged. He grabbed it and yanked it out from under the bear's foot.

Quarters were pretty close by that time. The bear must have felt the movement under his foot. He dropped the business of finishing Phillips, raised his head, and looked around over his shoulder at the newcomer.

He was a sight Fred Robinson won't be likely to forget for quite some time. He had been mauling Harry about the head, and he had bitten through the guide's felt hat. When he looked around at Fred he was champing his foam- and blood-flecked jaws on the hat, trying to rid himself of the thing. It was plain he wanted to clear the decks for further action.

Had Robinson pumped another shell into the chamber of the rifle after that frenzied snapshot as the bear charged? He couldn't remember. Had he replaced in the magazine any of the shells he had used? He didn't remember that, either. Was the gun empty in either the chamber or magazine or both? He didn't know. At the moment he had just one idea. To hold the muzzle of the rifle to the bear's head and snap the trigger.

Robinson guessed afterward that the front sight of his rifle was four feet from the head of the grizzly when he squeezed off the trigger. The estimate is probably a generous one.

The 200-grain slug struck just under the ear, and the bear went down as if hit by a lightning bolt, stone-dead in his tracks.

Harry lay under the bear, silent and inert. Fred rubbed snow on his face and worked over him for a couple of minutes, breathing a sigh of relief when the guide moved, flicked back to half consciousness.

Not that Harry's predicament was ended, by any means. In the first place the bear was lying squarely on top of him; and the bear weighed, by conservative estimate, 700 pounds. The pelt later measured eight feet one inch, from tip to tip; eight feet five inches across, which gives you an idea.

Besides, the guide was horribly mauled. The bear had bitten through the thick flesh on the inside of one leg—bitten the full length of his great fangs. He had driven the claws of his sound forefoot deep into the other leg, between knee and hip, tearing loose thick ribbons of flesh that hung down like tattered bloody rags.

Sometime in the fracas Harry must have reached up with his right hand in a desperate effort to fend off the grizzly's attack. For his pains the bear had bitten the index finger neatly off at the second joint, leaving it dangling by a thread of tendon.

The guide's head was in the worst shape of all. The grizzly had had Harry's whole head between his jaws. His lower fang went into the forehead just over the right eye, missing the arch of the eye orbit by no more than a quarter of an inch. To that margin Phillips probably owes his life. The smooth, round bone of the skull gave the bear no purchase for his powerful jaws. Could he have driven a fang into the orbit of the eye his chances of crushing bone would have been far better. Meanwhile, his upper fang had cut into the scalp above the forehead on the left side, gone to the bone and inflicted a slash three or four inches long.

Were the grizzly's powerful jaw muscles weakened by the shot that smashed into the bridge of his nose? Is Harry alive because the bear was prevented by wounds from exerting the full might of those great fang-studded jaws? Harry himself and Robinson and Buck say yes. Save for that earlier shot, unlucky as it seemed at the time, Phillips would have died there under the grizzly before Fred found and retrieved his rifle, they believe.

Robinson went to work to free Harry from his place under the dead bear. Try as he would he could not roll the bear off the man or move it enough to free any part of Phillips. Finally he managed to work one foot out. The grizzly was lying squarely on the other leg. Fred braced his feet against the bear's side and tugged at Harry's shoulders. Little by little he pulled the guide free. But the second foot came out from beneath the grizzly minus boot and sock!

Harry was still conscious, but he lacked the strength to stand. Fred proceeded to dress his cuts as best he could there on the mountain. First he cut off the finger that dangled by a cord. He hastily disinfected claw and fang wounds, using a small bottle of mercurochrome that Harry carried in his pocket. This checked the worst of the bleeding. Then began the slow, dread trek down the mountainside and across the valley to the horses.

Robinson had little hope that they would reach the horses with Harry still alive, that either animal would let him lift the guide into the saddle, reeking as he did of blood and bear, or that Phillips could endure the ride back to camp once he was in the saddle.

But they plodded on, a few yards at a time. When Harry grew sick and faint and wanted to give up, Robinson spurred him by complaints that he could never hope to reach camp alone, without the guide, with evening coming on rapidly.

They made it to the horses finally. Harry's mount, a wise, patient old cow pony, looked him over, sniffed the bear scent, and stood quiet as if he knew all about what had happened up there on the mountain. Buck commented later that this was one of the most unusual things he had ever known a horse to do. The average saddle animal fears bear smell as he fears death.

They rode into camp at dusk, with Phillips half lying across the saddle horn, shaken with cold, all but frozen in his bloody, sweat-drenched clothing, barely able to whisper "Bear!" when Buck asked him what had happened.

They laid him on a blanket in the cook tent, cut his clothes off, put hot rocks at his feet, and went to work in earnest on the bear wounds.

Picture that scene, there in the snowbound camp! Buck and Robinson and the cook working by candlelight. They sterilized the cuts one at a time with a powerful antiseptic agent that Buck carried in his kit, opening them up, cleaning them, taping the edges together.

All the cuts but one, that is. When they finished the job of first aid, an hour before midnight, there was one part of the work left undone. That was the severed finger. When Robinson had cut the dangling tendon, there at the scene of the scrap, it had contracted and drawn far back under the skin of finger stub and hand. With it, it carried inevitable contamination from the carrion-foul teeth of the bear. But it was too deep in the flesh to be opened up and cleaned.

They started Harry out for Jasper early the next morning with Colon, the wrangler. Herschel Neighbor, the second guide, had left before daybreak to push on ahead. At the Jasper Park boundaries lay a ranger's cabin. From their Neighbor could phone into town for a doctor and medical supplies to come out and meet the party.

Herschel made 28 miles to the ranger's cabin by four o'clock that afternoon and put through his call. Colon and Harry did half as well. They made camp in the snow that night. At three-thirty the next afternoon they reached the cabin. A half hour later a doctor rode in.

All in all, Harry Phillips was three nights and four days on the trail, getting down to the hospital at Jasper. And long before the end of the fourth day the contamination left on the torn finger tendon by the teeth of the grizzly was doing its work. Harry was delirious from that infected finger when the little train rode into Jasper.

It was six weeks before Harry saw the outside of the hospital again, and he was still pretty shaky on his feet. But he didn't feel like complaining much. By all the rules he should have checked out, back there on the north fork of the Burland or somewhere on the trail down to Jasper, and he knew it.

And ever since, he's always kind of figured that maybe the game laws of Alberta should be changed to let a guide carry firearms while he's guiding.

To which, from the depths of his heart, Fred Robinson echoes a loud and fervent amen. Those few minutes there on the shoulder of the mountain with Harry down under the bear weren't exactly a lawn party for Fred either.

Outdoor Life
November 1940

ROGUE ELEPHANT

by Capt. Patrick A. Meade

G agah jahat!'' The cry is rare, much less frequent in Malay jungle villages than that other dreaded warning, ''Amok!'' But when it does come, women flee from the stinging smoke of their mangrove-wood fires, men drop their spears or fishing nets and— snatching up children too small to run—dash for the flimsy protection of the kampong's strongest hut. Once in the shelter of its few clapboards and many square feet of bamboo, they raise their voices in unison, aided by frantic pounding on Malay drums and cooking utensils; and if the rogue elephant happens to be in fairly good humor, he will betake his huge bulk and vicious temper to wallow in their rice fields, or trample an acre or two of bananas to pulp.

But the rogue who visited the little kampong on the Straits of Malacca side of Gunong Pulai was not in good humor, and he strewed a dozen huts to the wind, trampling to death four unfortunate old Malays too indifferent or incapacitated to run for their lives.

Elephants are seldom seen in the vicinity of the Gunong Pulai, whose summit is a reservoir, the water supply for a gigantic fortress about 35 miles away at Singapore. Rubber estates surround Pulai on three sides, but the mountain itself is jungle-covered, and the dense tropical growth stretches far to the north. A road leading up the mountain from the southeast—made in haste by contractors' men—is boulder-strewn and rough, but a third of the way up, a little stream spurts from the rocks beneath a huge flame-of-the-forest tree. It makes an exotic picnic spot, and on the day the rogue elephant decided to run amok, I had taken some friends—a beautiful girl and her charming mother—out for a luncheon in the jungle. I also took along my bull terrier, Mike, a 12-gauge (for pigeons or a chance snake), and a sleek, maroon-colored new car.

The day was perfect, and so was the picnic. After luncheon, the

159

mother settled herself with a book while the girl and I went searching for dainty little blue-and-white "pigeon" orchids. We were perhaps 300 yards from the car when Mike growled low in his throat. He was trained to hunt wild boar, and when he turned back toward the car I knew that something must be amiss there. It was; for as Mike dashed back down the trail, the hoarse, squealing trumpet call of a wild elephant echoed through the trees, and an instant later I heard a crash, like cars meeting head on at 60 miles an hour. Unarmed and worried about my companion and still more so about her mother, I ran toward the sound, the girl behind me. Mike, however, was there a good first, and (with a courage which discounted size) had tackled the elephant—an elephant which had bumped my car completely off the road.

The brute was stamping around in the jungle, out of sight, and squealing with rage as Mike growled around his legs. The girl's mother was uninjured, and not overly frightened, for the elephant's attack had been very abrupt. The car, however, had its bright newness ruined forever; its spare tire had been wrenched off, both rear fenders smashed, and the rumble seat dented like a battered celluloid ball. Other parts had suffered too, but after giving the elephant time to move away, I got the engine started, and, with much maneuvering, got the car back on the road. Mike returned panting and happy, for hadn't he routed the lord of the jungle? I was trying to make things halfway comfortable for our return to Singapore when a kampong Malay came fleeing down the mountain.

He stopped when he saw us, and too excited and frightened to notice the damaged car, he blurted, "Allah be praised! A white man!" (A white man is the panacea for all native ills.) "Tuan, a gagah jahat has ruined my rubber trees and torn down my house!"

I clucked sympathetically and inquired, "Are your children and wife safe, Haji?" He looked bewildered and replied, "Allah know, Tuan! I was tapping rubber, and seeing that the elephant was truely a rogue, I ran for help. And God is my witness, Tuan, it is truly a rogue that you will shoot."

I told him I knew it was a rogue, and pointed to the car. The old Malay smiled and said calmly, "Now emphatically will Tuan want to shoot the elephant which is not only a rogue, but most surely mad!"

I assured him that nothing would give me greater pleasure, but

160

unfortunately I was weaponless. The Malay pointed to my 12-gauge propped against the battered running board, "But Tuan has a gun, a two-barreled one. Is the Tuan afraid?"

"Not afraid, Haji, but this gun is for birds, its shot are fine like seed." The distressed Malay, however, being a man of the jungle, could only believe that a white man, having a gun and refusing to help, must be frightened.

Suddenly I had an idea which would at least give the now destitute Malay moral support. Once I got the car down from the mountain it would be on a well-traveled road, not more than 15 miles from the city of Johore Bahru. The girl could drive in and telephone the Sultan, a man who'd forgo his chance of heaven for the opportunity to bag a rogue elephant. What is more, she could get the police department to locate my trackers and hunters. Samat and Mahat, in turn, could bring out my rifle and give me a crack at the brute. Perhaps I could even go hunting with the Sultan, and that would be something, for His Highness is a big-game hunter to be envied. However, as it turned out, there was no competition, for His Highness was away.

The two ladies were game, and I left them on the highway, with final directions for my trackers. A hundred yards beyond our picnic spot, no longer pleasant, the old Malay kebun (farmer) turned off the track into a pathway which led through thick matted jungle, a malodorous spot, with slimy black mud underfoot, mosquitoes which attacked with the enthusiasm of hornets, and leeches that came galloping over twigs to reach bare knees and open neck. But the ordeal was over in a quarter of a mile, and we came out of the jungle into the squatter's straggly two acres of puny rubber trees.

Apparently the maddened elephant had galloped straight down one row, for several trees of a good two-foot circumference looked as if they'd met an army tank. But the hut, once a really substantial affair, might well have been through a hurricane, for not even one of its piles was left upright. The Malay's wife, his four daughters, and ancient mother lamented loudly by the ruins, while his three sons looked on with Malay stoicism.

No one, however, had been injured, and I persuaded the boys, ranging in age from 10 to 16, to accompany me on the elephant's trail. Not that I needed assistance in tracking, for the holes left by the monster's feet were a foot deep, but the boys could relay messages and bring Samat and Mahat up to me by a more direct route. Confident in the ability of my 12-gauge to stop anything, the boys came willingly, and were only too anxious to overtake the gagah jahat so that they could see with their own eyes the avenging fire flash from the Tuan's gun!

The Tuan's anxiety however, was all the other way, and even now, five years later, I can still see every twist in that trail, every strange conformation in the trees, even the changing colors of the jungle, so closely did I watch for huge cocked ears and little pig eyes above wicked curving tusks.

It was two hours after I'd sent off the car that Daud, the eldest Malay boy, told me we were nearing kampong, on the west side of the mountain, which was only a half hour by trail from his father's rubber land. Following the elephant had taken almost an hour and a quarter, so I sent the youngest boy back to meet Samat and Mahat with a message. Ten minutes later, the jungle opened to present a most gorgeous view; in the distance the blue waters of the Straits of Malacca; in the immediate foreground, sweet-scented magnolia and yellow mimosa trees, and some blue-and-white flowing bushes; behind them, coconut and oil palms under cultivation, and near them the dull green leaves and bright yellow fruit of gold bananas. A heavenly, prosperous-looking spot. "There," said Daud. "Behind those meranti trees is the kampong of Mat Slaman."

A moment later we heard the wailing of women, and then saw a ruined village. The maddened elephant had really run amok there, charging back and forth among the huts. A dozen huts had been destroyed, four people dying in them, and three of the ruins were ablaze, threatening the portion of the kampong that had been left standing. As we arrived, the frightened Malays were just beginning to come back from their hideouts in the jungle.

Ignoring the almost overwhelming disaster, Mat Slaman, a graying, dignified man of splendid carriage, came forward with true Malayan courtesy to make me welcome and offer coffee, which, honoring tradition, I accepted. The damage to his huts could be repaired in a few hours, for the materials were at hand in the jungle, but aside from the loss of life—soon forgotten by the fatalistic Malays—the real loss was to the kampong's most profitable crop, a large grove of cultivated cottonwood trees. There it seemed as though the brute elephant had maliciously tried to ruin the trees which the Malays venerate—"Do not their pods shelter the souls of virgins?"—trees whose harvest of kapok represented the kampong's one cash crop.

Sulong, Mat Slaman's eldest son, joined us. He was apparently the only person who'd had a good look at the rogue, and he spoke of it with awe. "Wah, Tuan, he is truly a rajah. Old, perhaps seventy years, and his tusks are as thick as my waist, and long—hei!" The rogue had headed as if to circle the mountain, and the Malays agreed that he would probably cross the river and continue northeast toward the plains. That meant 50 miles or more of trailing, but it suited me. I could meet Samat and Mahat, and get into clothing more comfortable than lightweight shirt and shorts, I was still picking repulstive, blood-filled leeches from my body.

I met my trackers, and determinedly took up the trail. The monster, leaving a train of willful destruction, had circled to within eight miles of Johore Bahru. At one place he had smashed back and forth across a Chinese farmer's sweet-potato field; at another, he butted through log pigpens, killing some of the swine and scattering the remainder. We almost came up with him at a point where he had charged a car driven by one of the Danish planters but missed.

Two days, a week, passed and I was ready to give up, for with that solitary exception, he was always a day ahead. Again, however, he doubled eastward, and crossing the railway for the second time he pulled down a telegraph pole and butted a store shed onto the tracks. Then perversely he followed the rails back toward Johore Bahru. We learned later that he had taken a stand in the middle of the track and delayed the Singapore express for 15 minutes. Another 20 miles, and two Malay rattan cutters said they had seen him only two hours before. They had been cutting rattan, when suddenly the elephant appeared in a rage. He had squealed, flung up his trunk, and danced that peculiar little "two-step" which all elephants affect when about to attack. And then, as the Malays ran, he seemed to forget them, and turned quietly back into the jungle. "But, by Allah, he is a giant!"

All that day, tired and exhausted, we struggled through swamp, oozy, black, snake-infested swamp, and to add to our troubles, the rogue chose to follow the highway which cuts the country north to south. And, of course, with Samat, the one-eyed old reprobate, consulting his charms, we elected to turn in the wrong direction.

Then, with all the cussedness of his nature, the gagah jahat got lonesome and came back to look for us! We'd shot a hog deer, and decided (after a good 70 miles of man-killing travel) to rest all day Friday, which is the Malay Sunday. So we ate, washed our clothes, and lazed. Coffee was steaming for our evening meal (delicious coffee for which Mahat had walked 10 miles, and with the aid of $5 persuaded a Chinese bus owner to drive nearly 40 miles more), when suddenly Samat's eyes simply goggled. Turning quickly I saw an elephant standing 50 feet away between two clumps of bamboo. His nearsighted little eyes were plainly visible and his trunk was snuffing in air laden with the strange odor of coffee. We sat petrified, for, with the exception of a towel, I was naked, and my rifle hung on a tree fork, but within reach.

The brute snorted, took a few steps forward, and we dived for the jungle. The rogue saw the movement and squealed that harsh, fighting, nerve-rasping elephant trumpet call. But Mahat saved us, for even as he jumped for cover he snatched a knot of blazing damar gum from the fire and threw it. The knot burst, so he said, into countless flaming embers on the rogue's head. At any rate, the leviathan made off, venting his fright and rage, and we heard the crashing and snapping of limbs for at least five minutes after he had gone.

It was useless to follow, for he wouldn't stop for perhaps an hour, and daylight would be gone by that time. Once recovered from our scare, however, the sight of his wrinkled black hide, scarred with the marks of a hundred battles, gave us encouragement to go on, even if opinions did differ about the state of his tusks. Frankly, I hadn't noticed them, but Samat, who'd been the first to see the brute, claimed that the tusks were long, thick, and in perfect condition. Mahat who had actually stood and faced him, said they were cracked and yellow with age; not worth the trouble of cutting out and carrying back with us.

We had to bag the beast first, however—a task I began to think was beyond our power. The next day I was sure of it, for we found that the cunning old bull had slept within two miles of us! He had fed leisurely, cracking down three palms to get the hearts, and finishing with a dessert of papayas and jack fruit. We followed his trail, watchful and wary, and shortly after noon we came up to a stream in which he had immersed himself, and playfully blown water which still dripped from the trees.

Rogue Elephant

Samat, a wise tracker, suggested we take time out to rest before going on to tackle the gagah, which, he believed, was only a few hundred yards ahead. Samat was right, but there was something more than elephant in front of us, for with startling suddenness, the bad-tempered old rogue trumpeted a challenge, and something bellowed a reply. There was a crashing sound, another enraged squeal from the elephant, more crashing, and a booming, hollow thump. A moaning bellow followed the terrific thump, and we surmised correctly that the rogue elephant had come in contact with another jungle menace, a deadly old bull saladang, vicious with hatred, who had been driven from his herd. So with the safety of my Indian Express .465 off, we crept forward eagerly, but with caution.

The bull saladang was lying, with entrails trampled out, a few feet from a muddy wallow, but to our surprise there was no sign of the elephant. The country ahead was open marshland, only sparsely covered with stunted growth, and we closely examined every inch of it with our eyes. I was just about to speak when Mahat grasped my arm and pointed. Thirty feet away the mud in the wallow billowed, an ear flapped, and the old rogue elephant whistled with contentment as he foundered about.

Some movement of ours alarmed him, and with a grunt and a sucking sound from the mud, he heaved himself up with surprising speed, looking, as slime slithered down his hide, like some fabulous prehistoric monster rising from another world. Free from the dwarfing influence of the jungle, the elephant was monstrous, but his tusks, grotesquely hung with green swamp weeds, were both broken and cracked by age and battle. We stood motionless, and as the rogue "felt" the air for our alien presence, he faced us almost squarely. Slowly I raised the rifle, and in the fraction of a minute the whole jungle appeared to quiver into silence.My sights came to bear. The rifle exploded, the light breeze carried back cordite fumes, and the recoil jarred me to the toes.

The elephant teetered, but his trunk went up over his head, and a blast of fury shook the air. Why doesn't he go down? Samat shouts, and the elephant thunders toward him. Quick, a heart shot—it may stop him. He's almost on Samat! Thank God the bullet in the left barrel is soft-nosed—the first was hard.

Now the rifle booms again—the elephant goes down plowing the ground. He falls flat, one leg kicking absurdly.

Eight days of trailing around a 40-mile circle, 80 miles through swamp, jungle, and plantation under tropical heat and chilling, tropical rain torrents. Eight days of merciless thorn, and at least one narrow escape from the fangs of a king cobra, and all for two shots at a barn door! Now, looking down on the great majestic form, I forgot the rogue's depredations, and thought only of the pity of having to destroy him.

Samat began to cut portions of the elephant to sell to Chinese "doctors." Mahat unslung the camera. "Take photo, Tuan?"

Hell no! I wanted a drink and a bath!

Outdoor Life
June 1941

THE GREAT JONESBORO PIGEON SHOOT

by Jim Carmichel

T he whole thing got started when Bob Jenkins' second-oldest daughter was accused of shoplifting a brassiere at Modene and Mabel's Discount Variety Store.

Bob (whose full name is Robert E. Lee Jenkins), like most folks who live on the lower end of Washington County, took his daughter's troubles to Fry (for Friedman L.) Bacon, a lawyer of some local repute. Fry Bacon is one of the last of that dwindling species of attorneys once admitted to the bar after a period of having "read law," but with no other formal training. This shortcoming has been of no noticeable difficulty to Fry Bacon, who describes himself as a champion of poor people's causes, and in return for legal services, has been known to take chickens, coon hounds, and enough odd parcels of land to make him the county's biggest property owner.

Not one to let textbook law interfere with a good courtroom battle, Fry Bacon's favorite tactic is to open his Bible to some random page, wave it in the faces of judge and jury, shout that there is no higher law than the law of God, then have the jury get down on its collective knees while he leads the jurors in prayer for his dear misguided client, who has just recently been washed in the blood of the lamb and aims to spend the rest of his life doing kind deeds and "helping out widder women."

Fry Bacon was just the man to represent Robert E. Lee Jenkins' daughter.

In Fry Bacon's opinion the theft of a brassiere was a rather delicate subject and hardly one to be discussed before a courtroom audience. The word "brassiere" was abhorrent to him under such circumstances, as was the diminutive form "bra," so he substituted "set of briars,"

167

thumping his fists to his chest to indicate their approximate purpose and his own apparent meaning.

The case did not go well for Fry Bacon. His assertion that the poor girl was feeble-minded did not produce the desired effect, nor did his pleas that the lass was ''with child'' by a stranger last seen two years before. Seeing no hope in this line of defense, he turned to attack the two eye-witnesses as ''godless sinners and short-skirted harlots'' and was just warming to this line when it happened.

Six tons of pigeon manure came cascading through the courtroom ceiling. It covered the jury, it covered the godless harlots, it covered Hizzoner the judge and it covered Fry Bacon. It covered them with six tons of dry, crusty, choking pigeon droppings that had been accumulating in the courthouse attic for decades, straining at the ceiling rafters and needing only the shock wave of Fry Bacon's rhetoric to set them free.

''Ladies and gentlemen of the jury,'' Fry Bacon is reputed to have said when the dust cleared, ''behold the wrath of the Lord.''

The case was dismissed and the courthouse closed for six weeks because, as one Jonesboro wag put it, ''The wheels of justice can't turn in that stuff.''

The episode occurred not without some warning. About 15 years earlier, Bill Bowman, a leading Jonesboro humanitarian, had noted that the pigeons had so gummed up the courthouse clockworks that each hour was lasting about 80 minutes. The matter had been brought up at the City Council meeting, where Virgil Meeks suggested that the additional time was probably a good thing and the clock should not be tampered with. The Council agreed and voted 11 to 1 to leave the clock alone.

But the collapse of the courtroom ceiling meant something had to be done. The first order of business was to clear out the mess, and that in itself brought about a political scandal which almost brought down the county government. The lowest bid to haul away the pigeon manure ran into some thousands of dollars, enough to cause a countywide financial crisis, but at the last minute Mort Screeb, who owned a tomato farm down by the Chucky River, stepped in and said that the stuff was great tomato fertilizer and that he would haul it off for nothing. His one condition, however, was that he be allowed to take it as he needed it, which, questioning disclosed, might cover three or four years. In the end a cleanup crew was hired to cart it off, but the ensuing political fight, with Screeb screaming kickback, produced a shakeup in Washington County politics which continues even to this day.

Despite all the uproar a few cool heads noted that nothing was being done about the pigeons. They were as happy as ever, perching on the belfry railings, roosting in the clockworks, building more nests, hatching chicks and contributing hourly to another avalanche.

The county's first step was to hire professional exterminators. They rigged a cannonlike affair which made a burping noise guaranteed to frighten pigeons and starlings and other winged creatures. The Jonesboro pigeons loved it. It would burp and they would coo, and in winter they warmed their feet on its outstretched muzzle. Obviously, stronger measures were called for. That's when I arrived on the scene.

Jonesboro is not quite like anyplace else on earth. It's a beautiful little town nestled in the wooded valleys of East Tennessee. It was once the capital of the lost state of Franklin, was home to a scrappy young lawyer by the name of Andy Jackson and now, after 200 years, is one of the best preserved towns of its kind anywhere. No power or telephone lines ensnare its streets, no parking meters clutter its curbs and old-fashioned street lamps cast a warm glow on brick-paved sidewalks.

On the town square is the county courthouse, where dwell Jonesboro's pigeons. Though completed in 1912 it is still called the "new" courthouse by most of Jonesboro's citizens who well remember the "old" courthouse, and probably the one before that.

Stray dogs, camels and pack mules eventually find their way home, and it is no different with wandering Jonesboro-ites. After several years of living in the West and exploring lands far beyond, I returned to Jonesboro to spend my declining years near the poor dirt farm where I grew up.

Citizens of Jonesboro seldom leave town except in a state of acute disgrace, so it was naturally assumed when I left that there must have been substantial reason. This meant I was eyed with some suspicion when I reappeared on the village green. But I opened up a downtown office just as bold as brass, looked up old girlfriends and settled back in place as easily as a pup taking a nap. Whatever crimes or indiscretions that vivid imaginations may have conjured to account for my departure were apparently forgotten.

It was a comfortable reunion but alas, too good to last. When I moved into my second-story office directly across from the courthouse and laid eyes on all those grinning pigeons lined up on the balcony I knew fate had caught up with me.

No one could dispute that the courthouse needed to be rid of the pigeons, and it was equally clear that the only way to do it was to shoot them. Their clock-tower fortress was apparently impregnable to all other forms of attack. But until my arrival no one had possessed both the will and the means of dealing with them. My office window provided the perfect sniper's roost. Destiny surely planned the whole thing.

As discreetly as enthusiasm permitted, I passed the word that I wouldn't mind taking a few potshots at the pests "just to keep my eye in practice." And just as discreetly the word came back that it was my "bound civic duty to rid the town of the damnable beasts." Even the sheriff, H. H. Hackmore, who is in charge of courthouse maintenance, stopped by to bestow his blessing.

Second only to the speed of light is the blazing speed of Jonesboro gossip. In no time at all everyone knew that a big-game hunter had come to do in the courthouse pigeons.

The distance to the peak of the clock tower was 41 yards, and the choice of weapons was my old pump-up pellet rifle. I figured this was the only safe equipment for the job even though it might handicap me a bit. I didn't know just how much of a handicap this rifle would be until I tried adjusting the aperture sight for a 41-yard dead-on point of impact. The pellets hit everywhere except dead on, with the group sizes ranging upwards of 12 inches.

I'd made the mistake of announcing that I would begin knocking off the pigeons on the following morning. I say mistake because when I arrived at my office opposite the courthouse, pellet rifle in hand, a crowd of onlookers had already gathered in the street. It was going to be a memorable day in Jonesboro, they reckoned, and they wanted to see it happen. There was a smattering of applause as I entered the ancient building, and I heard Harry Weems, who runs Harry's Men's Shop downstairs, offering to cover all bets. I wish I could forget the whole thing.

Filling the rifle's air reservoir with 10 full strokes of the pump handle, I fed a pellet into the chamber, and taking a rest on the windowsill, leveled the sights on a particularly plump pigeon. The crowd below held its breath. *Plufft* went the air rifle, *splat* went the wayward pellet on an ornate piece of contrete scroll work, *coo* went the pigeon. I'd missed clean. A chuckle rippled through the throng.

Feverishly I pumped the rifle and fed another pellet. *Plufft, splat, coo.* The chuckle became a collective guffaw. *Plufft, splat, coo*; again and again I tried. No results. "Hey Carmichel," someone shouted from below, "if them was lions they'd be pickin' their teeth about now." *Plufft, splat, coo.* Even the pigeons joined in the fun, waddling over to the roof's edge for a better view of the whole sorry spectacle.

By then my audience was drifting off by twos and threes, telling each other it was the biggest disappointment since Jack Hicks' hanging was called off in the spring of 1904. Harry Weems paid off his losses and my disgrace was thus complete.

That day I called Robert Beeman, the country's leading dealer and importer of quality air rifles and accessories, and ordered a German-made Feinwerkbau Model 124 air rifle and a supply of special pointed pellets. The FWB-124 is the hottest thing going in hunting-type air rifles. It gives a muzzle velocity of better than 800 feet per second (close on to a .22 Rimfire Short) and is accurate enough to hit a dime—or a pigeon's head—at 41 yards. "Send it airmail," I told him. "I've got to salvage my reputation."

Revenge would be mine, I told everyone, describing the fancy new air rifle I'd ordered. But sometimes the airmails fly slowly, and it was weeks before the FWB-124 arrived. By then the whole town was laughing about the "wonderful pigeon gun" that existed only in my imagination.

But it did arrive, and my first few test shots showed it was more accurate than I had dared hope. Topped off with a 10X scope and zeroed dead on at 41 yards, it cut a neat little group about the size of a shirt button.

The next morning a small crowd of onlookers gathered to watch the next chapter in Carmichel's disgrace. Even the pigeons seemed interested, and about 20 lined up on the balcony railing to see what was happening. I started on the right end of the row and worked my way to the left.

The first bird toppled off with scarcely a flutter. Its neighbor noted its demise with idle curiosity but no particular concern. When the next two or three went over the edge the others began to get somewhat curious about what was happening and cooed at the stricken forms with some amazement. In fact, as more pigeons fell, the remainder reacted with increasing amazement, those on the left end having to lean far out from their perches, wings aflutter, in order to watch the peculiar behavior of the brethren.

The first run was 14 straight kills with Harry collecting bets like mad. The pigeons still hadn't figured out what was going on, but apparently they thought it best to go somewhere else and give it some thought. That day's tally was 27 pigeons and a few stray starlings. Next day would be even better.

But next day disaster arrived in a totally unexpected form. I was brewing a pot of tea and had just killed the first pigeon of the day when "Shorty" Howze, Jonesboro's seven-foot policeman, charged into my office and presented me with an official complaint lodged by one of the townspeople. According to the unnamed plaintiff, I was "molesting Jonesboro's beloved pigeons."

"C'mon, Shorty," I protested, "you've got to be kidding. Everybody wants rid of those pigeons. You told me so yourself. And besides, I have the sheriff's O.K."

"I know," Shorty replied. "The courthouse is county property and you can shoot over there all you want to. But the chief says when you shoot across the street you're violating Jonesboro air space. So the complaint stands."

"Who complained?" I asked.

"I'm not allowed to say."

"I know, but tell me anyway."

"That crazy-acting woman that just moved into the old Crookshanks place."

The one that has all the cats and makes her husband walk the dog at two in the morning?"

"That's the one."

"Thanks for telling me."

"By the way," he said, stopping at the door and glancing at the air rifle by the window, "that's one hell of a pigeon gun."

Except for an occasional guarded shot, the rifle stood unused. The pigeons flourished and grew fatter, and life in Jonesboro trudged through an uneventful winter. By spring I'd all but forgotten the ill-fated affair when a really splashing event brought the pigeon problem back into brilliant focus. The leading character was none other than one Judge Hiram Walpole Justice. It seemed that Judge Justice, all decked out in his new tailor-made blue suit, had just handed down an important decision and was on the courthouse lawn discussing it with some reporters when a pigeon swooped down and scored a bull's-eye on his jacket. Thousands saw it live on TV.

The judge turned on his heel and stalked back into the courthouse, muttering something about the futility of "holding court in a chicken house." That afternoon Judge Justice was in my office learning the finer points of shooting courthouse pigeons with an FWB-124.

Every morning thereafter, the judge would declare a recess at about 10 o'clock and rush over to my office to blast a few pigeons, giggling fiendishly every time one plopped on the pavement. Hizzoner became a very fine marksman.

This had been going on for about two weeks when one morning Shorty, backed up by the mayor and two constables, crashed into my office and waved a warrant at the backside of the judge. "Aha," yelled the mayor. "We know what you've been up to, Carmichel. This time we've got you dead to rights."

With his judicially robed backside to the door, the judge was kneeling on the floor and taking a careful aim with the rifle resting on the windowsill. So intent was he that he didn't even look up.

"That ain't me," I said, stepping out of the washroom. "That's Judge Justice. And if I was you I wouldn't bother him right now."

All worthy projects must end, and by late summer the judge and I had pretty well wiped out the pigeon population, firing something near 1,500 pellets in the process. In all probability the whole thing would have reached a happy conclusion had it not been for one of those freak, clod-dissolving August cloudbursts. The creek overflowed its banks, poured into the streets of Jonesboro, and for the first time in history, flooded the courthouse basement where two hundred years of moldy Jonesboro records are kept. The devastation to the voting records in particular was total. Wiped out.

An official inquiry was launched in order to discover the cause of the unprecedented flooding, and the final ruling was:

"One Jim Carmichel, a citizen of Jonesboro, is known to have shot pigeons on the courthouse roof and thereby stopped up the gutters and drainpipes, thus contributing to the flooding."

There's a new crop of pigeons living in the clock tower now. I can see them looking this way. . . .

(All statements of fact in the story you have just read have been checked and found accurate. Certain names and dates have, however, been altered to protect wrongdoers.—Ed.)

Outdoor Life
March 1980

THE CHABUNKWA
MAN-EATER

by Peter Hathaway Capstick

T he safari season was over and I was puttering around camp, taking care of the last-minute details of tagging trophies and sorting and packing equipment when I heard from the district commissioner of the area, who had sent a runner with a note wedged in a cleft stick asking me to come on my single-side band radio as soon as I got it. When I had the aerial rigged after breakfast, he answered my call immediately. We went through the usual amenities, the thin-red-line-of empiah voice hollow over the speaker. I asked him what was up.

"Sorry to bugger your holiday," he told me, "but something's come up. . . . I thought you might be able to help me out. That bloody Chabunkwa lion chopped another Senga last night. The Tribal Council is screaming for action. Suppose you might spare a day or so to pop over there and sort him out? Over."

"Stand by, please," I answered. We both knew that man-eating lions didn't usually get sorted out in a day or so. I lit a cigarette from the flat thirty-pack of Matinees. Well, I reasoned, I'm stuck. He must have already cleared it through my company or he wouldn't have known I was free. Also, one just doesn't turn down official requests from district commissioners, not if one wants to hang on to one's professional hunter's license. I reached for a pencil and pad.

"Right, Cyril," I answered. "What are the details? Over."

"Bugger hit the village just this side of the Munyamadzi—know it?—around midnight last night, so far as the report goes. Grabbed a young man sleeping off a beer bust with two others, but neither of his pals awoke. Smells like that same chap who ate the other bunch over at Chabunkwa, about five miles from this village. We don't have any

Game Department people in the area and it'll be a few days before we can get somebody up from Valley Command or Nsefu. Can you give it a try before the trail cools? Over.''

"Roger, Cyril. Roger. I'll leave in an hour. Shall I give you a radio sched at eight tonight to see if anything's new? Over.''

He reckoned that would be a fine idea. We went through the usual jolly-goods and signed off. I whistled up Silent and told him to get cracking with the normal katundu for a three-day trip. Less than an hour later we were boiling through the growing heat and billowing dust to the village of Kampisi.

Kampisi looked like most villages in Zambia's Eastern Province— shabby and dusty with a ragtag collection of snarling curs and tired-looking people, hordes of spindle-legged children who would not reach puberty. We were greeted by the headman, a born politician who always wore eyeglasses and carried a fistful of ballpoint pens despite the fact he could see perfectly well without glasses and couldn't write a letter. Status symbols are as important in the African miombo as they are on Park Avenue. He treated all within earshot to a tirade on the lack of government protection from the horrors of the bush. I asked him why in hell the three men had been sleeping outside when there was a known man-eater in the vicinity.

"The young men thought it was too hot to sleep inside their kaia, Bwana,'' he replied. "Also,'' he said, shuffling the dirt with a big toe, "they were a little bit drunk.'' He shrugged with typical African fatal-ism. Most Africans believe it can never happen to them, something like the attitude of front-line troops. The millet and sorghum beer the tribes brew and drink keeps fermenting in their stomachs until the celebrants pass into a comatose sleep wherever they happen to lie down. In this case the price of the binge wasn't a headache, but death.

The headman pointed to the north when I asked him in Fanagalo where the lion had carried his kill. Silent whistled for me, and I walked over to see the pool of dried blood on the crusted blanket where the man had received his fatal bite. He had backtracked the lion's stalk, showing where he had lain watching the village, how he had stalked the sleepers, and where he had begun to drag the body. I loaded my .470 Evans double-express rifle with soft-points and stuck another clump of the big cartridges into various pockets of my bush clothes where they wouldn't

176

rattle against each other. Silent started off on the now cold trail carrying the water bag, a pouch of biltong (wind- and shade-dried meat), and his long spear.

The afternoon sun seared our shoulders as we followed the spoor into the bush and finally found the spot in the *conbretum* where the lion had settled down for his meal. The prints of the hyena were over those of the cat, and the most we could recover was a tooth-scarred chunk of lower jawbone and some splinters of unidentifiable bone. Silent wrapped the pitiful fragments in ntambo bark fiber and we started back to the village. Too late. There was no point in continuing to follow the cold trail since darkness was only an hour off and we both knew the most heavily armed man is no match for a lion's stealth at night.

Arriving back at Kampisi about dark, I had two hours to kill before my radio schedule with the D.C. I fished out my flask of Scotch and poured a hair-raising shot into the little, scratched plastic cup while Silent recruited men to cut thorn for a *boma*, or as it is called in East Africa, a *zariba*, a spiky barrier or fence to keep out nocturnal unpleasantries. I felt the first lukewarm slug burn the dust from between my teeth and form a small, liquid bonfire in the pit of my stomach. It was that sundowner or three that made you forget the saber-toothed tsetse flies and the pain in the small of your back, like a hot, knotted cable from too many miles bent over tracking. Four wrist-thick sticks of the biltong washed down with a cool Castle Pilsner from the condensation bag on the Land Rover's bonnet completed my dinner. I sent one of the tribesmen to fetch the headman, who came over to my fire. In a few curt sentences I gave him the succinct impression that anything found wandering around tonight would be shot as the man-eater, so he'd better keep his boys on the straight and narrow. He looked hard at the two asparagus-sized cartridges in my hand and decided that would be a fair idea.

The commissioner came on the radio right on schedule to report everything quiet, so far, from the other villages. "Keep on it, Old Boy," he told me.

I did not think the man-eater would kill again tonight because of the size of his meal the night before. Still, I knew that there had been cases of lions killing as frequently as twice the same night and that, anyway, man-eaters have an uncanny way of showing up where least expected. To be on the safe side, I would sleep in the open car with the big rifle against my leg. Not overly comfortable, to be sure, but those two barrels contained better than 10,000 foot-pounds of wallop, which gives a man considerable peace of mind. I'm not the squeamish sort, but when you have just finished putting what is left of a man in a coffee tin for burial, it does give pause for thought. I had hunted man-eating cats twice before this experience: the Okavango man-eater, a famous killer-leopard, and a lioness who had developed a sweet tooth for Ethiopians. I had come close enough, theoretically, to being a statistic on both occasions to never again underestimate a man-eating feline.

I rigged the mosquito netting and took my weekly malaria pill as Silent maneuvered the extra thorn bushes across the barrier. The humidity hung about like a barber's towel, and sweat poured from my body. After 15 minutes of tossing, I took another bite at the flask and dozed off shortly after.

You don't have to live in the African bush surrounded by dangerous or potentially dangerous game very long before you develop a sixth sense that may mean the difference between life and the alternative. After enough experience, you find, your brain never goes completely to sleep, but, like an army posting sentries, keeps partially awake while the main body sleeps. A parallel may be found in the case of the new mother who awakes instantly at her infant's faintest cry. This reflex seems better developed in humans than in most big game, who have few if any natural enemies. I have walked up to within a few feet of sleeping lions, elephants, and rhinos, who never noticed me. But then, what do they have to fear?

I don't know what awakened me a few hours later—perhaps a sound I didn't remember hearing, but more likely that sixth sense of apprehension. I sneaked my eyes open but saw nothing in the pale moonlight filtering through the tall acacias. I lay listening for long minutes but decided it must be only nerves. Just as my eyes closed, the night was slashed by a shriek that would curdle Bearnaise sauce. Three more unearthly screams followed. I grabbed the rifle and electric torch, pulled the thorn fence away, and dashed barefoot toward the screams. The beam showed nothing as I pounded through the village until I came to a hut at the far side with the door hanging from a single leather hinge. A gibbering man was inside, his bloodshot eyes wide as poached eggs with terror.

I flashed the light around the interior of the kaia. No blood. The walls seemed intact, as was the roof. The soft snapping of Silent's fingers attracted my attention back outside the hut. In the beam of the light was clear evidence of a scuffle, the smooth earth torn by striations of long claw marks. Bending down, I defined the clear pugmark of a big, male lion. I went back into the hut. The man was still staring in horror, mumbling gibberish. Silent entered with my flask, and we were able to get a gagging shot down his throat. Finally, he calmed down enough to tell us what had happened.

He had awakened when his wife stirred to a call of nature. He told her not to go outside, but she insisted. Anatomically unequipped, as was he, to perform the function through the door, she had stepped out into the night, and the lion had immediately nailed her. The man, named Teapot, heard the struggle and the first scream and bounded off his mat to the door. His wife had reached it and was gripping a crossbar that formed a frame for the lashed-on tshani grass. He recoiled in terror as he saw the lion pulling her by the leg until she was suspended off the ground between his mouth and door frame. Suddenly, the upper hinge had broken, and the woman lost her hold. The lion immediately swarmed over her upper body and, with a crush of fangs, dragged her quickly off.

I looked at my wristwatch. The scratched, old Rolex said two hours until dawn, perhaps just about right to permit the lion to feed and get careless. We might be able to stalk him while he was actually eating his kill or intercept him on his way to water before he went to lie up for the hot hours.

"Chabwino, Bwana," commented Silent. "It is good. I think we will find this eater of people this day." I couldn't share his enthusiasm. Rooting man-eating lions out of thick cover is not my idea of good fun. Still, we had our best shot at him yet.

We took up the trail at half past five as the false dawn began to turn the trees into gnarled monsters. I felt that just as the day before, the lion would travel a few miles, then stop to feed, although after the meal he had taken the previous day, he couldn't have been terribly hungry. Silent ruled out the possibility of this being another lion; one glance at a set of week-old prints and my gun bearer could tell you that lion's favorite color as well as his probable political leanings. The tracks showed definitely that we were on the trail of the right lion.

The spoor led through thinning, winter-dry bush studded with thorn, scrub *mopane*, and towering anthills for a couple of miles, then turned off to the dense riverine vegetation that bordered the shallow Munyamadzi for about 500 yards of depth along each bank. I had tried hunting lion in this cover before, harrying them through the jungles of waxy, green *conbretum*, a dense, house-high scrub that grows like a beach umbrella with the handle cut off, in hope of getting my clients a quick shot as the cats crossed the open channels between the heavier clumps. It was hard, dangerous hunting that I had quit rather than risk a client's being chewed up. Half the time was spent on hands and knees peering under the dense growth for a patch of tawny hide, hoping, when you saw it that it wasn't attached to a growing halo of teeth hurtling at you in a close-quarter charge. Everything was in the lion's favor in this growth, and I hadn't kidded myself that the man-eater had left it. After all, he had already proven 10 times that he had no natural fear of man—the fear that can give the hunter an edge.

I thought about Paul Nielssen's mauling in the past year within this same strip of bush, about five miles upriver. A Spanish client, Armando Bassi of Barcelona, a fine hunter, had wounded a good-maned lion, but it had escaped into the thick conbretum before Paul could get in a finishing shot. As the professional, Paul was obliged to earn his $25 per day salary by following the lion and killing it. Nielssen put Bassi up a tree, as is standard practice, and went in alone after it with his double rifle, a .458 Winchester converted from a .450. The lion lay under a bush, after doubling back on his track in a short loop, and watched Paul track past. Nielssen later told me he heard a slight sound behind him, but as he spun to fire, the lion was on him and knocked him flat.

The infuriated cat grabbed Paul by the shoulder and sank his fangs through meat and bone, while shaking the puny human like a jackal with a mouse. For some reason the lion then turned on Paul's legs and began chewing, as I recall, on his left thigh. Armando Bassi, hearing the mauling, jumped out of his tree and ran blindly after Paul. Coming up, he shouted and yelled at the lion to draw its attention and blew the cat's head into pudding with his own .458. Lord, give us more clients like Armando Bassi! Paul owed the man his life and escaped crippling injury, although he suffered a broken femur and a collection of stitches that would have done a Bond Street tailor proud. An animal that can and does

180

kill Cape buffalo with a single bite doesn't waste much time sorting out a mere human.

As we approached the thick cover, Silent and I stopped to peel off our bush jackets lest they scrape against a branch or thorn giving away our presence or position. We left them behind with the water bag after I removed the cartridges from mine. Entering the green tangle, Silent moved just ahead of me in a low crouch, his eyes on the spoor and his spear held in front of his body like a lance. It is normal between a hunter and his gun bearer/tracker that the first spoors while the other covers the possibility of an ambush charge. It's impossible to hunt and track at the same time. The safety was off the .470 and the night sight, an oversized bead of warthog ivory, which doesn't yellow like elephant ivory, was flipped up for fast sighting in the deep shade. We drifted slowly through the bush listening for the crunch of bone or a low growl as the lion fed in the leafy stillness. The damp, soft soil muffled our stealthy walking on the outsides of our feet, the quietest way to stalk, as we slid through the mottled murk with pounding hearts, ringing ears, and stomachs full of bats.

My mind went over the lion charges I had met before: the quick jerking of the tail tuft, the paralyzing roar, and the low, incredibly fast rush, bringing the white teeth in the center of bristling mane closer in a blur of speed. If we jumped him and he charged us, it would be from such close quarters that there would be time for only one shot, if that. Charging lions have been known to cover a hundred yards in just over three seconds. That's a very long charge, longer than I have ever seen in our thick central African hunting grounds. In tangles like this, a long charge would be 25 to 30 yards, which gives you some idea of the time left to shoot.

Ahead of me, Silent stiffened and solidified into an ebony statue. He held his crouch with his head cocked for almost a minute, watching something off to the left of the spoor. The wild thought raced through my skull that if the lion came now, the rifle would be too slippery to hold, since my palms were sweating so heavily. What the hell was Silent looking at, anyway?

Moving a quarter of an inch at a time, he began to back away from the bush toward me. I could see the tightness of his knuckles on the knobby, thornwood shaft of the spear. After 10 yards of retreat, he pantomimed that a woman's hand was lying just off the trail and that he could smell the lion. The soft breeze brought me the same unmistakable odor of a house cat on a humid day. Tensely I drew in a very deep breath and started forward, my rifle low on my hip. I was wishing I had listened to Mother and become an accountant or a haberdasher as I slipped into a duck walk and inched ahead. I was certain the lion could not miss the thump-crash of my heart as it jammed into the bottom of my throat in a choking lump, my mouth full of copper sulphate. I could almost feel his eyes on me, watching for the opportunity that would bring him flashing onto me.

I lifted my foot to slide it slowly forward and heard a tiny noise just off my right elbow. In a reflex motion, I spun around and slammed the sides of the barrels against the flank of the lion, who was in midair, close enough to shake hands with. His head was already past the muzzles, too close to shoot, looking like a hairy pickle barrel full of teeth. He seemed to hang in the air while my numbed brain screeched SHOOT! As he smashed into me, seemingly in slow motion, the right barrel fired, perhaps from a conscious trigger pull, perhaps from impact, I'll never know. The slug fortunately caught him below the ribs and bulled through his lower guts at a shallow but damaging angle, the muzzle blast scorching his shoulder.

I was flattened, rolling in the dirt, the rifle spinning away. I stiffened against the feel of long fangs that would be along presently, burying themselves in my shoulder or neck, and thought about how nice and quick it would probably be. Writing this, I find it difficult to describe the almost dreamy sense of complacency I felt, almost drugged.

A shout penetrated this haze. It was a hollow, senseless howl that I recognized as Silent. Good, old Silent, trying to draw the lion off me, armed with nothing but a spear. The cat, standing over me, growling horribly, seemed confused, then bounded back to attack Silent. He ran forward, spear leveled. I tried to yell to him but the words wouldn't come.

In a single bound, the great cat cuffed the spear aside and smashed the Awiza to the ground, pinning him with the weight of his 450-pound, steel-sinewed body the way a dog holds a juicy bone. Despite my own shock, I can still close my eyes and see, as if in Super Vistavision, Silent trying to shove his hand into the lion's mouth to buy time for me to recover the rifle and kill him. He was still giving the same, meaningless shout as I shook off my numbness and scrambled to my feet, ripping away branches like a mad man searching for the gun. If only the bloody Zambians would let a hunter carry sidearms! Something gleamed on the dark earth, which I recognized as Silent's spear, the shaft broken halfway. I grabbed it and ran over to the lion from behind, the cat still chewing thoughtfully on Silent's arm. The old man, in shock, appeared to be smiling.

I measured the lion. Holding the blade low with both hands, I thrust it with every ounce of my strength into his neck, feeling the keen blade slice through meat and gristle with surprising ease. I heard and felt the metal hit bone and stop. The cat gave a horrible roar and released Silent as I wrenched the spear free, the long point bright with blood. A pulsing fountain burst from the wound in a tall throbbing geyser as I thrust it back again, working it with all the strength of my arms. As if brain-shot he instantly collapsed as the edge of the blade found and severed the spinal cord, killing him at once. Except for muscular ripples up and down his flanks, he never moved again. The Chabunkwa man-eater was dead.

Ripping off my belt, I placed a tourniquet on Silent's tattered arm. Except for the arm and some claw marks on his chest, he seemed to be unhurt. I took the little plastic bottle of sulfathiozole from my pocket and worked it deeply into his wounds, amazed that the wrist did not seem broken, although the lion's teeth had badly mangled the area. He never made a sound as I tended him, nor did I speak. I transported him in a fireman's carry to the water, where he had a long drink, and then I returned to find the rifle, wedged in a low bush. I went back and once more put the gun bearer across my shoulders and headed for the village.

Silent's injuries far from dampened the celebration of the Sengas, a party of whom went back to collect our shirts and inspect the lion. As I left in the hunting car to take Silent to the small dispensary some 75 miles away, I warned the headman that if anyone so much as disturbed a whisker of the lion for juju, I would personally shoot him. I almost meant it, too. That lion was one trophy that Silent had earned.

The doctor examined Silent's wounds, bound them, and gave him a buttful of penicillin against likely infection from the layers of putrefied meat found under the lion's claws and on his teeth, then released him in my care. We were back at the Senga village in late afternoon, the brave little hunter grinning from the painkiller I had given him from my flask.

I snapped a couple of pictures of the lion with the self-timer and began to skin him. I would later report that the hide had spoiled and was not taken, so I wouldn't have to turn in more than the ears to the Game Department, which claims all unlicensed trophies. Actually, I had it salted and presented it to Silent, who believed that sleeping on it would bring back much of the romance of his youth. When I dropped him off at his village, near my safari camp, his fat, young wives seemed to concur as they bore him off to his hut with much giggling.

The Sengas retrieved the body of the lion's last victim, which was about half eaten. That night, back in my own camp, I took a long bath and sat smoking in the tub, with a tall glass of man's best friend at my elbow. Only now did I realize how close I had come to being the Chabunkwa lion's eleventh victim. My side was starting to turn a lovely black and blue where the lion had hit me, but whether it was from a paw stroke or just the 450 pounds of impact, I didn't know. Academic at best. In this kind of business you learn to remember close calls only for what they taught you, not for how they might have turned out. I took away one lesson for sure: The next time a district commissioner asks me for a favor, I'm going to have a severe attack of radio trouble.

Death in the Long Grass
St. Martin's Press, New York 1977

MY LAST GRIZZLY

by Dan Ludington
AS TOLD TO
James Doherty

I should have cut and run clear out of Alaska that snowy October morning nearly 10 years ago when Jerry Luebke kicked open the door of my lodge at Summit Lake. Unfortunately, my crystal ball wasn't working. I hadn't seen the big guy in weeks, and anyway I'd always pictured fate as a frowner, which Jerry certainly was not. He was grinning giant in a size 44 wolfskin parka—an old friend with whom I'd shared many a campfire.

Now, 10 years is usually enough time to take the edge off the memory of any run-of-the-mine day. For me, however, this was to be no ordinary day. Jerry's first words—delivered after my two kids, Milton, then four years old, and Rendy, two, had been shooed off his knee—come to me as clearly now as they did a decade ago.

"I hate to tell you this, Dan," he said laconically, "but you and Maxine are about to have visitors. If not today, then tonight for sure."

As foreman of the Alaska Road Commission camp at Paxson, a wide spot in the Richardson Highway about 150 miles southeast of Fairbanks, Jerry was a sort of ambulatory newspaper for 20 or more roadhouse operators who, like myself, depended on highway traffic for a living. If he said visitors were on the way, I could believe it.

My place, Moochigan Lodge, sat on the edge of Summit Lake, a stone's throw from the highway and nine miles north of Jerry's homestead at Paxson.

"Why the sad face?" I asked. "After all, a little late-season business would be the next best thing to an early spring." I meant it, too. The

185

summer of 1949 had come and gone like a running deer. Worse yet, it promised to be a long, cold winter.

"It's nobody you know," Jerry replied. "I'm talking about that old sow grizzly that's been raising cain around Paxson for the past couple of weeks. The one with the cub. You've probably heard about 'em already."

This was some of the best grizzly country in Alaska. We knew it and so did swarms of sportsmen who regularly made our lodge their hunting headquarters.

Here, the Richardson Highway bisected a panorama of low, brush-covered hills laced with blueberry thickets. Fishing was excellent in dozens of nearby lakes and streams. Annually, the caribou herds drifting past provided a ready source of meat for lean-bellied predators.

But a killing frost had denuded blueberry bushes for miles around in mid-August that year and reports of marauding bears had been only too common. Indian summer had been frozen in its tracks, and the area's population of big game had grown hungrier and more ill-tempered with each passing week.

"Anyway," Jerry continued, "the sow and her cub have moved up to your neck of the woods. They're hungry, Dan. They've been prowling the old fish camps, and the sow's a big one. She's buffalo-colored and mean." A recital of the grizzly's depredations followed.

According to Jerry, the sow and her cub had been busier around Paxson than a colony of beavers. Garbage cans, ever a favorite target, had been ransacked nightly and a number of food caches violated.

It wasn't until Jerry told of actually being chased by the grizzly, however, that I became alarmed. With Maxine hanging on every word, he recounted an incident that had taken place the previous evening.

Dusk was coming on, and Jerry had been working in the clearing behind his cabin at the edge of the road commission camp. Suddenly, with no more warning than a sneeze, the sow had charged from a nearby clump of brush.

From her position on the back porch, the big fellow's wife screamed a warning. Jerry looked up, found himself cut off from the cabin, and legged it for the camp bunkhouse. He'd won the race by a whisker.

I digested the tale in silence, then shrugged in a poor attempt to conceal my misgivings. But Maxine wasn't fooled.

186

My Last Grizzly

"I just thought of something," she exclaimed. "Dan killed a caribou last week. The meat is hanging outside the kitchen door right now, like an invitation to supper."

I had to grin, remembering the day not too many years before when I'd suggested to Maxine that she learn to hunt. Just then she was outguessing her teacher.

"And the wind, Dan," she continued excitedly. "It's been in the north since yesterday. The old sow is bound to have caught the scent. She'll be here about dark like Jerry says. Wait and see."

"Maybe," I said, "and maybe not. Anyhow, with this fresh snow on the ground the two of them shouldn't be hard to track."

Jerry nodded agreement. Without a word, Maxine crossed the room and plucked my .401 Winchester autoloader off its pegs. That model was discontinued in 1936, but I had mine rebuilt around 1939. If my wife was worried as she handed me the rifle, she didn't show it.

Throughout my 22 years in Alaska I'd killed my share of bears, and I guess Maxine had confidence in my ability. It still gets me when I realize how she was forced to revise her thinking before dark.

It was snowing lightly when Jerry and I left the roadhouse. We climbed into his pickup and headed south along Richardson Highway. I remember turning in my seat as we rounded the first curve. Maxine was waving good-bye from the roadhouse door.

"Last report I had," Jerry said, "the sow and her cub were poking around near Fish Creek. Might be a good place to start looking." Then, as an afterthought, "Dan, that old devil will go about 800 pounds, and she's just itching for trouble. How about postponing this deal? I'll take tomorrow off and we'll make a hunt of it."

I shook my head. Jerry's recent, narrow escape had convinced me of something that made killing the bear quickly imperative. It was my guess that the animal was nursing an old wound.

I told Jerry that in my opinion someone armed with a small-caliber rifle had taken a shot at the sow. As her wound festered, her temper had followed suit until she became hostile and constituted a real menace.

In all the years I'd been in Alaska, and while acting as a big-game guide, I'd never heard of a healthy bear charging a human being. As a rule, the average bear—any variety, any size—is sociable enough when left alone. Though he'll go out of his way to keep your scent in the wind, the odds are long he's not looking for more than a nodding acquaintance. On occasion, I'd even run bears out of my way with rocks and sticks, or just an ear-splitting banshee yell.

Though he shared my suspicions about the sow, Jerry made one last attempt to stall off my search. Again I rejected any delay. While he eased the truck through the snow, I strained my eyes for bear sign.

Funny, I thought, how a first snowfall can change the look of a countryside. Yesterday the brush had seemed visibly thin, like a blanket of twisted wire laid across the hills. Today, it was thickly padded with the white down payment of an early winter.

We'd gone a little over a mile when I signaled for a halt. Near the mouth of a small culvert that ran beneath the highway I'd spotted a welter of tracks.

"Could be some trucker stopped for water," Jerry said, "but let's have a look."

He pulled the truck off the road and we climbed out. From 20 feet away you could read the sign like a book. The footprints were big and comparatively fresh. The telltale cub tracks were right there beside the big ones. Following them toward the low ridge that paralleled the road would be easy.

I felt a surge of excitement as I climbed to the top of the pickup, and, between the intermittent flurries, scanned the white slope with my binoculars. I remembered other winters when I'd hunted and trapped these hills alone. Every dip and rise in the landscape was back-of-the-hand familiar.

Right now, however, my quarry was at least one ridge away. The glasses revealed no sign of life on the nearest hillside.

I jumped to the ground. Without a word, Jerry climbed into the truck, backed it farther off the highway, then pocketed the key.

"What's the big idea?" I asked.

He shrugged, and the wolfskin parka wrinkled comically around his neck.

"I'll climb to the top of the ridge with you and have a look around," he said. "Might see something moving on the other side."

The bears had broken a wide trail, and walking was easy. A light snow was still falling, and I judged the temperature to be a comfortable 10 degrees.

My Last Grizzly

On the summit of the ridge we came across droppings to which the snow had already begun to adhere. This, and the amount of snow that had collected in the tracks, convinced us the sow and her cub had a good three-hour head start. Their trail angled slightly across the valley below, then rose again to the next low ridge about half a mile away.

By now, Jerry's conscience had begun to get the best of him. His road-clearing gang faced a long, tough day, and more snow was definitely on the way. With a final warning about watching my step, he waved good-bye and started back the way we had come. I continued on.

Within minutes, the snow began to thicken noticeably. An hour or two of this and the trail would be obliterated. I picked up the pace.

By now, however, something else had begun to disturb me. Beyond the shadow of a doubt, the sow and her offspring were headed for my lodge. Mentally, I projected their route. By nightfall, it would bring the pair to my back door and the ripening caribou meat that even now must be wafting its mouth-watering scent across the hills.

By the time I'd panted to the second ridgetop, the valley beyond was curtained completely by the snow. It fell in long, sullen waves from the lowering sky and all but hid the line of brush about 10 yards below the ridge crest where the tracks ended.

I stopped and thought the matter over carefully. The chances were good that a mile or more still separated me from the two grizzlies. The tracks were filling up. The snow made the binoculars useless, and plunging blindly into the brush was out of the question.

The sow was man-wise and mean. In all likelihood she was still traveling. On the other hand, she might have caught my scent and doubled back under cover of the storm to stalk me.

Later—while mulling things over in a hospital bed—I would conclude that this moment of hesitation probably saved my life. Had I turned back, the sow would have nailed me from behind, unseen. Plunging ahead would no doubt have proved equally fatal.

At any rate, I was standing there, cold and undecided—my binoculars in one hand, my rifle in the other—when the sow exploded like a four-footed thunderclap from the line of brush not 30 feet away. Her deep-throated roar ripped through the silence on the ridge. Instinctively, I let the binoculars fall on the strap around my neck, swung my rifle in the grizzly's direction, and yanked the trigger. In the split second that should have preceded the blast, I glimpsed the sow's crazy red eyes and hair standing ramrod straight along her back. Then I experienced the sickest, most all-gone moment in my life.

For the first time since I'd bought the .401 back in 1932, the auto-loader failed to fire. Instead of its usual, death-dealing bellow, the rifle responded to my trigger pull with a dry, harmless click. Desperately, I pumped another shell into the chamber just as 800 pounds of rock-hard, crazy-mad grizzly slammed me to the ground.

Luckily, my binoculars broke the force the sow's first swipe at my chest, made with a right paw the size of a football. But despite the protection of the glasses and four or five layers of heavy clothing, her claws laid open my chest as neatly as a surgeon's knife—and I didn't feel a thing. As I staggered backward, I managed to crack the sow a solid blow on the nose with the butt of my rifle. She snapped viciously at the weapon, but I hung on. It was my only hope, and I knew it.

Then I was on the ground, and from my worm's-eye view the bear looked as big as a mountain. Methodically, she began making mince-meat of my left arm, and when I yelled in pain she snapped at my head.

In the years since, I've relived that moment 1,000 times in my dreams. Without fail, the memory of the grating sound the sow's teeth made across my skull is enough to awaken me in a cold sweat. And always I wake up kicking, just as I was kicking when it happened.

By now, though only a few seconds had elapsed since the bear struck me, I felt as if I'd been flat on my back for an eternity. And while I kicked and screamed and cursed, I kept thinking what a lousy way this was to die. I thought of Maxine and the kids—Maxine with another baby on the way and me in hock to my blood-soaked eyebrows. The more I thought of it the harder I kept digging my size 12 boots in the sow's belly.

Then, as if annoyed at the time it was taking to put me away, the grizzly bit through my face from the center of my nose to my right temple. The blurred image of her oncoming fangs was the last thing I ever saw through my right eye.

The pain inside my head mushroomed to killing proportions, and I fought frantically to retain consciousness. The temptation to drop my rifle and grab my head was almost overpowering. But I was staking my dwindling chances on the gun—and finally my opportunity came.

Annoyed at my incessant kicking, the sow, which had transferred her attentions from my head to my left leg, eventually backed off and grabbed my right leg above the offending boot. In that single, redeeming instant, I pointed the rifle at her broad chest and pulled the trigger.

I saw the hair blow straight up on the grizzly's back as 250 grains of lead crashed completely through her. She dropped my foot and reared upward a few inches, her forepaws off the ground. Her death roar and that of the rifle sounded almost as one. She flopped on her belly at my feet—lifeless.

I fell back in the snow. It seemed terribly quiet all of a sudden, though my ears still rang. Then the realization began to sink in. The bear was dead. I'd won. I was alive!

I said it over and over to myself, five, maybe six times, I couldn't believe my luck. Like a fighter on the verge of being knocked out, I'd thrown a desperation haymaker and connected.

A moment later, reality in the form of a 100-foot-high wall of pain put things back in sharp focus. When the spasm passed, I staggered to my feet.

Now that it was all over I was scared. Thank God, I thought, Maxine can't see me now.

I put my right hand on top of my head. My scalp was literally in ribbons. A large piece of skin was draped across my good eye, and I eased it upward gently. It promptly tumbled down again, triggering a fresh flow of blood. I ripped off what was left of my undershirt and wrapped it around my head. With only my right arm usable, it took a bit of doing.

The grizzly had given my left arm a thorough going over. I surveyed the mess impersonally, as if it belonged to someone else. One glance convinced me that even if I made it to a doctor, the shredded arm would have to come off.

As a souvenir of the blow that knocked me down, I had three deep claw cuts across my chest. I remember marveling at their neatness. Six inches higher and the swipe would have been fatal.

But it was my lacerated left leg that concerned me most. It was on fire with pain, and I faced a long hike back to the highway. Just above my left ankle the blood was pouring from a big hole where the bear had got in some of her final licks.

I cautiously shifted my weight to the leg. The bone appeared to be intact, but the movement was sheer agony. I groaned—both in pain and at the thought of the distance I had to travel.

Suddenly, I noticed I'd begun to shake. That's right, I thought, go ahead and panic—panic like a damned tenderfoot, out here in the middle of God-only-knows-where, and you've had it.

Then, from force of habit, perhaps, I leaned down to pick up my rifle. That was stupid. I awoke, probably only moments later, with my face buried in the snow, smothering.

That did it. Time was running out. I lurched to my feet, and, without so much as a backward glance at my dead attacker, went reeling down the trail.

My attention focused on only four things during the next terrible hour and a half. The first was a snappy debate with myself about the wisdom of taking a shortcut to the highway. I abandoned the notion quickly in favor of returning the way I'd come. At least one person knew the route I had taken and would look for me along the trail if I failed to show up.

And I recall seeing the brush move along the trail and imagining it was the cub. You're an orphan now, little guy, I said to myself. Old Man Winter will get you, sure as hell.

Next, somewhere along the way, I looked down at my right hand and saw it still clutched the rifle. Angrily, I flung it into a snowbank. Packing all that extra weight, I thought. How dumb can you get?

Finally, I remember something flopping against my left cheek. Reaching across with my right hand I tried to brush it away. It was my mangled left ear, hanging by a thread of skin to the side of my head. Gingerly, I tucked it back beneath my blood-soaked turban. Doctors can do wonders nowadays, I thought. Ten to one they'll sew it back on.

A pain-racked eternity later, I staggered onto the highway at the exact spot where I'd left it. Luck was with me.

As I slumped to the ground, a freight truck was braking to a stop at the culvert. The driver, Lewis Clarke, was an old friend.

While he loaded me into the cab I mumbled details of my scrap with the grizzly. Louie kept saying something that sounded like "Good God," and shaking his head. We finally got going north, in the direction of my lodge. I insisted we roll right past. I didn't want Maxine and the kids to see me like this. Anyway, the nearest doctor was at Big Delta Air Force Base 70 miles north, where the Richardson Highway joins the Alaska Highway.

The trip was a confused blur in my pain-occupied mind. I recall that we stopped at a roadhouse well beyond mine, and Louie passed the word ahead to the Army Alaska Arctic Training Center, which also occupied the base and ran the hospital. He called Maxine also and told her I'd been hurt. She promised to go at once to Fairbanks where I was eventually to be taken.

An Army ambulance met our truck some miles south of the Big Delta intersection. At the base I was given sedatives and first aid, then placed in another ambulance that headed for the hospital in Fairbanks in a blinding snowstorm.

In the 50 miles between the towns, the ambulance got stuck four times in king-size drifts. It was early evening before Dr. William Smith of the Fairbanks Medical and Surgical Clinic got me on his table.

In the hours that followed he took more than 200 stitches in my face, scalp, chest, arm, and leg. He managed to save the arm I'd given up for lost, and to reattach my ear. My right eye, however, was beyond repair.

Ten days later, I was bound for Seattle and a succession of operations spread out over a period of six months. I was fitted with a plastic right eye. Today, 10 years later, I'm still trying to get used to it.

I've regained complete use of my injured arm and leg. The leg, by the way, gets a workout every morning. Immediately after rising I kick the head of a huge bear rug that decorates the floor of my bedroom.

Jerry Luebke made me a present of my ex-assailant's hide. The day after my epic one-rounder in the wilderness, he returned to the ridge, skinned out the grizzly, and recovered my rifle. As we suspected, the sow had been wounded once before—with a slug from a .25/20.

I can only theorize about the failure of my first shot. About a year after the battle, I went back to the scene and found the cartridge that had misfired. The primer was dented, but not deeply enough to ignite the charge.

I had taken the rifle from a warm room into the cold. It's possible that lubrication in the trigger spring mechanism congealed with the change in temperature. Also, some snow may have got into the warm breech and later have frozen. Either situation would have been enough to prevent the spring from sending the firing pin forward with sufficient force to fire the cartridge.

That grizzly, incidentally, was the last I've taken from that day to this. I'm now cook and camp manager for a contractor building storage tanks in Adak, and I don't do much hunting—just a little bird shooting now and again. The loss of my right eye makes it necessary for me to shoot left-handed, and that's no good for bears.

Outdoor Life
November 1959

NEVER TRUST A MOOSE

by Eric Collier

I should have known better in the first place. I was hunting mule deer in a tongue of fir and lodgepole pine forest that licks almost at the log walls of our home in the British Columbia wilderness, where I farm beavers and muskrats in their natural habitat. A November moon was waning, and three inches of snow blanketed the kinnikinnick and blueberry vines. The wind was faintly from the Arctic, the air tangy and crisp with a definite hint of more snow to come.

Now was the time I must go to work and stock our moss-chinked meat house against the hungry months ahead. In my country a deer killed in November stays frozen until the following April.

I found my buck—a three-pointer—bedded on the rim of a deep gulch, staring languidly into the westering sun, as bucks have been doing on late-November afternoons ever since there have been bucks. I shot him in his bed, dragged him out of the gulch, and gutted him. Then I put him beneath a fir tree to cool off. Next morning I'd come with a horse and pack him to the meat house.

Standing beside the steaming carcass, 30 yards from the rim of the gulch, I could neither see nor hear any movement below. True, a red squirrel shucked a cone from a fir tree, but squirrels don't count. Yet I had a sudden intuition that life was abroad down there in the bowels of the gulch, although why I don't know. But it was definitely there, and I bolted a cartridge into the breech of my .303 Ross, crouched back on my heels, and strained my ears and eyes.

A bull moose of full maturity weighs around 1,400 pounds on the hoof, and he may carry a rack of horns spreading 60 inches or better. It doesn't seem possible that so large an animal can move through timber as silently as a foraging lynx cat. But it can, and it does: A bull moose is often seen before it's heard.

Such was the case that afternoon. The horns came up out of the gulch first; a spread of 45 inches, I judged. Then the grotesque Roman nose, followed by the rest of the head. It was the kind of opportunity a trophy hunter dreams about but doesn't often get.

I wasn't interested in trophies, for I have yet to find horns that taste good in a stew. At that moment I wasn't even interested in moose. I don't like their meat, for I ate far too much of it during the gaunt years of the depression. And I'd left my camera at home.

It was a couple of seconds before horns, head, body and all four legs were up out of the gulch. Then, head high and nostrils testing the air, the bull moved stiffly toward me. That was odd, for he could see me crouching tensely by the body of the deer. By all rules of the game he should have wheeled and gone back into the gulch much more quickly than he'd left it. But he moved up to within 20 yards before he stopped and gazed at me intently, obviously unafraid. If I've every seen mayhem in a bull moose's eyes, it was in his.

For 33 straight years my everyday life has been spent here, and these woods had to provide me not only with a living but with recreation to boot. After all, when you're 100-odd miles from the nearest electric light you wouldn't recognize Clark Gable if you met him along the trail.

Anyway I'd think twice before digging into my jeans for the price of a movie ticket. But I'll spend hours in the hush of the forest, crooning softly to a suspicious bull moose, inching up, camera ready to snap a picture if I can get within 15 to 20 feet before he takes off. That's my personal moose hunting. I do it with a rather poor camera but if you don't like an animal's meat or want a trophy why hunt him with a gun?

Sure, I guide moose hunters in the fall, but my job is to find the bull; they take over from there.

I've been within 15 to 20 feet of more moose than I can tell you about—and got photos of almost every one—but up to the time of this story I'd yet to shoot my first bull or cow in self-defense. Several had got snooty enough, for if you work around a moose any considerable time it soon sheds its instinctive fear and distrust and begins talking back. When that happens you start looking at your hole card.

When a cow or bull has fight on its mind, there's a lot in its expression that isn't altogether sweet. The ears flatten against the neck, the mane stands up, and the whites of the eyes show. Usually there's only a single

196

soft grunt of warning, and then the animal moves forward and comes exceedingly fast. That's why I brought the .303 to my shoulder within a split second of the big bull's first show of truculence. Maybe I should have settled the business for good right then and there, and been spared the ordeal that was to come.

I know now that I'd have been forced to shoot if a yearling hadn't got into the act, because here was one moose that would kill or be killed. But the yearling temporarily solved the problem, paying a harsh price for doing so. I didn't know he was around until the bull suddenly pulled his eyes from me to stare questioningly and belligerently at something off in the timber.

I lowered my rifle and followed the line of this stare. At first I could see nothing except timber, but after another prolonged look I saw a yearling bull moving slowly toward the gulch. The little fellow wasn't doing any harm; just nipping the shoot of a red willow here, or rubbing his poor sprout of horns against a seedling fir there.

Feeding slowly toward us, he apparently didn't notice the big bull until he was within 30 yards of him. Then he tossed up his head and froze in his tracks. Somehow I wanted to yell, "Get the blazes out of here, you little fool, while the getting is good!" But it wouldn't have helped.

The yearling was oozing good nature, and it was as clear as the air you breathe that he just wanted to move up alongside the big bull and pass the time of day. As he started forward again I heard the big boy grunt. There was a weight of hidden warning in that grunt to anyone who understands moose talk. Again I was tempted to shoot but I couldn't make up my mind to. The old bull charged before I could decide.

Despite popular belief, a bull moose does far more fighting with his front feet than with his horns. True the antlers are used extensively, and sometimes with fatal effect when the heat of the rut is on. But at any other time of year it is the front quarters that throw the most lethal blows.

That yearling was worse off than any babe in the woods. By the time he came awake to what it was all about the big bull was almost within striking range. Then the youngster did something you'll not often see a sensible moose do. He wheeled and broke into a gallop. And a galloping moose is about as graceful as a knock-kneed man in a sack race.

I didn't even see the first blow, it flicked out so fast. But I certainly heard it connect. Crack! A sickening crack, too—one that could be heard from one end of the gulch to the other. The youngster stumbled and almost went down. Crack! I saw it this time. It was like the flick of a swamp adder's head. And the little fellow was down in the snow.

That's when I roared in instinctive anger. The right-front foot of the big bull was raised for another blow, but at the sound of my voice it went stiffly back into the snow. The bull half turned, staring angrily at me. Thus the yearling got his one chance for a getaway, and he lost no time grabbing it. Limping badly—I'm sure his hip had been dislocated—he came up from the snow and lurched away into the sanctuary of the gulch.

The bull moose continued his belligerent appraisal of me for a moment. Then he blew his nostrils, scratched vigorously at his right ear with his hind foot, shook himself, and moved slowly off into the thickets.

"You cantankerous old bum!" I yelled after him.

Old Cantankerous was as good a name as any for him, and he lived up to every syllable of it.

In my country moose browse the timbered ridges until the snow gets knee-deep, then come down to the beaver dams and pasture in the second-growth beaver cuttings. Usually this is not until Christmas or New Year, but that year Mother Nature showed the harsher side of her breasts, and by December 15 the snow was belly-deep to a calf, and the moose came drifting into the creek bottom. Old Cantankerous was among them.

I was kneeling down, building myself a mink set in the overflow of a beaver dam, and at first glance I didn't fully recognize him, although I knew I'd seen this bull somewhere before. He'd shed his horns, and that made a difference.

He was standing on the ice of the beaver pond 50 yards upstream, and had neither seen nor winded me. A beaver dam covered with sodden snow provides exceedingly treacherous footing, and my snowshoes were on the far side of it, 300 feet or so away. So was my Ross .303. When I finally recognized the bull, I cursed myself and began fruitlessly scheming how I could get across to the rifle without attracting his attention. But I decided it would be better to stay put until he moved off. I think I was scared of that bull.

I cautiously sank down behind the dam, wishing he'd go so I could finish my business. I wasn't looking for trouble that afternoon. After at least 15 minutes of indecision he smelled of the snow, belched, and veered up-pond toward a willow patch that would furnish his supper.

Never Trust a Moose

Christmas sulked in on a bloated full moon. Azure skies, and a wind out of the Yukon as sharp as porcupine needles. Spruce trees along the creek bottoms popping their useless protests. A little cross fox yapping on a mountaintop, beseeching the harsh land that had spawned him to give him food. Moose calves coming up from their beds in the snow at daybreak, with frosted hocks and ears; chickadees falling from the perches in the spruce thickets, little feathered bodies frozen solid while they roosted. Christmas, the birthday of our Lord; Christmas and 54 degrees below zero.

You don't trap mink, otters, or other fur bearers in weather like that; only the coyotes and timber wolves are abroad. And moose. Come rip-roaring chinook or searing Arctic blizzard, moose must eat. The lower the mercury, the more browse they must consume lest the body heat be extinguished within them. No shed or den for them; just the overhang of a spruce tree for shelter, virgin snow for a bed.

For myself, hibernating over a potbellied stove soon becomes irksome. Two or three days of it is all my stomach can stand. Then, cold or no cold, I must busy myself with some outdoor chore. While the cold snap lasted, running the traplines would be a dreary, useless business. So, having mastered the somewhat tricky art of handling a camera with mittens, I went to stalking moose. And by moose I mean Old Cantankerous.

And that brought me to New Year's Day. Thirty-six inches of snow, now, and warmer. Only 28 below. Gray, scurfy clouds scudding across the face of the sun; mink tracks again beginning to show in the seepage of the beaver dams. For that's another miracle of the beaver. No matter how bitter the cold, the water seeps through his dams and moves freely down the creek to keep its rendezvous with the river.

That afternoon the bull chewed his cud at the edge of a small meadow only half a mile from my cabin, and my mind was made up. I'd get a photograph. But now there was a nasty question that had to be solved. How could I handle camera and rifle at the same time? No matter how quick you are, it takes a second or two to drop the camera, unsling the gun, slip the safety, and bring the butt to your shoulder. A mature bull moose, murder in his eye, covers a deal of ground in just two or three seconds. I wasn't kidding myself; if Old Cantankerous were to charge, only powder and lead would stop him.

Had my son been at home the whole affair would have been simple.

He'd cover the bull while I took the photo. But he wasn't with us. The previous fall he'd traded the loneliness of the wilderness for a three-year hitch in the Canadian army. That day there was only my wife.

I broached the matter quite casually. "I believe we could get a picture of Old Cantankerous this afternoon," I told her. She knew all about him by this time and was under no illusion as to what I meant by "getting a picture." It meant stalking to within 10 or 15 feet of the big bull.

"We?"

"If you'd like to handle the camera while I cover with the gun?" I said, a little tolerantly. Perhaps I was hoping she'd say, "You couldn't get me within 400 yards of that brute!" Then maybe I'd have scuttled the whole idea.

Instead, she began pulling on her overshoes in a very matter-of-fact way. Which is what I should have expected, for we came into the wilderness together determined to enjoy the sunshine and endure the storm. Why should I think she'd deny me when I asked that she share my adventures with a moose?

While she was piling on sweaters and mackinaw I got her snowshoes from a shed and pummeled the leather harness soft. Next we checked the box camera. It held four unused negatives. I took the .303 Ross down from its peg on the wall and fondled it briefly, for that old gun has been with me since 1922.

"Ready?" I asked my wife. She was set to go, all 115 pounds of her, and seemed impatient to get this bit of business over with. I stared thoughtfully at the five 220-grain soft-points in the palm of my hand and hoped I wouldn't have to use one. I dropped the cartridges into the magazine and stepped into my snowshoes. "O.K.," I said.

A smooth trapping trail took us within 100 yards of the meadow. The bull hadn't moved; he was still out in the open, 15 yards from the brush. He half turned in his tracks as we came into view, watching us with seeming indifference. The approach across the meadow wasn't easy, for here the snow was 36 inches deep. Our snowshoes sank into it for some eight or 10 inches, and each time we lifted a foot three pounds of snow came up on the webbing. "Think you can manage it?" I asked.

"I think so," my wife said.

With me breaking trail, we moved cautiously to within 30 yards of the bull. He looked as big as a mountain, and he was watching us with bold intentness. I stopped and slid a shell into the breech of the .303 and pulled the moose-hide mitten from my right hand. Now there was just a thin woolen glove between my finger and the trigger. I stared at the old bull. As long as he stood with his ears well up and his mane down we had nothing to fear.

We slid forward again and now there was only 15 yards between us and the bull. I stopped and breathed, "How does he look through the finder?"

"I'll try one but another five yards would be better."

Another five yards! That would put her within 10 yards of a bull moose packing as much danger as a case of ditching powder. I was beginning to experience a gnawing uneasiness.

"Unbuckle the heelstraps of your snowshoes," I suddenly told her. Free of the straps she could still move forward, but, in an emergency, could slip quickly out of the shoes and dodge. She unbuckled the straps and looked up at me. "O.K.," I said. "Another five yards—but not an inch closer."

We never made it. The words had hardly left my mouth when I heard the old bull grunt. Both his ears flattened back against his neck, his mane bristled over his withers, and his eyes rolled to show a bloodshot white.

I sucked in my breath. "Quick—shoot now!" I said.

The camera came up against her chest and she looked down into the finder just as the old bull charged. A scream forced itself from her lips. "You shoot!" she cried.

Even in the flick of time it took for the gun to jump to my shoulder, for my eye to look down the sights, he was almost on top of her. It had to be a brain shot; no other could possibly drop him before his front feet began pounding my wife to a pulp. A good many thoughts might have hammered at my brain in the moment. I might have been cursing myself for exposing her to this danger in the first place. I might have thought of the 100-mile trek with sleigh and team to a doctor.

But there was only one thought, and it was more of a prayer: that the .303 wouldn't miss. I held my fire deliberately since there would be no time to reload. Somehow I managed to keep the pressure off that trigger until he was 10 measured feet from her snowshoes. Then I held right between his eyes and tripped the trigger of the Ross. A brain shot, I'd said—it had to be a brain shot. And, thank God, a brain shot it was. He was dead when he hit the snow.

Slowly, almost reluctantly, my eyes rose to meet those of my wife.

The fear that had been in her lingered in the tenseness of her face, the pallor of her cheeks, the dilated pupils of her eyes. And it was a fear of which she need never feel shame. To see Old Cantankerous standing and chewing his cud would tingle the roots of your hair; to see him charging was a vision of hell itself.

I looked down at his body, still quivering in death. My thoughts went back to the gulch and the yearling, to those other moose he had quarreled with as they approached his feeding spot. I thought of the long winter days ahead when I'd be away from home on some distant part of the trapline, and my wife there alone. True, I had killed a bull moose out of lawful season, and while game laws are necessary to the preservation of wildlife, there are isolated occasions when breaking them does far more good than harm.

My wife had rebuckled the heelstraps of her snowshoes and started toward me when a thought flashed through my mind. I held up my hand. "Wait," I said. "I want a photo of you right there where you were when he went down."

I moved forward, took the camera from her, and backed up a couple of snowshoe lengths. I was about to take the picture when she asked, "Did you wind it?"

"Wind it!" I almost shouted. And as the words sank in, I asked in amazement, "You mean there's a photo of him charging?"

"I think so," she said.

There are a good many things in the life of one who follows the forests and watersheds for a living that I cannot properly explain. How she was able to keep her eyes on the camera, hold the thing steady, and press the button when 1,400 pounds of rage was almost on top of her is one of them.

Outdoor Life
September 1953

MORE ELEPHANT STORIES

by John Taylor

You don't have to be a crack shot to be a successful elephant hunter—a very mediocre marksman can still kill elephant. I do not pretend to be any Deadeye Dick or lay claim to any fancy degree of marksmanship; yet I kill nearly all my elephant with a single shot apiece. That is not necessarily superlative skill. It is just that I do not get all steamed up; I do not attempt to squeeze the trigger until I am certain of at least anchoring my beast—no matter what it is—if not instantly killing it. Steadiness and patience are of much greater importance than actual marksmanship. After all, you must have noticed that most elephant are shot within 25 yards and that I refer to 40 yards as a very long shot. So it is, at elephant.

In the Asenga country the grass is the trouble. There are oceans of 10- to 12-foot elephant grass, and the herds seem to spend most of their time in it. I have heard it described as maddening. But there are swarms of elephant there in the right season.

When I got into the Asenga country the thought that instantly jumped into my mind was: Now if only I had a kind of house decorator's ladder, how easy it would be. Why I should have thought of that particular type of ladder I don't know—I've never been a house decorator myself, nor used such a ladder. But there it was. Moreover, there was plenty of bamboo growing in the district, so it was a fairly simple matter to make a usable ladder though its not having any hinges made it a somewhat rickety affair. Still, with the two men who carried it steadying it when I climbed to the top, it was quite practical. I used it with great success. But I considered it preferable to use a small-bore rifle rather than one of my more powerful weapons because I was afraid the latter might send me flying from my perch on the top of the ladder if the fellows who were supposed to be steadying it got bored with the proceedings, as they almost inevitably would when the shooting had been going on for some time and they were unable to see what was happening; and also because I found that the elephant were not alarmed by the report of the small rifle to the extent they were by the heavier one. Sitting on top of the ladder with my shoulders just level with the tops of the grass I would wait for an elephant to raise his head sufficiently or move into a place where the grass had been trampled down a bit. Then it was merely a case of slipping the little slug into his brain. He would drop instantly and disappear in the grass—there wouldn't be a sound out of him. Consequently, his pals wouldn't know that anything had happened to him: because they couldn't see him fall on account of the grass, and because there was no commotion to alarm them, the whiplike crack of the small-bore being something they hadn't heard before. I have shot as many as seven like that without having to move my ladder; and then about half an hour later killed another five out of the same herd from a different position. The principal difficulty I experienced when using this method was to decide if an elephant were worth shooting or not. Frequently I would get only a fleeting glimpse of his tusks; sometimes I could not even get that.

I picked up the spoor of a pretty big herd in Rhodesia and followed them over the Tanganyika border when they crossed. I caught up with them in one of those places you dream about with everything in your favor: There was a fair-sized clearing in the light, open forest with a mud wallow in the middle of it and a couple of dusting places close by. Halfway between the fringe of the forest and the mud wallow was a small anthill with a couple of forked trees growing out of it. These afforded adequate cover for me and my gunbearer, for the trees broke up our outline—making us invisible provided we kept still—yet in no way interfered with our view of the herd or impeded quick handling and exchange of rifles. An ideal spot. The anthill was perhaps 40 paces from the mud wallow and 20 to 30 paces from the two dusting places.

We sighted the herd when we were fully 150 yards away. The elephant were thoroughly enjoying themselves; slapping dollops of mud onto their shoulders and backs with a satisfying clop, as happy as children making mud pies; others, having had their mud baths, were scraping the bare ground of the dusting places with one huge forefoot, then sucking up a trunkful of the dust and puffing it over heads, necks, shoulders, and behind huge ears, for all the world like women completing their toilet.

One very big bull, which I guessed was the leader, had had his bath and shampoo and was now doing nothing under the trees. All this reminded me of a veritable "elephant playground" I had once found in a district to the north of the Zambezi. I had been hunting with but moderate success for some three or four weeks and was wondering to myself which of all the various districts known to me would be the best right now. I knew I ought to be doing better and would do better if I could just hit upon the right district. Having made up my mind, I decided to give this section one more day. I had noticed a large circular patch of extraordinarily dense bush with a good deal of heavy timber growing in it. Elephant paths led toward it, but so far I hadn't had occasion to examine it. Each time I passed that way I was following spoor which did not lead directly into it. I now decided to have a look at the place and see what it was like inside. But the local natives were horrified at the idea of entering. They declared the place was haunted—though they didn't know by what—and that anyway the elephant would certainly kill any human being who was foolish enough to enter. When I told them I had every intention of entering, they did everything in their power to try to dissuade me. They were really concerned about it. This one sent for that one, and he sent for someone else, until I had all the elders of the district around me. They told me what they thought were horrifying tales of the savagery of the elephant if their chosen playgrounds were ever violated by man. They assured me that elephant which might well be afraid of me and my rifles elsewhere would be very different animals if I attempted to look for them in their playground.

I didn't doubt there was a good deal of truth in what they said; but nevertheless I wasn't worried. The elephant could be as savage as they liked, but their savagery wouldn't be a match for my fine rifles—at least I hoped it wouldn't. It would all depend on the type of bush I found inside. If the place were, as the local men said, a kind of playground, then I had a hunch I would find it open once I succeeded in getting through the outer ring of bush.

But that same outer ring was an extremely nasty proposition when I came to tackle it. In all my wanderings only once or twice have I come across anything quite like it. I was following an elephant path which led directly toward it, but when I came to enter I found that the bush—not thorn—was as thick and dense as a box hedge which has been allowed to grow wild. It was utterly impenetrable except along the zigzag tracks made by the elephant themselves. The bush was about 15 feet high, and I found that I would have to get down on hands and knees to get along the little tunnel which was all that could be seen of the "path" because the bush closed up entirely from a height of about three feet up. The big gray beasts could brush through this as easily as I could brush through a field of wheat; but a man could not. I had a look at one or two other entrances, but they were all the same.

When I signified that I was about to enter the local men again tried to dissuade me, and when they saw that I wasn't listening to them they flatly refused to take another step. They said they would wait under a shady tree, but that they never expected to see me again. I asked my two gunbearers if they were coming with me or if they would rather wait outside. Their snorts of disgust at the notion that they should wait in safety while I went forward alone were masterpieces. Nevertheless, it wouldn't do to be careless. These local men weren't cowardly and there was no doubt about their fear: I had a hunch it wasn't all bugaboo. Moreover, we'd look pretty foolish if we met a herd coming our way as we crawled along on hands and knees trying not to let the muzzles of the rifles pick up sand.

In fact, I didn't entirely like it. True, there wasn't much likelihood of our meeting elephant coming our way at that hour; but it was pure surmise on my part that we were going to find better going ahead. For all I knew to the contrary there might be only an occasional small clearing around some of the larger trees. But having once started it was obviously out of the question to turn back—I just had to see what was in front.

We crawled along, swearing and dripping with sweat from every pore, for what seemed like two or three ages. And then suddenly, and without the slightest warning, we found ourselves on the edge of what looked like an old English park that had gone to seed a bit. Only in place of the few scattered deer that you would have seen once upon a time in an English park, here elephant were scattered about. Just elephant and nothing else. The dense bush had ceased as abruptly as it had begun. It must have been about 150 yards thick—though we had zigzagged much farther than that—and looked for all the world as though it had been planted around that park the way a hedge is planted around a garden. But this hedge had never known a gardener's shears or clippers.

There were great shady trees here and there and small clumps of evergreen bush, and away down in the center we later found a spring of cool water gushing out between two large boulders. It ran into a deep clear pool which the elephant used for drinking purposes, and then into a few shallow pools which they used for mud baths. There were dusting places close by and, as we afterward discovered, salt licks also. It was a delightful place, and completely private. The short green grass almost deserved the name "sward"—at least at first glance.

There were elephant drowsing under the trees, others drinking and blowing water over themselves, and cows washing down their youngsters; others again were slapping mud on themselves or powdering themelves with dust. All were perfectly happy and right out in the open. They obviously assumed they were quite safe in here. It seemed a shame to violate the peace of the place; yet one day's shooting wouldn't do much harm, and it might be many years before I visited it again.

There were not so many elephant, probably not more than 40 to 50, altogether. But it seemed as if there were many more because they were all over the place and right out in the open in a way you seldom see them nowadays except, perhaps, in some national park where they never hear a rifle speak. The glade seemed full of elephant. It was roughly circular and perhaps a quarter of a mile across.

We moved quietly around to our left, keeping close to the hedge, and so up along it to a spot where I could see two big tuskers under a shady tree. They were about 75 yards from the hedge, and there was a fair-sized anthill with a small bush growing out of the top of it roughly halfway between them and the hedge. I made for it. Taking up a position on top of the anthill, with the little bush to break up our outline, I opened fire. The two bulls collapsed in their tracks, and I reloaded the .400 myself instead of exchanging rifles, since no quick third shot was called for. The commotion that now ensued among the other elephant was truly remarkable; I have never seen anything quite like it. Some of them twisted and turned, this way and that, trying to spot the danger zone; others rushed here and there, trumpeting and screaming and adding to the general confusion. We stood quite still and watched them. There was one big old cow that appeared to be the leader of about a dozen other cows with a few half-grown calves among them and two or three immature bulls. I didn't at all like the purposeful manner in which she was looking for us. There

207

was no indication of panic about her; on the contrary, she set out to find us in the most deliberate and reasoned way, her companions following her. These old cows are sometimes very dangerous. Since the licensee never shoots them, long years of immunity give them an utter contempt for man, and it is by no means uncommon for them to kill the wretched owners of the "lands" when they go raiding and those owners try to drive them away. This old girl led her party right up to the two dead bulls and sniffed over them. Getting a whiff of the freshly spilled blood she suddenly wheeled around and loosed a shrill trumpeting blast. The result was extraordinary: every elephant in the glade suddenly froze in its tracks. There wasn't a sound or a movement.

Then slowly and quietly the old cow began to circle, her trunk snaking about, trying to pick up our wind. I declare she appeared to be tiptoeing. For a moment her companions remained still, then commenced to follow her. They circled to within about 25 yards of us, and it was quite obvious that it was only a matter of time before the old cow got our wind. It was equally obvious that she would then charge. I really ought to have shot her then and there and been done with it; but I hated to fire if I could avoid it because there were several other shootable bulls in sight and I didn't want to stampede them if I could help it. But since a charge was so imminent, I might just as well have dropped her without waiting for it. Possibly, I was interested in watching her methods.

Naturally I had kept turning to face the cow, meaning that my two gunbearers also had to move to be always in their correct positions; and just before she was due to get our wind, the old cow suddenly wheeled around and with a scream of rage came bald-headed for us. She must have seen some slight movement back over her shoulder in the way elephant can without your knowing they are looking at you at all—like hogs.

With her ears back she looked incredibly vicious. As she came, her party came too. I had no alternative but to drop her. My little Purdey brought her down without any fuss, and with one exception those with her halted. The exception proved to be another big old cow who, trumpeting shrilly, endeavored to press home the charge. However, my left barrel took her between the eyes. Exchanging rifles, I waited. For what seemed a very long time the other members of the troop just stood about, ears cocked and trunks up, unable to make up their minds what to do. I did not want to turn my back and walk away, for that might well have provoked another charge, and I certainly didn't want to waste any more ammunition on them. But these two shots had started the ball rolling again among the other elephant in the glade. They trumpeted and yelled and rushed around but didn't seem to get anywhere. No attempt was made by any of them to clear out of the glade, though there was nothing to prevent their going. Never have I seen elephant so excited. At long last the troop of cows in front of me wheeled and dashed off for perhaps 100 yards or so, and then halted again.

I once more took over the little .400, since it looked as though anything could happen here. There was a good bull standing all by himself about 120 yards away, and a convenient tree within some 30 to 35 paces of him. I decided to make for it. We had to cross the open to get there and would be pretty nearly in the middle of the glade when we did so. I got the tree between him and myself and signed to my men to walk in single file behind me. We had no difficulty in getting to the tree without the big fellow's seeing us. However, I noticed that at least two other tuskers had spotted us, though they did not seem to realize what we were. They had seen something moving, something that wasn't an elephant, and their suspicions were aroused. One of them started slowly toward us with his ears out but his trunk down; the other stood there, ears cocked and trunk up, staring hard and trying to make out what it was. There were about 80 or 90 yards between them: one of them out on our right about 75 paces away, and the other beyond the one we were stalking, and also some 75 yards away. I slipped up behind the tree, edged around it, and let drive. My bull dropped dead without ever knowing that a rifle had been fired. With the other two bulls so threatening, I immediately exchanged rifles. The one on my right rolled up his trunk and came on the heels of the shot. But his rush appeared to be somewhat halfhearted. He wasn't roaring, and he didn't seem to be coming at full speed. The other certainly meant business. However, he didn't start quite so soon. In fact, he didn't start until he saw the other one coming. He made up for lost time then; but I decided to take the one on my right first as I felt pretty certain that the carcass of the first bull, almost directly in his path, would prove disconcerting. Whether the one on my right was really charging or merely bluffing, I cannot say. Anyhow, I dared not take a chance—besides, he was well worth shooting. My bullet took him, too, between the eyes and, without waiting to see the result, I instantly swung on the second. As I did so he reached the body of the earlier kill and immediately lost all interest in me. His trunk, which he had rolled up under his chin, he flung up over his head. He made a frantic effort to slew around. As he must have been coming at around 25 miles an hour he had to heel well over to make the sharp turn he wanted. My left barrel took him through the shoulder before he had completed the turn and literally blasted him off his feet—there was no question about his charging. He had loosed the charging bull elephant's characteristic series of short roars—a tremendous volume of sound—up to the time he encountered the first dead elephant; the other hadn't made a sound of any sort.

I again exchanged rifles, for there was no telling what was going to happen now. The various other elephant in the glade seemed to go crazy, stark staring mad when they heard this shooting and heard the roars of the charging bull. One big fellow with only one tusk stood there blowing a long-sustained blast through his trunk. The others dashed madly around in the most senseless manner. One party came rushing straight toward us as though they intended to run us down. There didn't seem to be a really shootable beast among them, so I let them come on until they were about 30 to 40 yards away in the hope that they would pass. When it looked as though they were really coming over us, I raised the rifle with the intention of dropping the two leaders, because that would probably cause the rest to halt or swing outward. But it was not necessary to shoot. As my finger tightened on the trigger, of their own accord they pulled up and stood there staring at us. And then just as suddenly they wheeled around and dashed away again. My two men and I looked at each other with raised eyebrows, shrugged a shoulder, and grinned. We had had many strange experiences together, but today's performance beat anything we had ever seen.

I decided I would like to add that big old single-tusker to the bag. If I could get him I would be willing to call it a day. He was about 120 paces away standing broadside-on to me. It was an incredibly long shot at elephant; but I could get a beautifully steady shot from where I stood, and since there were several other beasts that would make a closer approach to the single-tusker difficult, I decided to have a try at him. My bullet got him through the shoulder and there was no need for a second. The other elephant in the immediate vicinity cleared, thereby enabling us to wander around and collect the tails of the slain. But those elephant farther off wouldn't go. They stood watching us as we went from one carcass to another. Every now and then one of them would take a step or two toward us but would not attempt to interfere with us. They had quieted after the shot that killed the last, the old single-tusker; but it was most unusual for them just to stand around like that in the open and not make the slightest attempt to clear out of the vicinity. There were some of them within 60 to 70 yards of us the whole time, until we came to make our way out of the glade. I acted as rearguard then, and just before I started to crawl I looked back and saw the elephant still standing where we had left them.

As we emerged from the hedge the local natives, who had been sitting under a shady tree listening to the shooting and trumpeting, came racing up to hear our news. They could scarcely believe their eyes when they saw we were all in one piece and had actually to handle the tails of the dead elephant before they could be convinced they were real and not figments of the imagination. Of course, they assured one another, I must possess some powerful spell, magic, medicine. How otherwise could I have emerged alive? And not only with a whole skin, but with elephant also! The thing was almost unbelievable—entirely unbelievable if it hadn't been for those freshly severed tails. They looked with genuine awe and admiration and respect at my two staunch gunbearers and pondered on the strength of my "medicine" that was sufficient to cover all three of us. This morning's work would be something to talk over for the next quarter century.

Whenever elephant hunters foregather and the conversation turns, as it inevitably will, to rifles, sooner or later someone will mention the great Karamojo Bell's name and refer to his phenomenal success with his beloved little 7mm Rigby-Mauser. (Bell's total bag amounted to 1,011 elephant, 800 of which he killed with the 7mm and some 200 with the .303 British.)

Time and again I have heard men declare that what one man can do can be done again: that Bell may have had, indeed must have had, physique and stamina above the average; nevertheless he was human and if he could slay large numbers of elephant and make a handsome fortune for himself with a small-bore rifle why shouldn't the speaker be able to do it also, provided he could get himself an unrestricted permit? I repeat, I have heard this said on numerous occasions; and although Bell's original book, *The Wanderings of an Elephant Hunter*, has long been out of print, his *Karamojo Safari* is still widely read, and I haven't the least doubt that many readers of it are asking the same question as that quoted above. In fact, I have myself received more than one inquiry in this connection. And the answer, of course, is easy: If the inquirer could put the clock back half a century or so, if he were as keen as Bell and as fit, and, most important, an equally fine marksman, then, if he hunted the same districts as Bell hunted and could win for himself the confidence and friendship and help of the local natives to the extent that Bell did, why, there is no very good reason why he shouldn't do as well as Bell did. But that if is a mighty big one.

You do not find mobs of old bull elephant right out in the open nowadays feeding and enjoying mud baths in broad daylight as Bell found them—remember, he was the very first man with a rifle among those elephant, and it was mighty seldom he lost a pricked or wounded elephant. It is true that he did occasionally hunt and kill in heavy forest, but it was lone bulls or pairs of bulls he was following. Not once does he mention tackling mixed herds with nervous cows and their young calves under such conditions. And although it is customary to speak of those elderly bulls as "having tempers in inverse ratio to the length of their tusks," and even Bell himself does do, with all due respect to the man I have always ranked as the greatest elephant hunter of all time, that is hyperbole. My experience has been that the aged, whether elephant or man, are not looking for trouble: All they seek is peace and quiet. There is comparatively little danger in hunting lone bulls or pairs of bulls provided you go about it the right way. Why, in my younger days I was advised to let the herds alone and hunt only lone bulls. (That I did not follow the advice is another story.) When Bell shot mixed herds, he did so in open-grass country where he could see if a cow's charge was meant or merely bluff.

It cannot be seriously disputed that Bell's skill with the rifle was far above that of the average hunter. He admits that his marksmanship was of an "automatic accuracy" in those days, and that when he was shooting at fast-moving birds or elephant "the conscious section of mind allowed the rifle a certain amount of lead, but the instant the projectile was started on its way the subconscious section took charge, corrected the rifle, almost invariably in a forward direction, and a clean kill would result. It was only when the subconscious aimer was not functioning that a miss would result . . . I caught but a fleeting glimpse of a disappearing stern. I succeeded in introducing a nicely judged bullet which, but for the above-mentioned subconscious aimer, would have passed harmlessly beneath the bounding lion. The correction in this case was high, with the result that he was caught on the spine just abaft the shoulders while on the rise.''

Well, I don't know how many hunters or sportsmen can claim such adventitious aid to their marksmanship. I wish I could! Bell, I consider, was one of those outstanding marksmen only one or two of which appear in a generation. The late Annie Oakley was just about at the peak of her career when Bell was starting out on his, and had he been a man of different caliber and concentrated on trick shooting instead of on elephant, he might well have become a serious rival to Little Sure-Shot herself.

But the point I wish to make is that when tackling mixed herds in dense bush, as one has to nowadays if one wishes the bag to grow, circumstances can and sometimes do arise in which the greatest marksman who ever lived could not be sure of extricating himself if armed with a small-bore rifle. These occasions are not frequent but they must not be overloked or forgotten: I have experienced them myself on several safaris and both know personally and have heard and read of several other hunters also experiencing them. Those who were armed with small-bores were either killed or badly mauled. Remember, it's not necessarily the elephant at which you're firing that constitutes the danger: The real danger may suddenly appear from some entirely unexpected direction and be right beside you before you have the remotest notion of its existence. It may have been there right along on the other side of a thick bush within trunk reach of you without your knowing.

There is another very important point to remember, and that is that the greatest marksman will occasionally misplace his shot. It may not occur very often, but where elephant in thick cover and small-bore rifles are concerned, it doesn't have to occur more than once!

Bell describes a hunt in West Africa. Not having hunted since before the war, he admits that he was a bit out of practice. Carrying a .318, he followed a big bull into some dense bush. He was close behind. Without

213

warning the bull suddenly swapped ends and came rushing back over his tracks. The range was very close. Bell snapped a shot at him but missed the brain. He says that he just had time to jump aside and put another shot into the elephant's heart as the brute rushed over the very spot he had been standing on a moment before. The muzzle of his rifle was within inches of the elephant's side as he fired.

Now Bell was much too fine a marksman to miss an African elephant's head at 10 yards' range; yet the elephant took not the slightest notice of the shot—a heavy bullet would have brought him to his knees. Then Bell's luck stood him in good stead by permitting this to take place in a type of bush which allowed him to jump to one side out of the elephant's way. But I know places, and I don't doubt Bell knows similar ones, in which the resilience of the bush would merely throw you back under the elephant's feet. It's a moot point whether being trampled underfoot by an elephant would be preferable to impalement on a tusk! I have no hankering to experience either.

Since I have repeatedly urged both orally and in print that no light bullet can possibly stun an African elephant if it misses the brain even by but a small amount (owing to the honeycomb formation of his skull, which dissipates the bullet's punch), and that only a heavy slug can hit a sufficiently powerful blow to have it transmitted to the brain, the question is certain to be asked: How do I account for the indubitable fact that Bell stunned many elephant with both 7mm and .303 rifles? And as any truly experienced hunter can tell instantly that Bell belongs to that select few—and all too few they are—who have put on paper their African hunting experiences and told us the truth and nothing but the truth, without allowing their imaginations to run away with them to the extent of inserting fictional adventures and observations for the benefit of the thrill lovers, there can be no doubt whatever of the accuracy of his descriptions. For instance, there was the occasion when he dropped a mighty tusker and climbed up on his back for reconnaissance while his man cut of the tail. Bell then jumped down and went on to kill a number of other tuskers, but after he had left that first big one recovered consciousness, got to his feet, and cleared off minus his tail without anyone's being the wiser until they failed to find him next day, although the mark where he fell was plainly to be seen. There can be no question that that elephant was truly stunned, knocked out—yet the rifle was a 7mm and the bullet only weighed 173 grains.

My answer is that Bell did not miss the brain, the elephant was not stunned by "having the bullet pass close to the brain," as Bell says. I contend that the bullet struck or entered one of the subsidiary areas of the brain but just lacked the necessary momentum to carry it on into one of the more vital regions. If this is admitted there would be no question of the shock's being transmitted to the brain for the excellent reason that it would have been administered to the actual brain itself, where a very slight tap would be sufficient to stun even an African elephant.

Pondoro: Last of the Ivory Hunters
Simon & Schuster, 1955

215

HOW TO SHOOT
THE BIRD OF PEACE

by Nord Riley

T he most popular game bird in the United States lives in town, dresses like a clergyman, has a reputation for piety and nonviolence, sings hymns, and has scriptural credits that range from Genesis to John. Heeding the New Testament injunction to love his enemy, he builds his nest in the hunter's backyard tree and from there seduces the man's family by dropping empty eggshells on his children and cooing at his wife. He sits with sparrows on telephone wires. He is a delicate quarter-pounder with pink feet and the facial expression of a nun. He runs like an old lady and in the air gives off squeaking sounds as though he hadn't been up for some time and needed oiling.

Since he looks exactly like his wife, he seems above carnality, and yet the millions that are shot each year are replaced and added to by a female whose slatternly nest never has more than two eggs in it. No other game bird comes to the table so often and in worse condition. He is utterly ignored by most cookbooks. With wine and cloves he is superlative, but he is usually fried. Eating him fried is like feeding on mummies.

He is the mourning dove.

He is also a fraud and an imposter. With an image resting on the work done for Noah during the high water by his Old World relative, the turtledove, and on his jobs as an artist's model to symbolize purity, peace, and hand soap, he has lobbied himself through 40 percent of the country's state legislatures as a songbird in need of legal guarantees against loss of life and limb. It's just one man's opinion, but I don't think he can sing. He can't even chirp. He keens. In graveside tones, he fills the suburbs from morn to night with a dirge of singular tedium.

Having spent my early years in North Dakota, a state under the

216

impression that a dove is a songbird, and having been confirmed in a church whose altar paintings had a limit of doves in them, I still—25 years later—feel funny when I shoot a dove. I get the feeling I've just bagged the chaplain.

No one, not even a resident of a state in which doves are fair game, is immune to the bird's reputation and appearance. A man taking up hunting for the first time should never start on doves. They'll ruin him. In recent years, I've persuaded three men to give hunting a whirl. It is testimony to my dull wit that I started them all on doves. None ever hunted again. The dove's gray, fragile gentility, his sweet face, and his familiarity took their toll on my friends' enthusiasm. And what really did them in was executing the wounded.

Jim Vance, a crony of mine for many years, joined a recent hunt. He'd never fired a shotgun before. He appeared to have a natural accuracy and was doing well until he trudged across a plowed field to Leroy Younggren, a veteran gunner. In his right hand, Vance cradled a wounded dove. He held it out to Leroy and said, "What do I do now?"

"Stomp on him," said Leroy, his mind on a bird coming in from the south.

"Stomp on him?"

"Either that or wring his neck."

Vance stroked the bird's brow and adjusted a ruffled feather as he weighed the alternatives. "I'll stomp him," he mumbled.

It was a bum decision. Stomping a dove in soft plowing is hopeless. After a few minutes, he shambled over to me. He was obviously shaken; the bird was disheveled. "I stomped the little fellow knee-deep," said Vance, "and every time I looked down, there he was looking back up."

"Do what I do," I told him. "Push in his forehead."

Vance fell back. "You're kidding!"

I explained that it is a harsh fact of hunting that wounded creatures must be dispatched with swift mercy. "A dove has a skull like a peanut shell. Push it in, and it's all over."

Very probably, we'd already lost Vance when I told him that, but when he tried to push in the forehead of his dove we lost him forever. It was plain bad luck; not one bird in 100 is like his was—an elderly cock with a skull like a filbert.

Since I left North Dakota and came to California, I've spent every

September 1—excepting those of the war years—hunting mourning doves and their plumper cousins, the whitewings. A quarter of a century of this has given me a chance to weigh the dove against the classic game birds of our land, the ducks, geese, pheasants, sharptails, and quail. I believe the dove deserves to be rated No. 1. No other bird gives a hunter such a wonderful run for his money or provides so much sport, adventure, conviviality, and great eating. It's time to unfrock the masquerader.

It is difficult for a man accustomed to quail to believe that a bird residing in his blue gum, balancing on his antenna, eating his boysenberries, and moaning incessantly is a legitimate game bird. He doesn't believe it until he finds the dove out in the country and tries to hold a gun on him. Then it becomes clear that *la dolce vita* has no effect on the fowl's native skills as a flyer.

The mourning dove is a master aviator. That slim body, long-tailed and scimitar-winged, is an artist's idea of grace. It's for going 70 miles per hour. It's for sideslipping, banking, corkscrewing, weaving and diving.

That ought to be enough, but the dove has another aerial antic—a flight of such eccentricity of speed that he appears to be drunk. A quail, a sharptail, a Hungarian partridge, or a pheasant jumps up, ascends to 20 feet, and wings off in a straight line at constant speed. Not a dove; there's nothing stodgy and reliable about him. He flies at 200 feet or at two, and his inconstancy kills you.

One of the most common and rewarding September spectacles is that of a single dove sprinting, stalling, darting, and turning as he weaves his way across 80 acres and through the shot patterns of a dozen hunters and then, with the bravado of a bullfighter, drops to earth and calmly eats his morning cereal. It's not unusual to hear hunters shout and clap at such a performance. He is very hard to hit, this bird, and he is missed more than any other.

A word about his meekness. Is there, in the entire country, another game bird that, upon espying a skirmish line of armed men ahead, neither ascends as does a duck nor darts into a bush as does a quail, but insists upon charging? A dove doesn't avoid danger; he simply revs up and plunges through.

That sweet face of his is a swindle, too, as much a swindle as that of the pheasant, which has the meanest-looking countenance of all the game birds. The pheasant also struts and beats his chest. But who is it that, when the going gets tough, sends his women up to attract fire and then pulls his head down and runs like a thief?

For years, it was my whim to shoot doves with a single-shot, full-choke 12-gauge. It was light, fit me well, and having but one round in it, made me take more care in shooting. Once (and only once) when doves were coming straight at me—favorite shot—I dropped 10 with 11 shots. Then, one sunny, 115-degree afternoon outside Indio, California, the forearm fell off that old Iver Johnson. I lashed it back onto the barrel with black friction tape. That done, I missed the next 17 birds. I was pondering whether to use the eighteenth shell on myself when Leroy Younggren, lounging in the shade of the next telephone pole, heard my oaths.

"You're starting to shoot funny," he said. "Are you having your usual sunstroke?"

September 1 on the Southwest deserts is generally the hottest day of the year. I am a middle-aged blond with skin that in many ways resembles cellophane. It's watertight but translucent. Sunlight comes right on through it and cooks me internally, much as a roast is cooked in one of those new infrared ovens. At one point, I turn magenta and begin to see a variety of spots—exploding stars, mainly—some of which I shoot at.

I checked my vision by staring at the ground. "No stars," I told Leroy.

"Gnats?"

At times when heat waves are bad and perspiration is heavy, I mistake a nearby gnat for a faraway dove and bang away at it. On this afternoon, a breeze had blown away my halo of insects. I walked over to Leroy. He is six feet four and thin enough to stand in the shade of a telephone pole and have enough left over for a guest.

"I'd better find out what's wrong quick," I said. "I'm running out of shells."

"Here comes one," he said. "Let me see what you're doing."

When the dove was in position, I fired. He flew on. Leroy sighed. "Ah, Riley, you do need constant care, don't you?" He reached over and, with his dampened forefinger, tapped down a shred of friction tape sticking up from my barrel. I had been using it as my front sight.

219

After that, I switched to my Winchester pump with a variable choke. Heeding the advice of those experts who insist that anything tighter than a modified boring is a waste of both opportunity and shells, I set mine at improved cylinder. With heavy shot, I found it uncommonly good on geese.

But when I turned it on doves, my average of two shells per bird sank to four to one. Three years ago, it slumped suddenly to six to one, but that was the year my pith helmet was loose. My first shot jarred it down over my eyes, and I found myself getting off my second shot in complete darkness. Last fall, I went back to full choke, and once again doves fell. Anyone else would have known better than to fire at them with an open boring.

Though he is classed as an upland game bird—and I suppose he is, because he can't swim—the dove differs importantly from quail, pheasants, grouse, and partridge. They are ground dwellers, live out their entire lives within a mile of home, are fast on their feet, prefer hiding to flying, and get dizzy at altitudes of more than 100 feet. A dove resides in a tree, walks as though his feet hurt, and takes to the air at the slightest provocation. High or low, near or far, he loves to fly, and in this respect he resembles nothing quite so much as a teal in a Prince Albert.

Like waterfowl, the dove follows aerial tracks in going out to eat and drink. This habit of his provides some of the most exhilarating pass-shooting a man can find. The trouble is, though, that a dove is also the smallest of upland game birds, with a body the size of a lemon and a neck like a wet macaroni. If he had a brain bigger than a grape seed, he'd have a headache. At 150 feet, which is a common distance in pass-shooting, a bird this size often flies right through the pattern of an improved-cylinder boring.

Jump-shooting doves from weed patches and stubble fields is also good, though prostrating, sport, and here again a tight choke is best. Doves don't hold for man or beast; they cut out with a rusty, quaillike clatter.

A fruitful dove hunt depends upon more than a full choke. There are several key requirements. The first is to hunt on the opening day of the season, which in California is usually September 1. There are millions of doves around then. But a week later, because of the hostilities and a drop in temperature, most of them are in Mexico. The second requirement is

220

to go where the doves are. Doves are everywhere, but concentrations of them are confined to certain areas, and the extra hours of driving it may take to reach these areas are worth it.

Our group goes 200 miles from the Los Angeles precincts, where most of us live, to the Mexican border section of the Imperial Valley. The veterans of this group have been making the trip for 30 years, but—well as they know those flat, fertile fields—they always send down a reconnaissance party a day ahead of the opening, for scouting is the third necessity for success with doves. Crops rotate, dove tastes are fickle. What was kafir corn last fall is now plowing; doves that swarmed over a field in the past have deserted it for one that seems identical.

In sum, if a hunter will make the effort to go to where the doves are the day before the season opens, locate a field the birds are using, be there at dawn, and fire at them with a full-choke gun, he'll have a great time.

The best explanation of the dove's preeminent popularity is quite simple; he provides the ordinary hunter with something to shoot at. In many regions, good duck hunting is available only to those who belong to costly clubs, and the daily limit may be as low as two. Many farmers charge for hunting pheasants on their land, and a reasonably good shot can, in California and other states, get his limit of two cocks with two shells. Quail prefer private property. Grouse are scarce.

But our gray and melancholy groaner is around by the millions. Because he loves to fly, and because he has no game refuges, he is the one bird the ordinary hunter can readily get a shot at. Thousands of dove hunters do their shooting from country roads.

Though the limits on doves—37 in Arizona, for example—read like those for ducks in the 1900's, and though most hunters seem to limit out on opening day, the dove isn't going the way of the auk and bison. He is more than keeping up. In California, the daily limit was recently hiked from 10 to 12. This seems impossible for a bird that lays but two eggs (a bobwhite lays 15). Here again, the bird is deceitful. She lays two eggs all right, but in some areas she does it four times a year. And when her daughters are six weeks old, they lay their first two eggs. Add to this dogged reproductiveness the fact that perhaps half the dove population lives in the suburbs, thus remaining safe from crows, magpies and other rural egg fanciers, and it becomes clear that hunters can shoot doves with a clear conscience.

221

Another captivating thing about doves is that they are cheap and fairly comfortable to hunt. Most dove hunters appear to have been dressed by the Salvation Army. I, for example, am annually mistaken for a bleached bracero. All the dove hunter needs is enough clothes to keep from being arrested, a gun, and lots of cheap, low-base 7½'s and 8's. No boat, no hip boots, no thermal underwear, no camouflage jacket, no waterproof pants, no hand warmer. For decoys he uses bodies of the fallen, for a blind the shade of a tree.

This is also a sport for the old, the sedentary, and the ramshackle. Our group includes two recent coronary victims, both of whom shoot from campstools and send out either a dog or a relative to pick up the dead.

For many of the ink-stained wretches who toil in cities, the opening of dove season has become a social event. It provides the first blast of the hunting year, and, since dove hunting is no good after the opening, everybody shows up for the opening. Our little posse runs to about 25 men, none of whom see each other except on the first two or three days of September. Edgar Bergen flies down. Chill Wills and Cannonball Taylor drive down together. Rip Torn flies out from New York.

Our most treasured member is the sales director of a brewery. He brings down several kegs of medical supplies—on tap—for our dispensary, a room of the motel set aside for the sunstruck, the parched, and the neurotics like me who insist they have holes in their patterns. When all of us and the thousands of other groups hit the fields together, the result is rather like an armed uprising during Mardi Gras.

Once the birds are bagged, ignorance and stubbornness take over. Everyone I know insists on cleaning his birds soon after he shoots them. This almost always at about 10 A.M., when the temperature is 110 degrees. The hunters have been up since four, they've fired at least 50 rounds, they are sore in the shoulder, hot, and thirsty. Yet they all have this compulsion to pluck and draw. Somewhere, somehow, they have been persuaded that, unless a dove is immediately shorn of the feathers that protected him and relieved of the organs that made him work, he won't be fit to eat a few hours later.

I suspect that women, either high-school hygiene teachers or wives, are to blame. Women know nothing about game and hate to cook it, but they are hell on germs, ptomaine, and meat that isn't bright red. Men, who seldom cook, tend to take their wives' word on culinary matters. In

222

my opinion, the man who sits out in the scorching, fly-ridden air and cleans doves is a misguided, unwholesome litterbug. The birds are going to be tougher, the chances of decay may well be greater and the hunter leaves on his host's field a fetid mass of feathers, feet, heads, and entrails. A sane sportsman would get out of the sun, return to his quarters, put his doves in a cool place, and have a glass of beer. Both parties will be improved.

A week in the refrigerator does wonders for doves—they all grow tender, and none spoil. I've brought home hundreds, left them intact in the icebox for a week, and never lost a bird to spoilage. Cleaning a chilled dove is infinitely less distasteful than cleaning a hot, fresh one. Viscera and feathers go into the garbage can. No flies, no odor, no litter. That's sanitary.

Should you pluck or skin? I say skin. Most people pluck. Because of my age and physical dilapidation, I no longer fistfight about it; I have subsided to a roar. I have noted that none of the pluckers cook; they just pluck. I cook—30 or 40 doves a year. To give the pluckers a fair roll, I've cooked doves with their skins on and their skins off. It's no contest.

There are three sound reasons for skinning doves: 1) It's faster and easier; 2) doves are often too gamy in taste for many people, and the gamy taste is in the skin; 3) if the dove is cooked in a liquid, as he should be, the skin is unappetizing to many a diner's eye. I have a dreary hunch that those who pluck also fry. God forgive them.

Around our house in Manhattan Beach, California, are a good many cookbooks. The general ones all have sections dealing with quail, pheasants, grouse, ducks, geese, and even mudhens, but they utterly ignore the commonest game bird in the country. Even some of the cookbooks devoted exclusively to game omit doves. Harry Botsford's commendable *Fish and Game Cook Book* has dozens of good recipes for everything from woodcock to squirrels but not one for the mourning dove.

Confronted with a dozen unfamiliar, maroon-breasted little bodies and unable to find any directions for cooking them, most women become irritable and fry. This bit of inside information I gathered by interviewing the wives of my hunting companions. From them I got some pretty emotional statements, one of which—"I hate doves!"—was unanimous. Another—"I cooked them once and, so help me, never again!"

—was very popular, too. All declared, one way or another, that doves were tough and strong. And, indicating the depths of their desperation, most of them asked me how I cook mine.

Well, madam, the recipe that has worked well around here for 20 years isn't at all complicated. First you leave the doves in the refrigerator for a week, then you skin them. That done, you melt between an eighth and a quarter of a pound of butter (a good oil will do, too) in a heavy skillet. Add to this a couple tablespoons of finely chopped onion and a chopped clove of garlic. Flour and season the doves lightly and brown them, keeping the heat low to prevent burning the butter and blackening the onions.

When the doves are a light brown, transfer them to a Dutch oven or covered casserole dish. Into the skillet pour a cup of claret or Burgundy, swirl it around, and, with a spoon, pry loose all the stuff that has stuck to the bottom. Pour this, plus a cup of hot water, over the doves. Add three or four cloves, a two-inch slice of orange peel, a pinch of nutmeg, and cover.

Put the vessel in the oven at 300 degrees or on top of the stove over a low fire. Cook for 45 minutes or more, adding more hooch as the need arises. Cooked this way, all the doves will be tender, moist, delicious, and not gamy. Figure two or three doves each for the ladies and three or four for the bucks. My wife, who loves game, prefers doves cooked this way to any bird in the business.

Outdoor Life
July 1966

WOLVES DON'T LIVE BY RULES

by Frank Glaser
AS TOLD TO
Jim Reardon

It was a cold clear March day at Savage River on the north slope of the Alaska Range. I was sitting on a hill watching a muskeg flat on which several hundred scattered caribou were feeding. A quarter mile below me, a coal ledge jutted from the 15-foot-high river bank, and a yellow seepage from it smeared the blue-white river ice. Five caribou stood licking at the stain.

I was looking for wolves, and idly I glanced at the five caribou from time to time as I swung my binoculars to scan the snow-covered land. After an hour of careful watching I saw a lone gray wolf trotting across the flat. Soon three others single-filed down the river to my left. Then another appeared on my right, picking its way upstream.

The five wolves were converging on the caribou at the coal seep.

The wolf on the flat trotted to the edge of the bank above the unsuspecting caribou and peeked over at them. Then it backed off to lie down and wait. The group of three wolves left the creek and disappeared into the spruces below me. I lost track of the fifth wolf.

I watched the five caribou. After about 10 minutes a gray wolf streaked out of the timber and grabbed a big cow by the flank. The remaining four caribou scattered as the frantic cow skidded and staggered, trying to shake the clinging wolf. She tried to jump from the slick ice to the bank but immediately fell, foundering on her side, the tenacious wolf still clamped firmly to her flank. Three of the other wolves appeared and swarmed over her, chopping and slashing.

And then, incredibly, she pulled free. All of the animals skidded on

225

the slick ice, but the frantic cow made it to the bank, humped her way to the top, and hooked her front legs over. The wolf on the bank met her head on, sinking his teeth into her nose. He hung on as the two of them rolled and flopped down the steep slope to the river ice.

A red stain spread across the ice as the five wolves killed the cow and started to eat.

Another March found me on the same hill, again watching scattered caribou and looking for wolves. Below, on the open flat, a lone cow was feeding. Three wolves, trotting single file with heads and tails down, started to cross the flat half a mile downwind of the caribou.

When they caught its scent, one of them, a big gray, immediately lay down in the snow while the others turned and loped into a nearby draw. After his partners had been gone a few minutes, the big gray wolf openly ran to within 10 yards of the caribou, sat down in plain sight, and started to howl.

The caribou stopped eating and curiously stared at him. She even walked toward the wolf, occasionally bounding nervously into the air. The two other wolves came into sight behind her, sliding along on their bellies like cats stalking a bird. Frequently they raised up and peeked ahead to see how close they were.

The caribou remained intent on the performing wolf in front of her. The gray wolf howled, trotted back and forth, and gradually worked closer and closer to the nervous but fascinated caribou. When the wolf was within 40 yards, it sat and howled continuously.

One of the stalking animals dashed from behind a knoll about 30 feet from the caribou, grabbed the animal's flank, and hung on. The two other wolves joined it in seconds, and the three of them quickly pulled her down.

There you have two common daytime hunting techniques used by wolves. I have seen as many as six wolves play the decoy game—they're very good at it. Sometimes, however, wolves simply run their prey down.

One April, again at Savage River, I saw a cow moose on the skyline, running and continually looking behind her. Five wolves soon showed up on her trail. I grabbed my rifle and ran up to an open sidehill from which I thought I might be able to take part.

The moose ran into a dense patch of spruces, the wolves right behind her. After a while she came into the open, with the wolves jumping and biting at her and then leaping back as she tried to strike them with her hoofs. They were too far away for me to interfere, so I sat and watched through binoculars.

She made a game fight of it. As the wolves slashed at her, leaping in and dodging back, she stood on her hind legs time and again, running at them, pawing and striking with her front hoofs. But finally the wolves simply pulled her down.

When I got there, they had eaten a few pounds of the hindquarters and had left. That animal was slashed and bitten all over the body, and pieces of hide as big as a man's hand had been peeled off. The moose was heavy with calf. I have seen pregnant caribou cows killed the same way.

As a private trapper and a government wolf hunter, I have observed wolves in Alaska since the late 1920's, when—for the first time in this century—they became common in Alaska's interior. The more I learn about wolves, the less I like to generalize about their hunting methods and other habits—wildlife doesn't live by rules.

I have read many incorrect statements about wolves. Two in particular that many people believe are that all the wolves in a region join forces each night to hunt, and that wolves invariably hamstring big-game prey.

Actually, wolf "packs" are almost always family groups, sometimes containing as many as two or three generations. However, during breeding season, when different families combine, I have often seen groups of 30 to 45 wolves.

At Savage River I was awakened early one March morning by the howling of several bands of wolves. I got up, dashed out with a rifle and binoculars, and located three bunches.

As I watched, all three came together on a big flat. I'd guess that there were three or four families.

Suddenly all of those wolves appeared to pile on one wolf, and the growling and yipping carried for miles in the still, cold air.

I saw how I could get within rifle range by working through some timber. As I hurried along I pictured in my mind six or seven dead wolves and a bunch of crippled ones, and I figured that a lot of hides and bounty money were going to come my way pretty easily.

But my dreams were shattered when I got within rifle range. All the wolves had left but two, and those two were mated. Not one injured wolf could I see. In the years since, I have found that wolves seldom seriously injure one another when fighting.

The largest bunch of wolves I have ever seen numbered 52. I had a good 45 minutes to count them. Fifty were black, and two were gray. The peculiar thing about these wolves was that they were together in October. Ordinarily the big packs form only during breeding season in February or March.

Except during breeding season, strange wolves are not welcomed into a family. I once watched, for some time, a pair of wolves that had a den with a bunch of pups in it. The family group also contained four other adult wolves, which might have been brothers and sisters, parents, or even grandparents of the mated pair.

One day—when all six adults were lying about, sleeping after a night of hunting—a big gray wolf, strange to the group, showed up on a ridge and trotted casually toward the den.

One of the adults saw the stranger when he was 100 yards away and immediately ran toward him. The five others were right behind. The first wolf struck the stranger with a shoulder, knocking him over. Before he could recover, all six of them had him, holding him from all sides.

There was no snapping and letting go as you see in a dog fight—each of the six simply grabbed the visitor and hung on, stretching the wolf out and banging him against the ground.

After perhaps 30 seconds of this, they all suddenly let go and stood back. The strange wolf got to its feet, hobbled down the ridge a few hundred yards, and lay down. I didn't see him in the area again.

Wolves are doglike in much of their social behavior, and it isn't difficult to take advantage of some of their habits.

When I first started to trap on Savage River in 1924, I noticed that my sled dogs refused to pass up the few scattered clumps of grass that were exposed on the high wind-blown ridges. They simply had to lift a leg to every clump, and they'd go far out of their path to reach one of these "signposts."

The next summer, I planted about 70 clumps of high grass on the ridges I trapped. I dug holes about six inches to the south of each clump and set spikes there to which I could fasten traps. When winter came and trapping started, I simply set the traps in the holes and covered them with dry dirt.

228

Wolves, like my dogs, would get the urge to raise their legs to these isolated clumps to leave their sign. As they did so, they stepped into my traps.

These were efficient wolf sets, and I also caught many foxes in them. An occasional wolverine or lynx would visit these clumps of grass, too, and I'd have their skins in my cache by spring.

I love the sound of a howling wolf, and after hearing it for years I found that I could imitate it. Often in the 1930's, on quiet evenings at my trapping cabin at Savage River, I would step outside and howl. If wolves were around, they usually answered, and they would frequently howl for hours as I dropped off to sleep.

I have called many wolves to within rifle range. Pups are especially easy to call.

Once, my calling had quite an effect on a superstitious Eskimo. On that occasion I had been sent to Golovin, on the Seward Peninsula, to try to take some wolves that had been killing the Eskimos' reindeer.

One morning I awoke and heard wolves howling near where the deer were grazing. An Eskimo herder and I went up on a ridge and counted nine wolves about two miles from us.

Soon a lone wolf howled behind us. I answered him, and he called back. We talked back and forth for some time before I spotted him with my binoculars. He was working his way across a big flat. As I watched him, he'd howl when I did and then come closer.

We lost sight of him in some low hills, but I kept howling occasionally. Finally he trotted into sight out of a ravine about 50 yards away, went up on a high snowdrift, and looked around, trying to find the "wolf" he had been talking with. It was an easy shot.

For the rest of my stay there, that Eskimo herder was half afraid of me, and he passed his uneasiness on to other Eskimos in the area.

I have often watched wolves hunting and killing moose and caribou in the daytime. But more often I have heard them killing caribou at night and have seen the kills the following day.

In my experience, February through April are months during which wolves seem to kill the most big game. The wolf's breeding season starts in February, and family groups merge then as the unpaired young wolves select mates. When these large groups join forces, they make heavy kills.

229

When wolves and caribou were numerous at Savage River in the 1930's, I could sense when there was going to be a big kill. As dark came on, there would be a lot of howling; I've heard as many as four separate packs within a few miles of my cabin. After the preliminary howling, all would be quiet, and I could almost feel the tension in the hills.

When the evening kill was made, usually around 10 or 11 o'clock, howling would start again. At that time I'd usually be reading or finishing up a day's skinning. Often the howling continued for hours after I went to bed. This seemed to be especially true on dark moonless nights.

I often investigated on the day after such a kill. Ravens would be flying around the dead caribou, so they were easy to locate. I'd find from one to 15 carcasses.

When attacked by wolves at night, a caribou herd crowds together instead of scattering and running. It's easy for wolves to catch the terrified animals and slash open their flanks. The caribou's paunch falls out, he steps on it and drags himself away, and then he drops.

Almost invariably, all the animals killed in one herd will be within a few hundred feet of one another.

I think that the wolf is the brainiest animal in Alaska. He learns well, and he learns fast. A good example of this braininess is his reaction to being shot at from a small airplane.

In the early 1950's, wolves existed in large numbers on the Arctic slope north of the Brooks Range. Caribou were just recovering from a bad slump then, so the U.S. Fish and Wildlife Service, for which I worked as a predator agent, organized a wolf hunt with small planes from Umiat on the Colville River.

There are no trees in the area, so we could fly low with ski-equipped planes and kill wolves with shotguns loaded with buckshot, a technique that some bounty hunters and some sportsmen still use in Alaska.

Normally we searched for wolves at an altitude of about 400 feet. When we found a bunch, we'd make a circle a mile or so away, drop to within 40 or 50 feet of the ground, and then come in on them.

The wolves usually ran straight away in single file. We'd fly on their left, and the gunner would shoot out the right side of the plane, often at ranges of 20 or 30 feet.

Usually the first pass at a bunch of wolves was easy, and shooting was simple.

But the second pass was another story. By then the surviving wolves would have learned a lesson. Many of them would weave back and forth, at a dead run away from the plane, when we got within a couple of hundred yards.

Occasionally a really smart wolf would learn to dodge left every time the plane got close, so that he would be under the plane and out of the gunner's sight.

We buzzed one wolf that stopped on the edge of a high rim. The terrain forced us to come at him from above, and each time we neared he dropped off the rim and out of sight. When we were directly above him, he would be hard to find and even harder to hit. I fired eight or nine shots at that wolf as we made pass after pass over him for at least half an hour. Finally my pilot made a dangerous approach from below and pushed the animal into the open, where I got him with a clear shot.

The belief that wolves always take sick, crippled, or otherwise misfit animals doesn't always hold true. A wolf will take what is available, and he doesn't go out of his way to kill the weak. Wolves commonly kill stragglers, but though some of these animals are weak, others are not.

A wolf's teeth—the uppers fit on the outside of the lowers—work like a pair of shears. His jaw muscles are extremely powerful.

At one time, I had in harness a number of dogs that were three-quarters wolf. Their teeth were quite similar to those of wolves. They could hold a frozen rib of a moose or caribou in their front paws, feed it into the sides of their mouths, slice it off into quarter-inch pieces, and then grind the pieces into pulp.

A wolf can crack bones that even a grizzly bear can't break.

Some people are said to "wolf" food, and the word is appropriate in that context. I have opened the stomach of hundreds of wolves and have commonly found fist-size chunks of meat there. The bitch wolf feeds her weaned pups by regurgitating such chunks—I've often seen these pieces around wolf dens.

I think that wolves are unusual in their awareness of man. Even in wilderness areas, where they have little or no contact with humans, wolves have a pretty definite reaction to an encounter with man.

It has also been my experience that the wolf is the only animal able to recognize a motionless man for what he is. A bear, moose, caribou, or any other animal I know about in Alaska cannot recognize a motionless

231

man by sight alone, especially if the man's silhouette is broken by a rock, leg, or tree. But a wolf can.

Several times—when I have been absolutely motionless and wearing dull clothing, with the wind in my favor and my outline broken— wolves have approached, looked at me for a moment, and then whirled and run.

I don't regard the wolf as a coward, as do many people. Actually he's very brave.

I once watched two wolves drive a large grizzly from their kill. Another time, I saw a family of wolves drive three grizzlies from their den.

On still another occasion, in Mount McKinley National Park, I was watching a family of wolves feed on several caribou they had killed. They would sleep, feed a bit, and then sleep some more. Eventually a big dark grizzly ambled up the river bar, feeding on roots and whatever else he could find. Suddenly he got the scent of the dead caribou, whirled, and sat up, leaning into the wind. A moment later he took off at a run toward the carcass of the wolf-killed caribou.

Six wolves were lying near the dead caribou, and when that bear plunged into their midst, they scattered in every direction. One big gray ran off a few hundred yards, stopped, and howled. Four of the others gathered around her, and then the five of them trotted off.

The last wolf was a big black. He stood watching as the others filed off.

The bear sprawled across one of the carcasses, watching the wolves leave. Then the black wolf walked, stiff-legged, from behind the bear. As he neared, the bear glanced around but didn't move. The wolf walked as if he were on eggs—his tail straight out, his head straight—almost like a pointer on a hot scent.

When the wolf was about 10 feet from the grizzly, he leaped in and bit the bear's back, hard.

I clearly heard the bear roar as he lurched over backward reaching for the wolf. The wolf lit out downhill, with the bear hot on his trail. The bear gained, finally getting so close that he'd have had the wolf in another jump if the wolf—his tail held low and his hind legs spread— hadn't made an abrupt turn.

If was a beautiful maneuver. The bear actually rolled over in his attempt to make the turn. He was as mad as a hornet when he picked himself up. He turned, walked back to the meat, and found the wolf already there.

The wolf backed off when the bear arrived, and then he lay down about 20 feet from the grizzly. But soon he circled, tiptoed close again, leaped, and bit, and once more the bear chased him down the hill.

The wolf tired of the game after about half an hour, and he trotted off in the direction the other wolves had gone.

It's my opinion that the wolf has been called a coward because he is so shy of man and because he commonly hunts in a large group with the odds in his favor. But these facts demonstrate his intelligence to me.

A wolf can become lonely, I believe, if kept away from others of its kind. And a female wolf has pretty strong maternal feelings toward almost any pup. I used these traits to make $50 when a dollar was worth something.

It was spring at Fairbanks, and I was approached by a man named Van Bebber, who made a business of keeping and feeding sled dogs for people. A couple of months earlier, Van Bebber had acquired a three-year-old female gray wolf from a trader up on the Tanana River. The wolf was in a cage when he got it, and he had released it in a stout pen with 10- to 12-foot walls.

Van Bebber had a buyer willing to pay $200 for the wolf, but he had been unable to catch her and put a collar and chain on her. She was so violent when he tried to force her that he was afraid she would kill herself.

Since I drove wolf-dogs and was a trapper, Van Bebber reasoned that I was an expert on wolves. He offered me $50 if I could put a chain and collar on the wolf without hurting her.

It became obvious that the wolf was terrified of Van Bebber, so I asked him to leave. Then I took a three- or four-month-old pup of his, put it on a chain, sat down in the middle of the pen, and started petting the pup.

I spent the afternoon there. Once in a while I released the pup, and it would run over to the wolf. She would smell it, it would try to play with her, and she would respond halfheartedly.

While petting the pup I would howl like a wolf, and soon the female was answering me, with a real low howl. By that evening I'd had my hands on the wolf two or three times. But each time, she leaped back stiff-legged and her mane came up.

Next day I went into the pen with a choke collar in each pocket of my coat, plus a chain. I figured that if I could slip the collar over her head, I could snap the chain into it afterward.

She circled me one way and then the other, fast and nervously. Again I howled and used the pup as bait, and I got my hands on her. Twice I almost had the collar on her, but she leaped back.

The third day, the wolf was noticeably tamer and very fond of the pup. She obviously had looked forward to our return—her actions said so when we came in.

It was almost anticlimactic when I slipped the collar over her head and, a little later, snapped the chain into it.

The wolf's cruelty is not exaggerated.

One September day, I noticed a bull moose standing in the river near my cabin. The next day, he was lying on the bank with his head on the ground. I went over to see what was wrong with him and found that, though he was alive, he couldn't lift his head. Wolves had eaten 25 or 30 pounds of meat from one of his hindquarters. The suffering animal had been standing in water, trying to cool the feverish leg, when I had first seen him.

I shot the moose to end his suffering. Then I followed his back-trail to see what had happened. Five wolves had run and pestered him until he became exhausted and fell. They had eaten what they wanted and then had left—or perhaps they left because they heard my dogs barking or smelled my cabin.

Twice since then, I have found moose in similar conditions, both times in deep snow with a light crust that had supported the wolves but not the moose.

When wolves make a kill and are hungry, they'll usually drink some hot blood and then eat the hams. Sometimes they'll eat the tongue. A large number of wolves may eat an entire animal except for the skull and the very largest bones—and even these will often be cracked open so that the wolves can get the marrow.

There are a great many variables in the relationship between wolves and big game. Some wolves are much faster than others. The speed of big-game animals, even those within the same species, varies greatly.

It takes a large number of wolves to pull down a mature bull moose that has hard antlers and good footing. But two or three wolves can finish off the biggest bull that ever lived if he is antlerless and is caught in deep and crusted snow.

An animal in advanced pregnancy is vulnerable to wolf predation anytime. But the same animal at another time of the year might be able to run circles around the wolf, for the wolf is actually a relatively slow runner.

Because caribou are night-blind, one of any age or sex is highly vulnerable on dark nights. During daylight, however, practically any adult caribou can outrun wolves if he sees them in time. Wolves know this and hunt accordingly.

In the North, wolves depend more upon caribou for food than upon any other species of big game. Wolves exert strong influence on the caribou herds, especially young caribou.

In June 1940 in McKinley Park, Harold Herning, a park ranger, and I were eating lunch on a little hill overlooking a fork in the Teklanika River. In the V of the fork were 350 or so caribou, mostly cows, yearlings, and calves.

For several months previously, we had been observing a family of six wolves led by a small black female. Now, as we watched, these wolves trotted up the river and, upon smelling the caribou, dashed over the bank toward them. The caribou fled.

The little black female was much faster than the other wolves. She soon left them behind. Some 40 or 50 two- and three-week-old calves bunched up and dropped behind the main body of caribou, and the black wolf was soon among them.

She grabbed one calf by the middle of the back, reared up, shook it, flung it aside, and continued the chase. She bowled over the next calf with her shoulder. Before it could get up, she grasped its back, shook the animal three or four times, and dropped it. The third one was also knocked over.

The fourth calf happened to be in soft ground, on which a wolf is clumsy. The black female hit the calf, knocking it down, but at the same time she stumbled and rolled end over end herself. The calf was the first to get to its feet, and as it started to run, it accidentally bumped into the just-recovering wolf, knocking her flat.

That angered the wolf, and after half a dozen jumps she caught the calf by the back and raised it high in the air, shaking it. Then she slammed the calf down, put both of her front paws on it, and actually bit out large chunks, tossing them aside as fast as she could. The wolves didn't eat any of those calves. Each had bites through the backbone and into the lungs and heart.

Despite his savageness, however, I admire the wolf. He's a fascinating animal, and I'd hate to see him disappear.

Alaska has taken some steps toward making the wolf big game (see ''I Say Make Wolves Big Game!'' *Outdoor Life*, January 1968), thereby reducing the danger of the animal's being wiped out in our forty-ninth state.

The wolf is a trophy of which any sportsman can be proud. But my guess is that there won't be many wolves taken by trophy hunters. These fine animals are just too smart for that.

Outdoor Life
March 1968

LIONS DON'T COME EASY

by Jack O'Connor

P ractically everyone who has never hunted in Africa will assure
you that there is nothing to getting a lion. All you have to do, they
say, is drive around in a safari car for a few hours, looking over
various samples of the king of beasts. Then, when you find the kind you
want, one with a mane that exactly matches the pine paneling in the
rumpus room, you just step out and give him the business.

Yet I have just finished eight days of dawn-to-dark hunting—and only
this morning did I shoot my lion. Incidentally, I shot the seventy-eighth
lion I saw—an average of almost 10 a day. There are still plenty of them
in the best areas of British East Africa, but unless you are lucky you have
to rustle to get a good one.

The three of us—H. W. (Herb) Klein, M. C. (Red) Early, and I—first
started to think about a lion hunt back in 1950, when we were chasing
Dall sheep and grizzlies in the Yukon. Herb and Red, old friends of
mine, like to hunt and shoot and fondle a firearm as much as I do. Both
are husky Texas oilmen, and they have hunted everything from Texas
white-tail deer to Alaska brown bear. They are among the half dozen
hunters who have taken all varieties of North American wild sheep.
When you've accomplished things like that, you have to begin to raise
your sights a bit.

One night we were gabbing in our Yukon cook tent when Herb
suddenly said, "What do you say we take a whirl at lions in Africa one of
these days?"

"Sounds good to me!" Red grunted.

I said little, but all my life I had, like most American sportsmen,
dreamed of the fabulous game country that is East Africa—of the great,
black, truculent Cape buffalo; the fantastic wildebeest, which
looks like a cross between a mule, a deer, and a buffalo; the leopard; the

THE GREATEST HUNTING STORIES EVER TOLD

elephant; and many strange antelope. But most of all I had dreamed of someday knocking over a great-maned lion, the grandest of the cats, the epitome of all that is Africa.

The dream began to come true last fall, when *Outdoor Life* gave me the go-ahead on the trip. The three of us engaged the famous Nairobi outfitting firm of Ker & Downey Safaris, Ltd., and for months we were busy getting together rifles, ammunition, and photographic equipment, obtaining passports, and enduring injections for everything from cholera to housemaid's knee. Stories of the Mau Mau trouble gave us pause, but we discovered that the uprisings were confined to an area far from the hunting fields. Finally last June we met in New York and flew to Nairobi by way of London, Paris, Rome, and Khartoum in the Sudan.

Three and a half days out of Nairobi we were in our first hunting camp in northwestern Tanganyika with Don Ker and Myles Turner, white hunters, 26 native helpers—gun bearers, cooks, drivers—and two hunting cars and two big five-ton trucks. The camping equipment would knock your eye out. Nairobi outfitters cater to the carriage trade, and while we hunt we live in style.

As I write this, I am sitting at a portable typewriter in a clean, airy, and spacious dining tent. While I labor at one end of the table, Don Ker and Red Early are playing blackjack at the other. Herb Klein has just come in with a zebra and a Thomson's gazelle. Hot and tired after stalking the zebra, he is taking a bath in a folding canvas tub while his personal boy stands by with the towels. This is astonishing luxury for an old desert rat like me, who on most of his trips has been his own guide, his own cook, and his own skinner.

The amount of game we've seen has been fantastic. I have hunted from Mexico to Alaska, but in the 12 days since we left Nairobi I have seen more game than ever before. Yesterday we saw at least 10,000 zebras. Beautiful little Thomson's gazelles hop around in the tall grass like so many fleas; we've surely seen over a million of them. And hundreds of giraffes and ostriches; thousands of topi, wildebeests, and goofy-looking kongoni.

Game of some sort is continually in sight. Here you see a herd of gazelles, over there you see a few water bucks among the trees. Beyond the hill a zebra barks like a cocky little dog, and a dainty dik-dik, an antelope no larger than a rabbit, scurries through the grass.

238

The same armchair hunter who tells you that catching your lion is easy, also tells you that Africa is hot. Of course it is. That's why, when an acquaintance back in the States advised me to take an eiderdown jacket for early-morning wear, I thought he was balmy. But I took it along—and it's the most useful garment I have. We've been camping at about 5,500 feet. Nights are so cool we sleep under two or three blankets. And in the morning my jacket is as welcome as it was in the Yukon.

But back to the lions. We made our first camp near a donga, or dry streambed. Tents were being set up when Myles called to Herb and me. "Come here, pals," he said. "I want to show you something."

In the mud beside a nearby water hole were the big round pug marks of two lions. "A lion and a lioness," Myles told us. "Things look good!"

Actually they were even better than we had hoped.

After lunch we went out in the hunting cars, Myles with Herb and Red, and Don Ker taking me. We were not a mile from camp when Don suddenly put on the brakes. "See the lions?" he asked, lifting his binoculars to his eyes.

I jumped as if I had been shot, but I managed to follow the direction of his gaze. Across the donga, perhaps 150 yards away, and beneath a big thorn tree, were the silhouettes of a couple of lions. They looked just like the circus kind. Then my binoculars showed me lions all over the place—females, half-grown cubs, and a couple of young males with sprouting manes.

For whatever the reason, lions are not afraid of automobiles. Putting his four-wheel-drive hunting car into low, Don crossed the donga and in a moment we were up to our necks in lions. Those around the thorn tree posed like mamma, papa, and the children in an old-fashioned family portrait. More lions popped up out of the grass until there were 18 in all.

Breaking out my black-and-white still camera, I shot several pictures of them. Then I turned to color movies. One lithe and beautiful young lioness detached herself from the group, walked up to within a few feet of the car, and looked it over.

Reluctantly we drove away. This, I told myself, was going to be a cinch. I was even more convinced we were on the gravy train when we saw two more lionesses, shortly after. They were lying in the thin shade of a thorn tree right out on the hot, bright plain. One was devouring the carcass of a Thomson's gazelle she had killed, and when we drew up and

239

stopped she nervously picked up the dead Tommy and trotted away until she found herself another tree. She didn't know what the strange mechanical monster was, but she wasn't going to share her Tommy with it, that was sure.

That same afternoon I shot my first African game—a Tommy for us dudes and the white hunters to gnaw on, and a topi for the help. Each was a one-shot kill with an 87-grain bullet from the .257 Weatherby Magnum, and each was made at around 200 yards.

I figured I'd really have something to tell Herb and Red when I got back. I had actually seen some real live lions with hair, long teeth, and big red mouths. I had also actually shot a couple of funny-looking un-American antelope. Would the boys be burning with envy?

But when Don and I drove up to camp my small accomplishments faded into nothing, for there was Red gloating over the carcass of a big blond lion, while the native boys whooped and hollered around him in triumph. Just as the debunkers had said; there's nothing to shooting a lion in Africa. You simply drive around until you see the one you want.

Actually, Red had done just that. From a distance Myles had spotted a lion and lioness lying in the grass. Leaving the car half a mile away, the two men had made a long stalk, creeping along on their hands and knees through the tall grass until they were about 75 yards from the lions. Then Red eased himself up onto the convenient anthill, and when the lion raised its head above the grass he plugged it through the neck.

Easy? For him, yes. But Herb and I didn't shoot our lions the next day, nor the day after that. We didn't shoot any old he-lions on account of we didn't see any. We saw lady lions. We saw baby lions. We even saw young legal males which we passed up because they had small manes.

In East Africa, male antelope (which by all laws of logic should be called bucks) are called rams if they are small and bulls if they are large, and the very feline male leopards and cheetahs are called dogs. So Herb and I gagged up our reports to each other when we met at night. "Oh, the usual! Lots of ewe and lamb lions, but no old boar lions."

We went out at dawn, came in after dark. We covered country in the hunting cars. We glassed from the little rocky hills called kopjes and pronounced "copies." We explored dongas. We shot a few antelope to keep our help sleek and fat and our own bodies and souls together. But what we wanted was a lion apiece.

I got the first break. We moved part of the outfit a few miles from the place where Red had shot his lion and camped on a donga spotted with water holes every mile or so. The area was very dry and the high grass had been cured by the sun. All around us was the fresh, clean, delicious smell of natural hay.

A little scouting soon showed that the lions in the area were concentrated along this donga. They had cover in the brush along the watercourse, pools in which to drink, and plentiful game close at hand. Every night we could hear their grunting, coughing roars as they hunted. Water bucks, Thomson's gazelles, topi, impalas—all came down to water and paid their toll to the great lurking cats.

There are various ways of getting lions. One is to cruise around in a hunting car until a shootable specimen is spotted and then to stalk him afoot. In both Kenya and Tanganyika the law says that no game may be shot from a car or within 200 yards of a car. So even if you spot a fine trophy lion you have to drive on at least 200 yards before you can get out and begin your stalk.

Another way is to hit fresh spoor, or tracks, follow the lion to his lair, boot him out, and take your shot at him. Still another is baiting. You shoot one of the commoner antelope and drag it behind an automobile to leave a blood-scent trail. Then you tie the bait animal securely in a tree so that a feeding lion cannot drag it off into the brush. Perhaps a shootable lion will be attracted to the bait, and still be there when you come around at daylight. But more often the bait has been devoured by other visitors—buzzards, marabou storks, and hyenas. And when lions do come they are likely to be females and immature males that are not so wary of ambushes as the great maned lords of the jungle.

Don Ker elected to cruise in his hunting car, and we coverd a beat along the donga, stopping now and then to glass our surroundings or to get out to look for sign. We saw lions every day—sometimes a lone and beautiful female shining like gold in the early-morning sun as she lay full of antelope, replete, and happy, enjoying the warmth after the chill of the night at almost 6,000 feet. Sometimes we'd see two or three females or young lions together. Now and then they'd be sunning themselves, but in the afternoon they'd either be lying in the tall grass or bedded down in the thin shade of a thorn tree.

There were big he-lions about, no doubt of it. We'd see their tracks by the water holes. At night we'd hear their rattling low-pitched grunts, their full-throated, deep-chested roars. But when we went out at dawn they had gone back to their brush retreats. But sometime, somewhere, we'd be bound to see a trophy lion.

Then it happened.

One morning, just as the first clean, bright rays of the sun shone on bush and grassland, the lookout boy—his head through a hole in the car top—whispered that magic word, "Simba!" Across the donga, about 200 yards away, seated majestically on a big flat rock, were two big males, with a black and a blond mane respectively. My heart almost jumped out of my throat.

Calmly Don Ker, that old pro, stopped the hunting car, lifted his 7X35 Bausch & Lomb binoculars to his eyes, and took a look at the lions. "They're both worth shooting," he said calmly.

He drove on and parked the car some 300 yards away. Then Mr. O'Connor's personal whammy took a hand.

"Give me my three hundred," I told the gun bearer in the backseat.

That Weatherby Magnum is one of my favorites, a rifle I have described in these pages. It's a short-barreled, scope-sighted featherweight, so accurate it will keep five shots on a silver dollar at 200 yards.

So off we went. We dropped into the donga and presently came to a spot where I could shoot. The lions had become nervous. Apparently they had seen or heard us because when I sat down to shoot, they were on their feet.

The rifle was wobbling all over the place. My first shot at the black-maned lion got away from me. I missed, and off went the old boy into the bush. I worked the bolt rapidly, then swung over to the blond. This time the crosshairs settled down right behind his shoulder, and when I squeezed off the shot I expected old Leo Africanus to drop. Instead he gave no sign of being hit, turned his big broad fanny to me, slowly walked off the rock, and disappeared.

The only thing that could have happened, I told myself, was that I'd given the trigger a terrific yank and jerked my shot high.

As we sneaked back to the car I was about as low as I have been in all my life. I had dreamed for 40 years of killing a great-maned lion. Two of them had been tossed into my lap—and I had flubbed the opportunity like an excited schoolboy missing his first buck. I crept along trying to hide my head in my jacket. The gun bearers wouldn't look at me, and until we got into the car Don said not a word.

Then he turned to me. "Don't feel badly," he said. "Lots of people have missed their first lion—and they have missed at a lot less than 100 yards."

I said nothing. There was nothing to say. So off we drove. Presently Don stopped the car.

"We'll have to try baiting now," he told me. "See that kongoni over there, about 300 yards away? I'd like to have you shoot it."

The kongoni is a big, horse-faced antelope with short, twisted, cow-like horns and a gallop like that of a spavined plowhorse. Nobody loves the poor kongoni. He exists in multitudes but he isn't much of a trophy, and his destiny seems to be lion food and lion bait. This one stood under a tree asleep on his feet and with his head down. He was about 300 yards away and the shot should not be difficult with my souped-up .300 Magnum.

I held onto the tree with my left hand, rested the fore end of the .300 over my wrist, put the crosshairs on the center of the kongoni's shoulder, and touched one off. Not a darned thing happened except that—far away, through an avenue in the trees—I saw dust kick up. I felt even lower. I worked the bolt, squeezed off another careful shot with exactly the same result.

"Way high!" Don said gloomily.

"I'll try a 220-grain bullet," I said. "It shoots a lot lower."

I fed one in, held as before, shot, and down went the kongoni.

A great light dawned on me. Carefully I examined my .300. The continual pounding of the hunting car over rough country had loosened the guard screws of the rifle so that it took three complete turns to tighten them. The scope mount was so loose that I could rattle it with my hand. I tried a shot at 100 yards, and the bullet landed to the right and a foot high. Even the three screws in the scope base were loose. I had to remove the scope to tighten them, and the .300, of course, was out of action until I could sight it in again. I didn't have a lion, but I did have an alibi.

In the rack in the hunting car was my .375 Magnum, a Model 70 Winchester restocked by Griffin & Howe and fitted with a Stith 2¾X scope on a Griffin & Howe mount. I took it out, tightened the guard screws, then shot twice with the 270-grain bullet at a knot on a tree 100 paces away. One shot was in the middle of the knot, the other about one inch away. Here was my lion rifle.

I got another chance a couple of days later. We were cruising along early one morning when what should we behold about 200 yards away but two big blond lions strolling along as amiable-looking as two well-fed house cats, their big bellies—full of meat and water—swinging from side to side as they walked.

It would have been very easy to leap from the hunting car with cries of joy and to salivate at those two big cats, but the Tanganyika game laws and the long arm of Don Ker's conscience would not permit. We cruised slowly between them, as if shooting lions was the last thing in the world we'd think of. I even thrust my camera out of the car and shot a picture of one.

But when we got about a quarter mile away we grabbed rifles, dived into the donga, and ran like the devil after the lions. When we got to the spot where they should be, we stuck our heads over the bank expecting to see them. No lions. Their tracks showed they had done exactly what we had done. As soon as they were out of sight they had run.

So we took up the spoor.

For five miles we followed it, with Don, the gun bearer Thomas, and a Wandorobo tracker doing most of the work. I must say with pride, though, that two or three times I found the spoor when it was lost.

It was noon. We were hot, weary, and thirsty when we saw a little Thomson's gazelle standing just out of a brush patch into which the tracks led, and gazing at something the way a bird looks at a snake.

"He sees the lions," Don hissed at me. "Get ready!"

So into the brush we crept. But the lions saw us first and we became aware of them as bouncing silhouettes fleeing through heavy brush about 75 yards away. I brought up the .375 and had the crosshairs swinging along the chest of a lion when Don shouted for me not to shoot. Like all white hunters he wants no part of a wounded lion in heavy brush.

We chased the cats about 300 yards and saw them again across an open flat just before they disappeared into another brush patch.

"Shoot if you think you can land one right!" Don yelled.

"Hell, I couldn't hit an elephant right now," I said as I gasped for breath.

So back we turned, again defeated. We had now spooked four big-maned lions and we were really loused up.

244

The next day, not far from where we lost those two, Herb Klein polished off a big blond male, probably one of the two we had muffed. Don and I continued to see lady lions but no males.

So back we went to our first camp, where Red had shot his lion. We held a conference and decided to try two more days for my lion. Since Herb and Red had killed not only lions but leopards—something for which I had no license—it was time to move on to other territory for other game.

The next morning we saw a big pride of 18 lions, including two young maned males. The temptation to bop one was pretty strong. That afternoon we put out a kongoni bait and chopped in two a big eland which Herb had shot the day before.

It was gray dawn the second day when Don and I drove out in the hunting car to inspect our three baits. When we could see the first one Don said calmly, "There's something on the kongoni—a lioness, I believe." He lifted his glasses. "No, it's a lion."

My own binoculars went to my eyes. I saw a very respectable maned male, young but shootable and a better lion than most Americans come back from Africa with. "I'll settle for that baby," I said.

Don kept the glass to his eyes.

"We've got two more baits to look at," he told me, "and I'd hate to have you go back with a second-rate lion like that one."

"You wouldn't hate it half as much as I'd hate to go back without any lion," I told him. "My best friends wouldn't speak to me."

"Well, maybe he'll be here when we get back," he said.

"You're the doctor!"

Off we went. The second bait had not been touched, but when we got to the third we could see that a lion had been eating on it and below it in the dust were the big round tracks of a male.

We parked the car away from the kill and got out. "He hasn't been gone from the bait for more than a few minutes," Don whispered. "He's bound to be close by."

We had hardly gone 300 yards through the tall grass and thin brush when the Wandorobo boy whispered, "Simba!"

Now luck was with us. A bit less than a hundred yards from the lion was a big anthill that would give us cover from the stalk and a rest to shoot from. Slowly, quietly, hardly daring to breathe, we crept up on his nibs. I poked my head over the hill. There was the great lion. He was

245

sitting in grass so tall that only his head and neck showed, nervously looking in the direction of his free meal, half of Herb's bull eland. His shaggy, majestic head and thick mane shone golden in the early-morning sun.

Cautiously I poked the big .375 over the top of the anthill. I rested the fore end on my left hand and the crosshair in the scope came to rest rock-steady against his burly neck. I squeezed the trigger so gradually that the rifle seemed to go off by itself.

As the 71.5 grains of No. 4064 powder exploded and drove the 270-grain soft-point bullet into the great cat's neck, all hell broke loose. Roaring like a fiend possessed, the lion tossed his great tawny body clear of the grass in his dying convulsions. I have heard many a wounded grizzly roar in his death agonies, and it's a blood-curdling sound, but I have never heard more racket than that big lion made.

We rushed forward for the finishing shots, and I was so excited that if Don hadn't restrained me, I think I would have tried to stab him to death with my pocketknife.

We stood over him. We gloated. We measured. We admired.

He was a beautiful lion. His great sandy body was as smooth and round as a sausage. His blond mane was heavy, shaggy, long. Don Ker told me he probably weighed 500 pounds, and was one of the largest lions he had seen in 27 years as a white hunter. From the tip of his nose to the last joint of his tail he was nine feet, seven inches long as he lay there.

All in all, he was some lion, and of all the trophies I have taken, the only one that has given me a greater thrill was the first desert ram I stood over, almost a quarter of a century earlier and half a world away.

Outdoor Life
November 1953

I HAD TO HAVE A MOOSE

by Olive A. Fredrickson

The canoe was a 30-foot dugout that the Indians had "given" me. They'd be along in the fall to claim payment in potatoes.

It had been hollowed out from a big cottonwood with a hand ax, but the tree wasn't straight to begin with, and the canoe had inherited the character of its parent. Otherwise the Indians would not have parted with it. As a result it was not only heavy and unwieldy but also so cranky you hardly dared to look over the side unless your hair was parted in the middle.

I was in the stern paddling. My six-year-old daughter, Olive, was wedged firmly in the bow. Between us were Vala, five, and the baby, Louis, two. We were going moose hunting, and since there was no one to leave the children with, we'd have to go as a family.

We weren't hunting for fun. It was early summer, and the crop of vegetables I had planted in our garden was growing, but there was nothing ready for use yet, and we were out of food.

The moose season wouldn't open until fall, but at that time British Columbia game regulations allowed a prospector to get a permit and kill a moose any time he needed one for food. I was not a prospector and, anyway, I had no way to go into town for the permit unless I walked 27 miles each way. But my babies and I were as hungry as any prospector would ever be, and we had to have something to eat. I was sure the good Lord would forgive me, and I hoped the game warden would too, if he found out about it.

So one hot, windless July day—shortly before my twenty-eighth birthday—when fly season was getting real bad, I called the youngsters together.

"We've got to go try to kill a moose," I said. I knew the moose would

247

be coming down to the river on that kind of day to rid themselves of flies and mosquitoes.

I had never shot a moose, but necessity is the mother of a lot of new experiences, and I decided I could do it all right if I got the chance. I got Olive and Louis and Vala ready, loaded them into the big clumsy canoe, and poked four shells into my old .30/30 Winchester Model 94. I jacked one into the chamber, put the hammer on half cock, and started upstream against the quiet current of the Stuart River.

It was a little more than a year after the June day in 1928 when a neighbor, Jack Hamilton, had come to our lonely homestead 40 miles down the Stuart from Fort St. James, in the mountain country of central British Columbia. He had a telegram for me from the Royal Canadian Mounted Police at Edmonton, and had to break the news that my husband, Walter Reamer, a trapper, had drowned in Leland Lake on the Alberta-Northwest Territories border. Walter's canoe had tipped over in a heavy windstorm.

That was almost 40 years ago, but I still remember raising my hand to my eyes to wipe away the fog that suddenly clouded them and Hamilton leading me to a chair by the kitchen table.

"You'd better sit down, Mrs. Reamer," he said.

I looked around at my three children. Olive, then only five years old, stood wide-eyed, not quite taking it all in. Vala was playing with her little white kitten, and Louis lay on his back, reaching for his toes. What was to become of them and me?

Olive leaned her head against my skirt and began to cry softly for her daddy, and I felt a lump in my chest that made it hard to breathe. But that was not the time for tears. If I cried, I'd do it out of the children's sight.

"Will you be all right?" Jack Hamilton asked before he left.

"I'll be all right," I told him firmly.

All right? I wondered. I was 26 and a homesteader-trapper's widow with three little children, 160 acres of brush-grown land, almost none of it cleared, a small log house—and precious little else.

That was just before the start of the great depression, the period that Canadians of my generation still call the dirty thirties. There was no allowance for dependent children then. I knew I could get a small sum of relief money each month, maybe about $12 for the four of us, but I did not dare ask for it.

I Had to Have a Moose

Olive and Louis had been born in Canada, but Vala had been born in the United States, as had I. I was afraid that if I appealed for help, Vala or I or both of us might be sent back to that country. In the very first hours of my grief and loneliness, I vowed I'd never let that happen, no matter what. It was the four of us alone now, to fight the world of privation and hunger, but at least we'd stay together.

My father had been a trapper, and my mother had died when I was eight. We had been a happy family, but always poor folk with no money to speak of. And after I married Walter, his trapline didn't bring in much. I had never known anything but a hard life, but now I was thankful for it. I knew I was more up to the hardships that lay ahead than most women would be.

I don't think I looked the part. Please don't get the idea that I was a backwoods frump, untidy and slovenly. I was small, five feet two, and weighed 112, all good solid muscle. And if I do say it, when I had the proper clothes on and was out dancing, I could compete with the best of them in looks.

There were a lot of moose around our homestead, some deer, black bears, wolves, rabbits, grouse, fox, mink, and muskrat. I decided I'd become hunter and trapper on my own.

We had a little money on hand to buy food with. We had no horses, but I dug potatoes, raked hay—did whatever I could for our few neighbors to pay for the use of a team. By the next spring, I had managed to clear the brush and trees from a few acres of good land.

Olive was housekeeper, cook, and baby-sitter while I worked outside. I planted a vegetable garden and started a hay meadow. I hunted grouse and rabbits, and neighbors helped out the first winter by giving us moose meat. We managed to eke out a living. It was all hard work, day in and day out, dragging myself off to bed when dark came and crawling out at daylight to begin another day. But at least my babies and I had something to eat.

Then, in July of 1929, our food gave out. I couldn't bring myself to go deeper in debt to my neighbors, and in desperation I decided on the out-of-season moose hunt. With the few odds and ends we had left, we could make out on moose meat until the garden stuff started to ripen.

We hadn't gone far up the Stuart in the cranky dugout before I began to see moose tracks along shore and worn moose paths leading down to the river. Then we rounded a bend, and a big cow moose was standing out on a grassy point, dunking her ungainly head and coming up with mouthfuls of weeds.

I didn't want to kill a cow and maybe leave a calf to starve, but I don't think I was ever more tempted in my life than I was right then. That big animal meant meat enough to last us the rest of the summer, and by canning it, I could keep every pound from spoiling. I paddled quietly ahead, whispered warning to the kids to sit still and keep quiet. The closer I got, the more I wanted that moose. She finally saw us and looked our way while I wrestled with my conscience.

I'll never know what the outcome would have been, for about the time I was getting near enough to shoot, Olive let out a squeal of pure delight, and I saw a little red-brown calf rise up out of the tall grass. That settled it.

The children all talked at once, and the cow grunted to her youngster and waded out, ready to swim the river. We were only 200 feet away at that point and all of a sudden she decided she didn't like us there. Her ears went back, the hair on her shoulders stood up, and her grunts took on a very unfriendly tone. I stuck my paddle into the mud and waited, wondering just what I'd do if she came for us.

There was no chance I could maneuver that cumbersome dugout out of her way. But I quieted the youngsters with a sharp warning, and after a minute the cow led her calf into deep water and they struck out for the opposite side of the river. I sighed with relief when they waded ashore and walked up a moose trail out of sight.

A half mile farther up the river we landed. I took Louis piggyback and carried my gun, and the four of us walked very quietly over a grassy point where I thought moose might be feeding. We didn't see any, and now the kids began to complain that they were getting awful hungry. I was hungry, too. We sat down on the bank to rest, and I saw a good rainbow trout swimming in shallow water.

I always carried a few flies and fishhooks in my hatband, and I tied a fly to a length of string and threw it out, using the string as a handline. The trout took the fly on about the fifth toss, and I hauled it in. I fished a little longer and caught two squawfish, and we hit back to the canoe.

I built a fire and broiled the rainbow and one of the squawfish on sticks. The kids divided the trout, and I ate the squawfish. As a rule

250

squawfish have a muddy flavor, and I had really caught those two for dog food. But that one tasted all right to me.

A little farther up the Stuart, we came on two yearling mule deer with stubby spikes of antlers in the velvet. They watched us from a cut bank but spooked and disappeared into the brush soon after I saw them. A little later the same thing happened with two bull moose. They saw us and ran into the willows while I was reaching for my gun. I was so disappointed and discouraged I wanted to bawl.

That made four moose we had seen, counting the calf, without getting a shot, and I decided that killing one was going to be a lot harder than I had thought. And my arms were so tired from paddling the heavy dugout that they felt ready to drop out of the sockets.

I had brought a .22 along, as well as the .30/30, and a little while after that I used it to shoot a grouse that was watching us from the bank.

I had about given up all hope of getting a moose and was ready to turn back for the long paddle home when I saw what looked like the back of one, standing almost submerged in the shade of some cottonwoods up ahead. I shushed the kids and eased the canoe on for a better look, and sure enough, I was looking at a young bull, probably a yearling. Just a dandy size for what I wanted.

He was feeding, pulling up weeds from the bottom and putting his head completely under each time he went down for a mouthful. I paddled as close as I cared, and warned Olive and Vala to put their hands over their ears and keep down as long as they could, for I had to shoot over their heads.

I put the front bead of the Winchester just behind his shoulder, at the top of the water, and when he raised his head I let him have it. He went down with a great splash, and I told the kids they could raise up and look.

Luckily for us, the young bull did not die right away there in the deep, muddy water. I don't know how I'd ever have gotten him ashore for dressing. When I got close with the dugout he was trying to drag himself out on the bank. My shot had broken his back. I crowded him with the canoe, feeling sorry for him all the while, and as soon as I had him all the way on dry land I finished him with a head shot.

I had always hated to kill anything, and by that time I was close to tears. Then I saw Olive leaning against a tree, crying her heart out, and Vala and Louis with their faces all screwed up in tears, and I felt worse then ever. But I reminded myself that it had to be done to feed the children, and wiped my eyes and explained to them as best I could. About that time a porcupine came waddling along, and that took their minds off the moose.

Dressing a moose, even a yearling bull, is no fun. I went at it now, and it was about as hard a job as I had ever tackled. The kids tried to help but only succeeded in getting in the way. And while I worked, I couldn't help worrying about my out-of-season kill. What would happen if I were found out? Would the game warden be as understanding as I hoped?

When the job was done, I built a small fire to boil the partridge I'd shot and a few pieces of moose meat for our supper, giving Louis the broth in his bottle. I felt better after I ate, and I loaded the meat into the dugout and started home. But it was full dark now, and I was so tired that I soon decided not to go on.

We went ashore, spread out a piece of canvas, part under and part over us, and tried to sleep. The mosquitoes wouldn't let us, and I finally gave up. I sat over the children the rest of the night, switching mosquitoes off with a willow branch. Daylight came about four o'clock, and we got on the way.

I'll never forget that early-morning trip back to our place. My hands were black with mosquitoes the whole way, and the torment was almost too much.

Joel Hammond, a neighbor, had given me some flour he'd made by grinding his own wheat in a hand mill, and the first thing I did was build a fire and make a batch of hotcakes. The flour was coarse and sort of dusty, but with moose steak and greens fried in moose fat, those cakes made a real good meal. Then I went to work canning meat.

That was the only moose I ever killed out of season. When hunting season rolled around that fall I got a homesteader's free permit and went after our winter's supply of meat. It came even harder that time.

The first one I tried for I wounded with a shot that must have cut through the tip of his lungs. He got away in thick brush, and I took our dog Chum and followed him. Chum drove him back into the river, and he swam across and stood wheezing and coughing on the opposite side, too far off for me to use my only remaining shell on him. Chum swam the river in pursuit, and started to fight him in shallow water.

Another neighbor, Ross Finley, who lived on the quarter section next

252

to ours, heard me shoot and came up to lend a hand. He loaded Olive and me into our dugout, and we paddled across to where the dog was badgering the moose. When we got close, Finley used my last shell but missed.

The bull, fighting mad by now, came for the canoe, throwing his head this way and that. I was scared stiff, for I couldn't swim a stroke and neither could Olive. I knew that one blow from the moose's antlers would roll the dugout over like a pulpwood bolt.

I had the bow paddle, and I moved pretty fast, but at that the moose didn't miss us by a foot as I swung the canoe away from him. He was in deep water now, and Chum was riding on his shoulders and biting at the back of his neck. The dog took the bull's attention for a second or two, and I reached down and grabbed Finley's .22, which was lying in the bottom of the dugout.

I shot the moose right at the butt of the ear, with the gun almost touching him. He sank quietly out of sight, leaving Chum floating in the water. The dog was so worn out from the ruckus that we had to help him ashore.

We tried hard to locate the dead moose. But the current had carried it downriver, and it was days before we found it. The carcass was lying in shallow water at the mouth of a creek, the meat spoiled.

There were plenty more around, however. We could hear them fighting at night, grunting and snorting, and sometimes their horns would clash with a noise as loud as an ax hitting a hollow log. In the early mornings I saw as many as five at one time along the weedy river shore. I waited and picked the one I wanted, and that time I killed him with no trouble.

The Stuart was full of ducks and geese that fall, and there were grouse everywhere I went in the woods. I had plenty of ammunition for the .22 and always a few .30/30 shells around, I canned everything I killed and no longer worried about a meat shortage. Life was beginning to sort itself out.

A few unmarried men came around and tried to shine up to me, but I wasn't interested. All I wanted was to get more land cleared and buy a cow or two and a team of horses of my own. The young homestead widow was proving to herself that she could take care of her family and make the grade.

But before the winter was over I had another crisis. By February most of our food was gone, except for the canned meat and a few cans of vegetables. We had used the last of the hand-ground flour that Joel Hammond had given me and were desperately in need of groceries. I had no money, but I decided to walk the 27 miles to Vanderhoof, on the Prince George-Prince Rupert railroad, and try to get the supplies we needed on credit. I knew I could pay for them with potatoes the next fall, for by that time I had enough land cleared to grow a bigger potato crop than we needed for ourselves.

I left the three children with the George Vinsons, neighbors a mile and a half downriver, and started out on a cold, wintry morning. I had a road to follow, but only a few teams and sleighs had traveled it, and the walking was hard, in deep snow. Two miles out of Vanderhoof I finally hitched a ride.

I didn't have any luck getting credit against my potato crop. Those were hard times, and I guess the merchants couldn't afford much generosity. I tried first to buy rubbers for myself and the kids. We needed them very badly, and they were the cheapest footgear available. But the store turned me down.

A kindly woman who ran a restaurant did well by me, however. She gave me a good dinner, and when I put her down for 50 pounds of potatoes, she just smiled and shoved a chocolate bar into my pocket. I saw to it that she got the potatoes when the time came anyway.

Another storekeeper told me that he couldn't let me have things on credit, but he gave me $2 in cash and told me to do the best I could with it. I knew where part of it was going—for the oatmeal and sugar I had promised Louis and Vala and Olive when I got home. But I couldn't see any way to pay for another meal for myself or a room for the night, and I walked around Vanderhoof thinking of how wet and cold our feet would be in the slush of the spring thaw.

I was about as heartbroken as I've ever been in my life.

Finally I decided to make another attempt. Some of my neighbors on the Stuart River traded at a store at Finmoore, 19 miles east of Vanderhoof. I also had a friend there, Mrs. John Holter. I'd walk the railroad track to Finmoore and try my luck there. At the time I didn't know how far it was, and I expected a hike of only 10 miles or so.

It was about dark when I started. The railroad ties were crusted with ice, and the walking was very bad. My clothes were hardly enough for the cold night, either: denim overalls, men's work socks, Indian moccasins, and an old wool sweater with elbows out, worn under a denim jacket.

I had never been brave in the dark, any time or any place, and I can't tell you what an ordeal that walk was. All I could think of were the hobos I had heard stories about, the railroad bums, and I was afraid of every shadow.

I got to the lonely little station at Hulatt, 15 miles from Vanderhoof, at midnight and asked the stationmaster if I could rest until daylight. I lay down on the floor by the big potbellied stove. It was warm and cozy, and I was worn out. I started to drift off to sleep, but then I began to worry about the children and the likelihood that if I was later in getting home than I had promised, they might come back to the house and get into trouble starting a fire. Things were hard enough without having the place burned down. I got up and trudged away along the track once more.

It was two o'clock in the morning when I reached the Holter place. Mrs. Holter fixed me a sandwich and a cup of hot milk, and I fell into bed. She shook me awake at nine o'clock, as I had told her to. Those scant seven hours were all the sleep I had in more than 36.

Mrs. Holter loaned me another $2, and I went to the general store and struck it rich. The proprietor, Percy Moore, stared at me in disbelief when I poured out my hard-luck story.

"You've walked from the Stuart River since yesterday morning?" he asked in amazement. "That's forty-six miles!"

"No, forty-four," I corrected him. "I got a ride the last two miles into Vanderhoof." Then I added, "I've got fourteen more to walk home before dark tonight, too."

The first thing he let me have, on credit, was the three pairs of rubbers we needed so desperately. Then he took care of my grocery list. Eight pounds of oatmeal, three of rice, five of beans, five of sugar and—for a bonus—a three-pound pail of strawberry jam.

I plodded away from Finmoore at 10 o'clock that morning with almost 30 pounds in a packsack on my back.

Three inches of wet snow had fallen that morning, and the 14-mile walk seemed endless, each mile longer than the one before. My pack got heavier and heavier, and sometime in the afternoon I began to stumble and fall. I was so tired by that time, and my back ached so cruelly from the weight of the pack, that I wanted to lie there in the snow and go to sleep.

But I knew better. After each fall, I'd drive myself back to my feet and stagger on.

To this day I do not know when it was that I reached our place, but it was long after dark. Chum met me in the yard, and no human being was ever more glad to fumble at the latch of his own door.

I slid out of the pack, pulled off my wet moccasins and socks, and rolled into bed with my clothes on. The last thing I remember was calling the dog up to lie at my feet for warmth. The children awakened me at noon the next day, fed me breakfast, and rubbed some of the soreness out of my swollen legs and feet.

Next fall, when I harvested my potato crop, I paid off my debt to Percy Moore in full, except for one item. There was no way to pay him, ever, for his kindness to me when I was broke and had three hungry children at home.

I was to make many more trips to Finmoore in the years before I left the Stuart, for I did most of my trading at his store. And when times got better, he and his wife and daughter Ruth often came out and bought vegetables and eggs from me. I remember walking back to his place the next year, carrying six dressed chickens, selling them for fifty cents apiece, spending the money for food and packing it home. Three dollars bought quite a heavy load in those days.

Outdoor Life
May 1967

SANTIAGO
AND THE LADY

by Jack O'Connor

The first time Santiago Romero saw me I was on my elbows and knees, my hind end up in the air, and I was blowing up an air mattress. I didn't get a good look at him at the time, but my wife did. She said that his eyes almost popped out of his head and that he turned pale—that is, if Santiago, who is largely Indian and quite swarthy, could turn pale.

Anyway, said Eleanor, his skin became yellowish with faint green overtones. For a moment she thought he was going to swoon and fall off his horse or clap his spurs into the steed's side and get the heck out of there. Apparently he thought he was seeing some strange ritual the gringos practice before they devour innocent Mexican vaqueros. He spoke not a single word of English and had never known an American.

Inadvertently I saved the day. I had heard the horses coming and was conscious out of the corner of my eye that one had a rider.

"Que tal, amigo?" I said between puffs. That's just about equivalent to "How goes it, friend?"

The sound of his own language apparently served to reassure Santiago. He dismounted, bowed to my wife, and said, "I am called Santiago Romero."

My wife said she was called la Senora O'Connor and that her esposo who was laboring on the bed was called Jack O'Connor.

"O-cone-nor," said Santiago.

"Call me Jack," I said.

"Djek," repeated Santiago.

"The same as Juanito in Spanish."

"Oh," he said brightening. "I then call you Juanito!"

257

We were in the process of making camp out in the Mexican desert perhaps 20 miles as the crow flies from the Gulf of California. The spot was locally known as the "tinajo," or tank. It consisted of a corral of gnarled mesquite, a windmill, and a big tin water tank. In the corral was a watering trough which range cattle used. Next to it was a mud hut in which lived the caretaker, his wife, and five children. His sole duties were to shut off the windmill when the tank was full and to shut off the tank when the watering trough was full; then to turn them on again. He was paid fifty pesos a month—at that time about $10.

Our own camp was in an adobe hut on a little knoll overlooking the corral. Near it was another hut where hay was stored. I had made a deal back at the ranch for hay, horses, and Santiago.

"Drive on up to the tinajo," Epifanio, the ranch owner, had told me earlier that day. "You can camp in one building and you'll have hay and water right there. I'll send a boy up with some horses."

While we blew up our mattresses and laid out food and cooking gear, Santiago stood around watching. Without being asked, he went down to the trough and brought back a bucket of water, then rustled a couple of loads of firewood.

He seemed to sense when my chores were done. "Would you care to mount a horse and take a turn with me?" he asked. "Maybe we could see some deer."

By that time it was midafternoon, but I tied my scabbard on a saddle, stuck my old .270 rifle in it, and Santiago and I took off. It was late in December and a storm was brewing. Great white clouds with gray bellies were blowing in from the gulf on a chill wind, and when they passed over the sun the gray desert was suddenly drab and cold. As Santiago and I rode along we could see the long tracks of the big desert mule deer and now and then the little heart-shaped tracks of white-tails. Occasionally we'd see where a herd of the little Southwestern pigs called javelinas had crossed our path, and we flushed a few coveys of Gambel's quail. Once we came over the crest of a hill in time to see a frightened white-tail doe running wildly through the cactus below us.

We'd made a long circle and were turning back toward camp when Santiago suddenly put up his hand. "Buros!" he said. He pointed across a wide valley to a hill thick with palo verde trees. I detected a movement, put my binoculars on it, and saw a long-eared mule-deer doe. Then I saw

Santiago and the Lady

another, and another—in all about half a dozen. Since the rut was just beginning, the does were probably a harem, and the buck, who had collected them should be around.

Then my hungry horse saw an appetizing ironwood branch above him. He reached up and yanked it off with a sharp crack. That did it. The does started to run, and out from behind a palo verde came a magnificent buck. He was in sight for only an instant as he cut over the low ridge to the left.

"Look at the buck! Look at those antlers!" muttered Santiago. "Let us go!"

He unbuckled his chaps, dropped them to the ground, and took off his spurs. Then away he went on foot, with me right behind him. How he knew exactly where the buck would head I'll never guess, but he did. We ran for a quarter of a mile, then pounded over a ridge. Immediately we saw a big doe come streaming by, not much more than 50 yards away. Right after her came the buck—big, dark, and fat—running with his nose up and his great antlers laid back.

I was, alas, in no condition to shoot after my sprint, but I managed somehow to get the wavering crosshairs behind the old macho's shoulder. I touched her off and the buck swapped ends. I shot again and he was down. The first 130-grain Silvertip had taken him high through the lungs and the second had broken both shoulders. The bullets went clear through.

I dressed the buck while Santiago went back to get the horses, and then it dawned on me that this desert buck not only had the best head—13 points—of any Mexican mule deer I had ever taken but that he was also the heaviest. When we got the four quarters to the locker they weighed 176 pounds. As he lay there he couldn't have weighed much less than 250. All in all, he was quite a buck.

"How big!" Santiago commented when he joined me with the horses. "Like a bull."

We got a riata on the big buck's antlers, threw it over a palo verde branch, and, with me hoisting and Santiago lifting, managed to get the enormous buck over Santiago's saddle and tie him in place. Then Santiago seated himself on the buck and led the way in triumph back to camp.

When we jangled up my wife had a fire going, green beans heating,

259

potatoes boiling, and a dozen quail browning in a big frying pan.
Santiago turned to me. "It is good," he said, "to bring along a woman to
cook the meals, to wash the dishes, and to talk to."

"Yes," I said, "it is good. Women are useful."

Most poor Mexicans are not hearty eaters. They never have much
more than enough to get by on and their capacity is small. Santiago,
though, was an exception. He devoured the crisp brown quail, remarking
that he'd had no idea the little birds were so good to eat, and savored the
boiled potatoes like an epicure with a truffle. Papas, he told me, were a
delicacy he had rarely eaten. The fluffy Dutch-oven biscuits, he said,
were equal to his wife's tortillas, and the canned peaches were a delight.
Ah, women! They were handy in a camp.

But the next morning Santiago did a double take. Following my usual
custom when on a trip with my wife, I crawled out of my sleeping bag,
built a fire, and put coffee on. Then I fried bacon, scrambled eggs, made
toast, and took my wife's breakfast in to her as she lay in the sack.

Poor Santiago was astounded. When I handed him his plate he was
brooding so heavily he could hardly eat. Later, after he had brought in
the horses, he drew me aside. "Tell me," he said, "in Estados Unidos
do all the wives lie abed in the mornings while the husbands arise and
cook the food?"

"Yes," I assured him. "It is an old North American custom."

"In Mexico it is not," he told me with great definiteness.

But other surprises were in store for him.

"Put a saddle on a horse for la senora," I directed.

"For why?" he asked.

"La senora this day must shoot a buck."

He blinked, swallowed a couple of times, then went over and picked
up blanket and saddle.

I'd discovered earlier that the extractor on my wife's .257 was broken,
so now the only functioning firearms we had were my .270 and a
16-gauge shotgun. Poor Santiago was fit to be tied when he saw me
putting my scabbard and rifle on Eleanor's saddle.

"For why, Juanito, you give the rifle to la senora and take none
yourself?"

"We have but one that is effective," I told him.

"But when we see the buck he must receive a ball!"

260

"La senora," I assured him, "is a good shooter."

So we rode off, Santiago in the lead, followed closely by Eleanor, and with me tagging along at the end.

We headed for a chain of low, brushy hills where, in previous years, I had always found white-tail deer—venados, the Mexicans call them. The sandy soil of every valley was dimpled with white-tail tracks, but no deer did we see. I could tell, though, that they were moving out ahead of our noisy cavalcade.

Finally I said to Santiago, "It is good for you and la senora to ride to the saddle ahead, get off, and tie your horses. I shall make a circle and perhaps frighten the deer so that you shall see them."

"It is good," said Santiago.

I waited until they were within a couple of minutes of the saddle ahead, then turned my horse and rode down into a brushy little valley. I hadn't gone a quarter of a mile when I heard the brush pop and two bucks—an old one with a massive head and a younger one of frying size—ran up on the hillside not over 75 yards away and stopped to look at me.

"Boo!" I yelled.

Startled, the bucks took off—in the general direction of Santiago and Eleanor.

A few moments later I heard a shot, then another. I rode around a point. I could see the two standing horses, but Eleanor and Santiago were not with them. Presently I saw them bending over a buck down in the little valley below.

I joined them, noted that it was the smaller of the two bucks, and heard Eleanor's story: The buck had run right into the trap (the big deer turned off), tearing by at about 200 yards. Eleanor swung the scope smoothly ahead of him and touched off her shot. The buck collapsed, hit squarely through the lungs. Then a desert gray fox, frightened by the racket, popped up clear cross the valley, a good 300 yards away.

"Behold!" Santiago said, pointing. "Una zorra!"

Eleanor leveled down on the fox and knocked it for a loop.

Santiago was still goggle-eyed when I got there. "Ah," he told me, shaking his head, "a good shooter is la senora."

So we started back toward camp.

Since we had our deer and there was now no need for quiet, Eleanor, whose knowledge of Spanish is limited but who does not worry about it, held the following conversation with Santiago as we rode along:

"Grass is green!" said Eleanor.

"Si," agreed Santiago.

"Cows eat grass."

"Si."

"When they eat much grass they get fat."

"The truth," said Santiago.

"When cows are fat they are very good to eat."

"Ah, how good!" he agreed.

"Tell me," he said, "in los Estados Unidos do many women shoot the rifle and kill the deer?"

"Ah yes," I assured him. "The North American women love to shoot. Many times they go to the mountains to hunt while the husbands remain in the home to care for the young."

"Can that be!" he gasped, shaking his head. "What a people!"

Presently we heard quail calling down by the water. One of the coveys that watered there was coming in. Eleanor, who dearly loves to shoot quail, came whipping out of the shack with her 16 under her arm, looking as glamorous as a dame can look in a wool shirt, cowboy boots, and a soiled pair of pants with a hole in the knee.

"Hear those quail?" she said. "I'm going down and shoot our supper."

"Why don't you go with la senora and pick up the corpses?" I suggested to Santiago. "While you do I shall remove the pelt from the buck."

"It is good," said Santiago.

I stood and watched. They weren't halfway down the hill when a bird buzzed off. Eleanor's gun came up. It went bang and the bird dropped. Santiago picked up the fluttering quail, then pointed to another scurrying along the ground about 30 yards away.

"Shoot!" I heard him shout. "Shoot before he flies."

Eleanor rushed in until the frightened quail took wing. She shot and it tumbled.

I went about the business of skinning the white-tail. While I worked, I could hear Eleanor's 16-gauge popping. Presently she and Santiago came back. In each hand the vaquero carried a cluster of quail.

Santiago and the Lady

"I got nine," Eleanor told me.

"Good going," I said.

Santiago had never seen any wing-shooting and I doubt that he'd ever seen a shotgun. "How good the shooter is la senora," he told me. "The quail it flies. Bang! It is dead. Another flies. Bang again!"

That night was New Year's Eve. We feasted on baked quail, broiled backstraps from the big buck, French-fried potatoes, and stewed tomatoes. For dessert Eleanor had whipped together a cherry pie and baked it in the Dutch oven. Then we toasted one another, friendship between the United States and Mexico, and anything else we could think of in a mild concoction of rum, sugar, water, and lemon juice. When the New Year came, we all hit the sack.

We packed up the next day to drive back across the border. Santiago had his horses ready for the 10-mile trek back to the ranch and he was wearing a jacket and a good pair of shoes I had given him. He had 50 pesos in his pocket. Yet he was forlorn.

"You go quickly," he said. "You should stay longer—two days, five days, a whole week. There are many deer and we could shoot them."

"But we must go," I told him. "In our house there is much to do."

"I have never seen a shooter like la senora," he said. "Bang, bang, bang—the deer, the fox, the quail. But it makes me sad to know that anyone so lovely has death in her heart. That should be only for the men!"

Outdoor Life
March 1953

263